WITHIN TIME
AND
BEYOND TIME

WITHIN TIME
AND
BEYOND TIME

A Festschrift for
Pearl King

Edited by
Riccardo Steiner & Jennifer Johns

LONDON   NEW YORK

First published in 2001 by
H. Karnac (Books) Ltd.
6 Pembroke Buildings, London NW10 6RE

A subsidiary of Other Press LLC, New York

Arrangement copyright © 2001 Riccardo Steiner & Jennifer Johns;
Introduction © 2001 Jennifer Johns; "A Language Game" © 2001 Marion
Milner; chapter 1 © 2001 Alain de Mijolla; chapter 2 © 2001 André Green;
chapter 3 © 2001 James Hood; chapter 4 © 2001 Riccardo Steiner; chapter 5 ©
2001 Ron Baker; chapter 6 © 2001 Eric Rayner & Dilys Daws; chapter 7 © 2001
Bernard Barnett; chapter 8 © 2001 Harold P. Blum; chapter 9 © 2001 Carlos A.
Crisanto; chapter 10 © 2001 Rose Edgcumbe; chapter 11© 2001 R. Horacio
Etchegoyen; chapter 12 © 2001 Anne Hayman; chapter 13 © 2001 Otto F.
Kernberg; chapter 14 © 2001 Leo Rangell; chapter 15 © 2001 Anne-Marie
Sandler & Joseph Sandler; chapter 16 © 2001 Hanna Segal; chapter 17 © 2001
Harold Stewart; chapter 18 © 2001 Clifford Yorke

The rights of the contributors to be identified as the authors of this work have
been asserted in accordance with §§ 77 and 78 of the Copyright Design and
Patents Act 1988.

All rights reserved. No part of this publication may be reproduced, stored in a
retrieval system, or transmitted, in any form or by any means, electronic,
mechanical, photocopying, recording, or otherwise, without the prior written
permission of the publisher.

British Library Cataloguing in Publication Data

A C.I.P. for this book is available from the British Library

 ISBN: 1 85575 270 0

10 9 8 7 6 5 4 3 2 1

Edited, designed, and produced by Communication Crafts

www.karnacbooks.com

Printed and bound by Biddles Short Run Books, King's Lynn

CONTENTS

ACKNOWLEDGEMENTS

The first acknowledgement must of course go to Pearl King herself, whose 80th birthday provided the inspiration to collect papers from many of those who have worked with her over the years, and who have come to value her thought and contributions, as well as developing great affection for her. Next, the contributors themselves, who sent papers so generously and promptly, with accompanying comments about their relationship with Pearl demonstrating how much she is valued. They have created the book in her honour. Our publishers have been efficient, pleasant, and helpful; without the encouragement of Cesare Sacerdoti, the book would not have happened, and his successors at Karnac Books—Oliver Rathbone, Leena Häkkinen, and Malcolm Smith—have offered much support and advice. Eric and Klara King of Communication Crafts were utterly efficient, prompt, and supportive in the final stages of preparation. As so often happens, we owe a great deal to Jill Duncan, of the Archives of the British Psycho-Analytical Society, for collecting the papers and initiating the preparation of the manuscript, and to the Librarian of the Society, Andrea Chandler, for chasing up references.

Riccardo Steiner and Jennifer Johns

ABOUT THE AUTHORS

Ronald Baker, Training and Supervising Psychoanalyst, British Psychoanalytical Society; Member, Royal College of Psychiatrists.

Bernard Barnett, Training and Supervising Psychoanalyst, Child Psychoanalyst, British Psychoanalytical Society. Chairman of the Education Committee. Formerly Chief Psychologist and Director of Training, Child Guidance Training Centre and Tavistock Centre. Special interests: psychoanalytic education, the theory of play, and Holocaust studies. Currently writing a book on the superego.

Harold P. Blum, Training and Supervising Analyst, New York University Psychoanalytic Institute; Executive Director, Sigmund Freud Archives. Formerly Editor-in-Chief, *Journal of the American Psychoanalytic Association*. Inaugural Sigourney Award for Distinguished Contributions to Psychoanalysis.

Carlos A. Crisanto, Training Analyst, Peruvian Psychoanalytic Society. Formerly President of the Peruvian Psychoanalytic Society; Director of the Institute of Psychoanalysis in Lima, Peru.

Dilys Daws, Child Psychotherapist. Honorary Consulting Child

Psychotherapist, Tavistock Clinic. Founding Chairman, Association for Infant Mental Health UK. Formerly Chairman, Child Psychotherapy Trust. Author, *Through the Night*.

Rose Edgcumbe, Psychoanalyst, Child Psychoanalyst, British Psychoanalytical Society. Previously trained with Anna Freud at the Hampstead Psychotherapy Course and clinic (The Anna Freud Centre). Special interests: the developmental disturbances of childhood; problems of technique in the psychoanalysis of children and adolescents. Author, *Anna Freud: A View of Development Disturbance* and *Therapeutic Techniques*.

R. Horacio Etchegoyen, Training Analyst, Asociación Psicoanalítica de Buenos Aires; Doctor Honoris Causa, UNSL Universidad Nacional de San Luis. Formerly President of the International Psychoanalytical Association; Chair of Psychiatry and Psychological Medicine, Universidad Nacional de Cuyo; President of Asociación Psicoanalítica de Buenos Aires. Author: *The Fundamentals of Psychoanalytic Technique*.

André Green, Training analyst, Paris Psychoanalytic Society; Honorary Professor, Buenos Aires University; Member of the Moscow Academy of Humanities Research; Member of the New York Academy of Sciences. Formerly President, Paris Psychoanalytic Society; Director, Paris Psychoanalytic Institute; Vice-President, International Psychoanalytical Association; Professor, Freud Memorial Chair, University College, London. Author, *The Tragic Effect; On Private Madness; La Folie Privée; The Fabric of Affect and Psychoanalytic Discourses; The Work of the Negative; La causalité psychique; Les chaînes d'Eros; Le temps éclaté; La diachronie en psychanalyse*.

Anne Hayman, Training and Supervising Psychoanalyst, British Psychoanalytical Society; Child Psychoanalyst. Formerly Chair of Scientific Committee, British Psychoanalytical Society; Hon. Archivist of the International Psychoanalytical Association; research psychoanalyst at Anna Freud's Hampstead Clinic. Retired after 42 years in analytic practice. Independent thinker, as reflected in the variety of her psychoanalytic papers.

James Hood, Member of the British Psychoanalytical Society, in private practice in London. Formerly Consultant in Child Psychiatry, Northwick Park Hospital, Harrow, England.

Jennifer Johns, Psychoanalyst, British Psychoanalytical Society, in private practice and in the Department of Psychotherapy at University College Hospital, London.

Otto F. Kernberg, Training and Supervising Analyst, Columbia University Center for Psychoanalytic Training and Research. President of the International Psychoanalytical Association. Director Personality Disorders Institute, the New York Hospital–Cornell Medical Center, Westchester Division. Professor of Psychiatry, Cornell University Medical College.

Alain de Mijolla, Training psychoanalyst, Société Psychanalytique de Paris. Founder and President of the International Association for the History of Psychoanalysis. Member of the Archives and History of Psychoanalysis Committee of the International Psychoanalytical Association. Director, International Dictionary of Psychoanalysis..

Marion Milner [deceased], Training and Supervising Psychoanalyst, Child Psychoanalyst, British Psychoanalytical Society. Author, as Joanna Field: *A Life of One's Own; An Experiment in Leisure; On Not Being Able to Paint;* as herself: *The Hands of the Living God; The Suppressed Madness of Sane Men.*

Leo Rangell, Honorary President of the International Psychoanalytical Association; Past-President of the International Psychoanalytical Association and of the American Psychoanalytic Association; Clinical Professor of Psychiatry, University of California at Los Angeles; and Clinical Professor of Psychiatry (Psychoanalysis), University of California at San Francisco.

Eric Rayner, Training and Supervising Psychoanalyst, British Psychoanalytical Society. Formerly Vice-President of the Britsh Psychoanalytical Society. Author, *The Independent Mind in British Psychoanalysis; Unconscious Logic.*

Anne-Marie Sandler, Training and Supervising Psychoanalyst, British Psychoanalytical Society; Child Analyst. Formerly President of the British Psychoanalytical Society; Director of The Anna Freud Clinic; Vice-President of the International Psychoanalytical Association. Author, with Joseph Sandler, *Internal Objects Revisited.*

Joseph Sandler [deceased], Training and Supervising Psychoanalyst, British Psychoanalytical Society; Child Psychoanalyst. Formerly President of the International Psychoanalytical Association; Sigmund Freud Professor in Jerusalem; Freud Memorial Professor and head of the Psycho-Analytic Unit at University College London.

Hanna Segal, Honorary Member, Training and Supervising Psychoanalyst, British Psychoanalytical Society; Child Psychoanalyst. Formerly President of the British Psychoanalytical Society; Vice-President of the International Psychoanalytical Association. Member of the Royal College of Psychiatrists.

Riccardo Steiner, Member of the British Psychoanalytical Society. Honorary Archivist of the British Psychoanalytical Society. Co-author, with Pearl King, *The Freud–Klein Controversies 1941–1945.*

Harold Stewart, Training and Supervising Psychoanalyst of the British Psychoanalytical Society. Formerly Consultant Psychotherapist at the Tavistock Clinic. Author, *Psychic Experience and Problems of Technique; Michael Balint: Object Relations Pure and Applied.*

Clifford Yorke, Training and Supervising Analyst, British Psychoanalytical Society; Child Psychoanalyst. Honorary Consultant Psychiatrist, formerly Psychiatrist-in-Charge of The Anna Freud Centre, and Director. Honorary Fellow of the Royal College of Psychiatrists. Fellow, American College of Psychoanalysts.

INTRODUCTION

Jennifer Johns

This book is dedicated to Pearl King, who is herself both an institution in psychoanalysis and also an intrinsic element in the development of our science and our different institutions for the last half-century. Pearl has been involved in so much that it is difficult to do justice to all her professional work, and the breadth of it can perhaps be assessed by noting the eminence and variety of the list of authors who have contributed to this book, people whose work—theoretical, clinical, organizational, or that which echoes her passion for the history of psychoanalysis—has been deeply influenced by hers, and who all immediately offered papers when the book was first mooted.

Internationally, papers have been offered by those who have most reason to know of Pearl's work from 1957, when she became Honorary Secretary of the International Psychoanalytical Association. Leo Rangell, an old friend, has chosen to write about moments of decision and action in mental life, emphasizing the unconscious nature of such choices and the range of unconscious responsibility; Horacio Etchegoyen about the validation of the clinical process, linking philosophical trends and psychoanalytic development; Otto Kernberg writes affectionately about his experience of observing the growth of love relations in later life; André Green also writes warmly of Pearl's historical contribution, about the conflict between a passion for history and the problems of psychoanalytic historical thinking; Alain de Mijolla about Pearl's contribution to the IPA's handling of the French psychoanalytic crisis in 1953–64; Harold Blum also addresses a question close to Pearl's heart—the analysis of the older patient—and Carlos Crisanto reflects on the ideas of one of Pearl's early colleagues, D. W. Winnicott.

Nearer to home, Hanna Segal has also addressed the analysis of the older patient, while Harold Stewart reassesses Freud's thoughts on narcissism in males and females; Clifford Yorke draws attention to some disquiet about modern developments, shared by Pearl and himself, notably the tendency to value the "here-and-now" over more traditional concepts of transference, while the Sandlers state their own different point of view. Eric Rayner and Dilys Daws in collaboration show the value of such collaboration, drawing on their work with varied colleagues. The breadth of Pearl's interest, particularly in psychoanalysis at different stages of life, is demonstrated by Rose Edgcumbe's contribution on the analysis of a young person, while Bernard Barnett, an analysand of Pearl's, writes about the Holocaust and its aftermath, especially in relation to the superego. Using as inspiration Pearl's encouragement of speaking out, Ann Hayman writes about psychoanalytic terminology and the ways that meaning can slide, leading to important but often unnoticed alterations in theory and practice. Pearl's interest in the work, lives, and interests of her colleagues is represented by James Hood's personal memoir on Ronald Laing. A moving contribution was made by Marion Milner, who was Pearl's second analyst, and who, rather than writing a paper, sent a poem dedicated to Pearl.

Nor has the totality of Pearl's personality been overlooked by the contributors—it is commented on directly in several chapters, notably in that of Riccardo Steiner, slightly surprised by her Englishness, writing about her as a dedicated historian and archivist, whose sensitivity, generosity, and sheer determination have enabled her, in addition to all else she has achieved, to build the monument that the Archives of the British Society represent.

Pearl has been described as the "English Analyst" and her background is certainly that, though far from conventional. Her early years were spent in Africa as the child of Christian Missionaries, who returned to live in East Anglia during her childhood. In the 1930s, while studying psychology and sociology, her political passions inflamed by the hardships of that time in England, by the Spanish Civil War, and by the spread of National Socialism in Europe, she discovered the importance of organizational politics, and during the war she worked sociologically in munitions and hosiery factories, where the importance of communication in industrial relations and in education became clear to her. She met and worked with others who were later to create the Tavistock Institute of Human Relations, and through the climate that evolved between all the members of that group she herself became interested in psychoanalysis.

She trained as an analyst after the war, her first analyst being John Rickman. After his death she worked with Marion Milner. Almost immediately after qualification Pearl used her organizational talents and capacity to think creatively in the interests of her own analytic institute, The British Psychoanalytical Society (BPAS), as well as becoming involved in the International Psychoanalytical Association. The BPAS was itself dealing with the political and theoretical fall-out of the Controversial Discussions, about which Pearl, together with Riccardo Steiner, later produced a masterly volume (King & Steiner, 1991). The consequent tensions, which developed in relation to the educational and organizational aspects and structure of the Society and which became politicized, called for the level of skill in negotiations and finding compromise without betraying principles that had served Pearl so well, initially in her industrial work and later at the Tavistock. She became a member of the Middle Group, with respect for both the individual members as well as the theoretical positions of each faction in the conflicted Society. With her passion for the study of professional development, she was well placed further to develop her remarkable creative capacity to discover ways of thinking and relating within the social setting that could be of use, and her contribution to the structure of the Society and in particular to its training, is unique.

Internationally, Pearl's contribution has also been immense and influential. The International Psychoanalytical Association owes much of its structure and procedures to her extraordinary capacity to understand and conceptualize institutional and organizational matters, and the principles governing the relationships between individuals, their local organizations, and the wider international identity. Baker particularly commends her "firm belief that if the association could evolve an appropriate social structure, morale would improve and in turn this would lead to raised standards and a lessening in the growth of dissident groups", which she stated when she proposed the new Statutes of the IPA at the Stockholm Congress in 1963.

A striking example of Pearl's capacity to understand, patiently observe, and contribute positively exists in regard to her involvement with the tensions and splits in the French psychoanalytic movement between 1953 and 1965, reported on by Alain de Mijolla. This painful and difficult period must have appeared almost impossible for the varied members of the IPA to comprehend, digest, and cope with, as it was for the French themselves, and it was only with the patience, tolerance, and preparedness to give generous and genuine credit to the passions of those who argued that any resolution was possible. In so far as the splits are in part healed, the attitude so typical of Pearl, together with her colleagues, must have contributed. Again, the understanding of the complexities of the internal, the personal, the relational, and the social aspects are what she specializes in and which enable her particular skills to potentiate change and development.

Pearl's own personal fascination is in fact with development, in her individual patients and the institutions she studies and works with, and with the individuals within those institutions. In 1982 she became the first non-medical president of the British Society, and, together with her vice-president, Eric Rayner, they persuaded colleagues to allow Associate Members to vote on most issues at Business Meetings. She objected to the "infantilization" both of students and of her more junior colleagues. She has written about many topics, including essays that include the influence of the social field as well as the internal world, and most famously about treating the older patient—work that has linked with that of others and that is complemented by the chapters in this book by Blum, Kernberg, and Segal—about research, about psychoanalytic education and learning processes, about analytic identity and its development through the life cycle of the analyst, including the relationship to the psychoanalytic organization, about the affective response of the analyst, and, of course, about history, her passion. Her approach to history is rooted in her study of the development and evolution of individuals together with their relationships and their institutions; she can always see the perspective of a situation and how it has come about. Her memory is incredible and is supported by her use of the archival material that she has so carefully collected and tended both personally and in the

Archives of the British Psychoanalytical Society. The Archives have grown and matured under Pearl's care into a research tool, a source of actual knowledge about how processes have developed and past decisions been taken, thus allowing fact to replace fallible memories, and it has been possible to clarify past thinking and avoid the repetition of mistakes. It is also an enormous and important international resource, and its methods of collating and storing material, devised by Pearl, are a model for similar archives worldwide.

It was from this mass of material, committee minutes, documents, and correspondence that she and Riccardo Steiner were able to put together and create their impressive work, *The Freud–Klein Controversies, 1941–1945*, published in 1991. In 1992 Pearl and Hanna Segal were the first two British psychoanalysts to be awarded the Sigourney Prize from the United States for "outstanding contributions to psychoanalysis". Pearl continues to work, research, and plan further publications.

Pearl is much loved in the psychoanalytic community, both in the United Kingdom and perhaps even more abroad. She has been involved in the training of perhaps more analysts than any other over many years. She is a great lady, and her contributions come from her energy, her enthusiasm, her wisdom, her kindness, warmth, and generosity, and her respect for the opinions of others, even when she disagrees with them.

It is with great pleasure and pride that this book is dedicated to her.

PEARL KING: CHRONOLOGY

1918   Born in East Croydon, Surrey, on 17 June (during a Zep-
            pelin air raid).

1941–1946   Qualifies as a Social and Industrial Psychologist; during
            the war, works in industry as a psychologist, later studies
            post-war rehabilitation. Meets ex-military psychiatrists
            and social scientists applying psychoanalytic ideas to
            organizational problems. Decides to train.

1946   Accepted by Institute of Psycho-Analysis (Training Ana-
            lyst: John Rickman).

1946–1950   Supervised by Marion Milner, Michael Balint, Donald
            Winnicott. Meets and is influenced by Sylvia Payne,
            Paula Heimann, Hanna Segal. Simultaneously works at
            the Tavistock Institute of Human Relations doing indus-
            trial research.

1951   Qualifies as analyst.

1953   With Michael Balint, organizes the London Congress of
            the International Psychoanalytical Association (IPA).

1954   Full Membership of the British Psycho-Analytical Society
            (BPAS).

1955   Recognized as Training Analyst.

1956   Hon. Secretary of the BPAS.

1957–1961   Hon. Secretary of the IPA.

1963–1967   Associate Secretary of IPA for Europe.

1964–1966   Deputy President of the BPAS (with Bion, later Winnicott, as Presidents). Works on new Constitution for IPA presented at Stockholm Congress.

late 1960s   As Hon. Secretary of the Training Committee of the BPAS, reorganizes, with Adam Limentani, the Training Committee.

1979   Presents paper, on treating older patients, at New York IPA Congress.

1981   Organizes Conference for Training Analysts at Madrid IPA Congress—all Training Analysts welcome, rather than two from each Society, as had been the case before.

1982   Elected President of the BPAS.

1984   Retires from Presidency, becomes Hon. Archivist of BPAS.

1991   Publishes, with Riccardo Steiner, *The Freud/Klein Controversies, 1941–1945*.

1992   Awarded, jointly with Hanna Segal, the Sigourney Prize for oustanding contributions to psychoanalysis.

Pearl is an Honorary Member of the British, Finnish, and Swedish Psychoanalytical Societies.

A language game

("What is mind? No matter"
"What is matter? Never mind"). Who said this?

"Mind the gap!" shouts the mechanical voice at the Embankment
tube station.
"Mind the gap!"
I do, I did, I never have fallen between the platform and the train.
I don't mind, it doesn't matter.
Or does it?
I do mind the gap between the rich and the poor.
And I do mind the gap between what I can dream of for the earth
And what we are doing to it.
Destroying the living matter on which we depend for life—
like the Amazon Forests.

And I mind that I did not think
It mattered that I did not mind
When we came to the
End of the matter
So that there were
No more gaps
To mind.

Body and Mind, two sides of the same coin you said?

I minded that I did not mind
That the matter did not matter any more.
But I do know that it is
Out of the gaps
That new things grow.

Marion Milner (London)

WITHIN TIME
AND
BEYOND TIME

CHAPTER ONE

Splits in the French psychoanalytic movement, between 1953 and 1964

Alain de Mijolla (Paris)

My Dear Pearl,

The French psychoanalytic movement has, in my opinion at least, two good reasons for being very grateful to you.

First, and importantly, because of your careful and amicable handling of the very difficult situation for psychoanalysis that arose in France in 1953–1965, at the time when you were Secretary of the Organising Committee of the International Congress of the IPA in 1953 in London, and later, even more importantly when you were elected Hon Sec of the IPA in 1957, holding office till 1961, and later in 1963–67 as first Associate Secretary for Europe.

You were then directly involved in all the secret and public bargaining which put a full stop to the chaotic situation created by the first French split in 1953. Many letters in the archives show your active participation and your relationship with Jacques Lacan (did you not remind me recently of his invitation to a tea-party with dancing?), with Daniel Lagache, Serge Leclaire, Wladimir Granoff, etc.

The second reason is more personal. Ever since the creation in June 1985 of the International Association for the History of Psychoanalysis, you have been an intelligent and faithful supporter of its work. You are among the very rare colleagues to have understood and encouraged so well our efforts to increase the work in the field of the history of our movement, of our ideas, of our institutions, of our place within the culture of our different countries.

I cannot forget your participation in the first International Meeting, in 1987, the discussion on the attitudes of the psycho-analysts during the Second World War, and your gift to the young association of the unpublished report of Rickman about the German psychoanalysts he met in Berlin just after the end of the war.

I also cannot forget your kind and confident help for all these years, and your wonderful work for the Archives of the British Psychoanalytical Society, which remains as a model for all of those who fight, as I try to do, to open the eyes of so many col-leagues to the necessity of giving future generations those ele-ments of the construction-reconstruction of the fascinating history that the world has lived since the first researches of Freud.

Fascinating history, as I recalled [Mijolla, 1982] in my short essay on the history of psychoanalysis in France, "full of sound and fury", often "signifying nothing". . . . For this book of hom-age to your action for psychoanalysis, I have chosen to recall some moments of a certain madness which occurred during the period 1953–1964 in France, which was known well to you. I only hope that this paper, for the translation of which I must thank some friends and colleagues, especially Riccardo Steiner, will not appear too much as a "tale told by an idiot", even if many re-actions of the protagonists of these tragi-comedies remain rather difficult to understand and explain.

Affectionately, as ever, My dear Pearl,
Your grateful

Alain de Mijolla
President of the International Association for the History of Psychoanalysis

* * *

"No claim is made for completeness. The picture is confused: the truth is not easy to find."

P. Turquet, Report on a visit to the SFP, Paris, 21 June 1960.

I t is pretentious to claim to be able to do justice, in the restricted space of a communication or a simple article, to one of the richest periods of the history of psychoanalysis in France, full of dramatic events, not forgetting those theoretical and clinical reflections the impact of which we still feel today. The demarcation in time that I have chosen can only be arbitrary, since the split in 1953 itself was determined by previous events, the complexity of which I can only roughly sketch. The split of 1964 was followed by the creation of new movements and new splits, such as that which gave birth in 1969 to the Quatrième Groupe OPLF, perfectly reflecting the line of continuity with the split of 1963. As for the multiplicity of events that developed between the two above-mentioned dates, it will only be possible for me to produce something akin to a grotesque image of what happened. The same has to be said where the published and presented work produced by the various trends that characterize French psychoanalysis are concerned.

I must refer the reader to the work already published on my subject,[1] and restrict myself to the rather modest role of someone who

---

This article is the repeat of a communication given to the Fifth International Meeting of the IAHP, on 23 July 1994, in Berlin. Destined for an international public, it is an attempt to simplify and summarize some facts that, while well known to French readers, are rather obscure for a foreign audience. It was first published in French in *Topique*, 57 (1995), pp. 271–290, and in German: "Die Spaltung in der psychoanalytischen Bewegung Frankreichs von 1953 bis 1964", in *Spaltungen in der Geschichte der Psychoanalyse* (Tubingen: Ed. Diskord, 1995), pp. 168–191.

[1] It is necessary to mention two special supplements of the Lacanian review *Ornicar?*, No. 7, published in 1976 (*La Scission de 1953*), and No. 8, in 1977 (*L'excommunication*), in which Jacques-Alain Miller presented for the first time some of the essential documents in this study. Later, further publications, also in *Ornicar?*, completed them. In 1982, I myself published some previously unpub-

acts as a sort of memorandum or guide to this work, which traverses a period particularly difficult to explore on account of the deep repercussions, affective as well as theoretical, practical, and administrative, that have left traces and injuries not yet completely healed. This fact does not allow for an exhaustive study.

Dr Turquet, then Secretary of the Investigative Committee that the IPA sent to France, wrote the sentence with which I introduce my chapter at the beginning of the report on the situation of psychoanalysis in France that he issued in 1960. We must keep his prudent warning in mind throughout this study.

In 1952 there was only one psychoanalytical Institution in France: the Société Psychanalytique de Paris (SPP), created in 1926. In 1953, five of its training analysts resigned and created the Société Française de Psychanalyse (SFP), but they were then excluded from the IPA and had to work very hard for ten years in order to be reinstated. However, their reinstatement was obtained through having to accept the exclusion from the IPA of two training analyst founders of the SFP—Lacan and Dolto. In 1964 Lacan was to create l'École Freudienne de Paris (EFP), which he only dissolved shortly before his death. After the dissolution of the SFP in 1964, those among his members who were recognized by the IPA regrouped in a new Institution, the Association Psychanalytique de France, which still exists today.

The characteristic of the first split in 1953, which made it truly a novelty in the history of psychoanalysis, consisted in the fact that it did not happen because of theoretical divergencies; rather, it was due to problems related to the training and diffusion of psychoanalysis in France and its control.

Heavy criticisms were made and discussions took place for years around these issues, and criticisms of Lacan's didactic analytic meth-

---

lished documents for the Société Psychanalytique de Paris in "La Psychanalyse en France (1893–1965)" (Mijolla, 1982). The commentaries and previously unpublished documents in the two works by E. Roudinesco—in 1982, *La Bataille de cent ans, Vol. 1,* and in 1986, *Histoire de la Psychanalyse en France, Vol. 2,* 1925–1985—complete these first studies. In addition to the testimonies of several protagonists in these dramatic events, I have benefited from the unpublished archives of the Société Psychanalytique de Paris and of the International Psychoanalytical Association (with the help of Dr Adam Limentani, Archivist of the IPA, and his successor, Dr Anne Hayman), from Dr Rudolf Loewenstein (Library of Congress, Washington), and Georges Mauco (Archives of the IPA).

ods became sharper and sharper, whereas the theoretical changes in his way of thinking that have introduced so many transformations in psychoanalysis were neglected or relegated to second place. Nevertheless, those changes were increasingly to attract the attention of the French public and were to lead to the creation of what has been called "The Lacanian movement", which became a separate school of psychoanalysis.

I have therefore referred to two splits, very different in their nature in spite of the line of continuity linking them. A generation of psychoanalysts separates them. Although the most senior were always active, and one has to remember that Lacan was constantly present during the development of this whole story, the protagonists have changed too, and new personalities have appeared on the scene.

There is another characteristic that needs to be noted: all those who supported the various institutions claimed to speak in the name of the "true Freud" and saw themselves as his true representatives. None of them—unlike Adler, Stekel, Jung, Rank, and Horney, to name a few—presented themselves as dissidents to a Freudianism judged obsolete. Those were, on the contrary, "Other", those who were to be constantly represented or defined as traitors who abandoned Freud's thinking.

Just very briefly I will have to mention here the slow penetration of psychoanalysis into France (see Mijolla, 1984), which Freud designated during the 1920s as "reticent" to his ideas. Psychoanalysis was used by certain young rather nationalist psychiatrists who wished to adapt it to the French way of thinking. They preferred not to depend on the IPA, which at that time was mainly dominated by the Viennese and Berlin analysts; neither did they like being controlled by Freud.

A Frenchwoman, Princess Marie Bonaparte—who, it must be remembered, was not a medical doctor, and who had come to be quite close to Freud during her personal analysis with him—played a fundamental role in founding the SPP in November 1926. Her wealth and international relationships allowed her to be a Mycaenas, and with the help of Loewenstein she managed to keep the young Society relatively loyal to Freud (Mijolla, 1988b). Nevertheless there was already a certain atmosphere oriented towards splitting, even before the Second World War.

At the beginning of the war, the Institute of Psychoanalysis created in 1934 was closed, and the documents were scattered; during the four years of Nazi occupation everything that could remind one of the "Jewish Science" was forbidden. Some analysts, such as Marie Bonaparte and Loewenstein, emigrated; others—for instance, Sacha Nacht—resisted the Nazis; still others served in the Army, like Schiff. Some, such as Leuba, Parcheminey, and Jacques Lacan, continued to practise psychoanalysis—or, rather, psychiatrically oriented psycho-therapies—more or less discreetly. Only René Laforgue would main-tain a relationship with the Goering Institute, the importance of which, and its long-lasting effects, was only understood much later.[2] Laforgue's activities were nevertheless known, and after the war he was labelled a collaborator by his colleagues. In spite of this, this charismatic man had several analysands of high intellectual quality, who always remained loyal to him, including François Dolto and Juliette Favez-Boutonier.

After the Liberation of France, a new group emerged, in addition to the group of analysands of René Laforgue and what was left of the first training analysts of the Paris Society. It was mainly formed by people who were in their thirties—Serge Lebovici, Pasche, and René Diatkine, among others. Most were Jewish and had been more or less active in the anti-Nazi Resistance, often in direct contact with the French Communist Party. They were attracted by the personality and ideas of Sacha Nacht, whose conduct and ambitions resembled their own.

Bit by bit, the SPP was recreated, with both its good and bad aspects; meanwhile a new phenomenon was developing. The Ameri-can Army had imported a new fashion to Europe, alongside chewing gum and nylon stockings: the fashion for psychoanalysis. This phe-nomenon was not confined to France, and the standards required to become a psychoanalyst were becoming firmly established by the IPA, henceforth with its centre of gravity in America. Most of the ideological direction came from those Jewish analysts who had emi-grated from Austria and Germany and, not without difficulty, per-haps, had become more American than the Americans. They well knew and recognized the help that the IPA had given them in helping to save their lives and protect their identities as psychoanalysts, and the recognition of this fact played a definite role in the insistence of many members of the future Société Française de Psychanalyse in

---

[2] This was only revealed by the discovery of regular correspondence in the Archives of Koblenz by Regina Lockot (cf. Mijolla, 1988a).

gaining international recognition. They could not avoid the thought that while living through a Cold War, menaced by the threat of Soviet invasion, they too might need to escape and would in turn need the help of the IPA. The Soviet Union appeared no less hostile to psychoanalysis than had the Nazis, and the danger was real: in 1948–49 there was the Berlin blockade and in October 1962 the Cuban missile crisis.

In post-war Paris many candidates applied for psychoanalytic training. Psychoanalysis seemed radically to question the old psychiatric and psychological ways of thinking and practice. A training Institute became necessary, as did a meeting-place and a library, since no psychoanalytic books or translations of Freud were available, the bulk having been seized and destroyed during the Occupation.

During those years the necessity for the collective responsibility of French psychoanalysis was underlined by a public trial. L'Ordre des Médecins, which was increasing the number of prosecutions of non-medical analysts for the illegal practice of medicine, attacked a member of the SPP, Mrs Clark Williams. Her trial was commented on widely in the press from March 1950 to April 1951 (though the verdict was not delivered until July 1953), and this posed the President of the SPP and likewise his eminent colleagues the problem of public accountability as to the qualities of a psychoanalyst.

In 1947 Daniel Lagache created the licence in Psychology at the Sorbonne, and this led many students to choose this path to becoming a psychoanalyst. However, the problem of their non-medical status remained unresolved. It was necessary to create criteria and standards of training in order to defend them against external attack. Written largely by Jacques Lacan, a "Doctrine de la Commission de l'Enseignement", from the SPP, was published in 1949. Even if, for the most part, a medical training was judged preferable, it was clear that in order to be credible, the French would have to abide by the international standards of the IPA.

All was in place, therefore, for the creation of an essential training and teaching organization, and the inevitable struggle for its control. As luck would have it, three men, all about fifty, each represented the elements of the struggle.

Of all of them, Sacha Nacht was the most senior member of the SPP. A Rumanian Jew who had come to France to study medicine, he strongly supported the establishment of psychoanalysis in an autonomous Institute but based on a medical model. His inspiration for this project came from the Institutes of Vienna and Berlin, which he had

known before the war. He wished to institute a "Diplôme de Psych-
analyste", integrated on a more or less long-term basis in a medical
training, and by this means to gain an honoured position for himself.

He was authoritarian, snapped in anger readily, and was nick-
named "the satrap", but had considerable prestige with a number of
young Jewish analysts, most of whom were his analysands.

The second, Daniel Lagache, was an academic trained in literature and philosophy before taking on the study of medicine. During
the Occupation he had continued to teach in the "free zone", at
Clermond-Ferrand, where the Faculty of Strasbourg had taken refuge
on fleeing the Nazi annexation. After the Liberation, he returned to
Strasbourg, but he was soon appointed professor at the Sorbonne in
Paris. Juliette Favez-Boutonier succeeded him, followed by Didier
Anzieu, thus creating academic links that played a role in succeeding
events.

Daniel Lagache was intelligent, but he lacked charisma and had
less presence than either of the others. His work recalled the rigour of
the academic; he liked neither Nacht nor Lacan, and the feelings were
mutual. His principal supporter was Juliette Favez-Boutonier, along
with her husband, Georges Favez, followed by a group of analysands
of René Laforgue.

Is it necessary to present the third man, Jacques Lacan? To recall
his idiosyncratic and original uses of contemporary ideas, his interest
in the domain of psychosis, especially the subject of his medical thesis,
paranoia, his links with Surrealism, his taste for provocation, even
mystification?

He went his own way, accepting psychoanalytic standards only
superficially. For twelve years he promised to maintain them but
obstinately continued on his own journey, convinced that since October 1952 he had finally found his own creative path in psychoanalysis.[3] At that time he was still a friend of Sacha Nacht and was witness
to Nacht's remarriage in July 1952. A year later, they no longer spoke
to each other, and they never met again; both died thirty years later.

* * *

---

[3] An unpublished letter from Jacques Lacan to Rudolf Loewenstein (Archives
of the Library of Congress, Washington) allows us to specify the date as 12 October
1952.

To describe the train of events in 1952 in a few words: it essentially concerns those factions struggling for control of the Commission d'Enseignement at the very heart of the Institut de Psychanalyse, the statutes of which had been under lengthy discussion. This body was to have the power to select candidates for training, to open or close the portal through which it is necessary to pass in order to gain a psychoanalytic career.

Sacha Nacht, still President of the SPP after four years, wanted to become Director of the Institute and President of this important and powerful Commission. He preferred to leave the care of the SPP, reduced to the status of a simple learned Society, to others, primarily Jacques Lacan, whom he had chosen as Vice-President.

Daniel Lagache, already frustrated at having seen the locality he proposed for housing the Institute overridden in favour of Nacht's choice of the Rue St Jacques, rebelled against such a concentration of power. At first, Princess Marie Bonaparte agreed with him, since she sensed Nacht's opposition to non-medical analysts. For a short while, Nacht was in a minority and resigned his post as Director; Lacan was temporarily to occupy the post until the Statutes of the Society were definitively in place.

Jacques Lacan was elected President of the SPP in January 1953 with a majority of one vote, enraging Marie Bonaparte, who judged him a "madman" and denounced his breaches of the standards of training analysis. These were to become more apparent with time. In the event, the statutes designated "neurobiological" and proposed by Sacha Nacht, who was about to become Director once again, were accepted after several amendments suggested by the Princess, and it then became necessary to make an exact count of all the applicants to the training in order to distribute them between the three planned cycles of study. Jacques Lacan turned out to have such a large number of candidates that it would have taken more than twenty-four hours per day to analyse them all according to the frequency and time required. Despite his repeated denials and promises of reform, his practice of "shortened sessions" could no longer be concealed.

The Princess "came on board", as she put it, and subsequently supported Sacha Nacht and his group in their increasingly virulent attacks focused upon Lacan.

However, behind the scenes, a movement rejecting the authoritarianism of Nacht and hoping to promote a more academic teaching of psychoanalysis was developing around Daniel Lagache, on account of his position and that of Juliette Favez-Boutonier; they hoped to gain the approval of the public authorities.

One might have seen, on the one hand, the creation of an Institute—a private society centralized in Paris and calling for the sole approval of the IPA—and, on the other, a "free Institute", supported by Professor Jean Delay, the powerful incumbent of the Chaire des Maladies Mentales et de l'Encéphale at the Hôpital Sainte-Anne, with the potential of developing within the University structures of Paris and the provinces and thus becoming integrated in the mainstream of French public teaching. Between the two stood Jacques Lacan, who promoted the idea of a predominantly medical Institute but was also inspired by the advice given by Freud in The Question of Lay Analysis.

In May 1953, shortly after the organization of Nacht's Institute was put in place, Lacan's attitude set a spark to the gunpowder. The students protested. For the most part they were senior psychiatrists and psychologists holding important posts, and they could not endure being treated as children and submitted to what they saw as the pernickety requirements of the directorate. Meetings, debates, and motions followed each other, and Jacques Lacan was unable to avoid joining in, since—as one has to remember—a significant number of the protesters were still using his couch. Others vociferously pointed to this as countertransferential acting out, and also to a scandal that was all the more shocking since Lacan was still President of the SPP.

All the same, despite promises to change his ways, Lacan was challenged, following a defiant motion against him at a meeting of full members of the SPP on 16 June 1953. He resigned from the post of President immediately. Daniel Lagache spoke next, but, in a dramatic move, read a letter of resignation signed by himself, together with Juliette Favez-Boutonier and Françoise Dolto, at the same time announcing the creation of a new institution, the "Société Française de Psychanalyse" (French Society of Psychoanalysis). Jacques Lacan, while the others wanted to take him with them, had, because of his wish not to create a split, only been warned of this proposal on the previous evening. He then also declared his resignation from the SPP. The next day a public announcement was broadcast by the new SFP, making return impossible.

The secessionists had not considered that their gesture would exclude them from an IPA, which did not recognize any but the constituent societies. Sacha Nacht and Marie Bonaparte hastened to underline this and intervened with Anna Freud, as well as the members of the Executive Committee. An inquiry that was to last more than ten years thus began, starting during the Eighteenth International Congress in London at the end of July 1953. A Committee of Enquiry was set up. This was the first, although not the last, and was composed of Phyllis Greenacre, Jeanne Lampl de Groot, Mrs Hedwig Hoffer, and Donald Winnicott.

In the document proclaiming the founding principles of the Société Française de Psychanalyse, it was claimed that there was no discord of either theory or practice between the secessionists and the original Society, a statement that permitted the irony of Jean Clavreul in 1963, in the name of the Lacanians. Nacht's authoritarianism and a difference in the conception of psychoanalytic training were denounced as the only causes of the split.

This statement, however, constituted a deceit of considerable measure, since behind the screen of arguments about his technique, Jacques Lacan still followed his own path and thought. I have already mentioned his letter of 12 October 1952 to Rudolf Loewenstein. He claimed to have found his own method of psychoanalytic research, in a contemporary study of Freud's ideas: "I believe that some things have come to maturity for me both in my experience and in my thinking." He knew himself to be superior; many pupils were to follow his teaching, and he entered several years of intense creativity that would have prodigious mobilizing power, even for those of his enemies who wished to prove their own creative capacities. Each one would have to demonstrate himself as the most complete, the most Freudian of all the Freudians.

An early example of this theoretical development was represented by the lecture that Jacques Lacan gave at the end of September 1953 on "The Function and Field of Language in Psychoanalysis". His first Public Seminar followed little more than a month later, heralding a grand weekly ceremony that was to end only around the time of his death. It was at that time held under the auspices of Professor Delay's Psychiatric Clinic and focused on "Freud's Technical Writings", as an indirect response to the attacks on Lacan's own practice. A conference on "The Real, the Symbolic and the Imaginary" was to follow, completing the early elements of the Lacanian view of psychoanalysis, which was later to become richer and more complex.

However, Lagache could barely tolerate Lacan and became more and more hostile and suspicious of his teaching, which gained greater and greater resonance among the students, the young psychiatrists, and increasingly among those Parisian intellectuals who were attracted by the seductive new elaboration of psychoanalytic theories that they could follow, week by week.

In spite of this, and alarmed like many others at the prospect of finding himself isolated in France, Jacques Lacan supported all the initiatives of the Société Française de Psychanalyse to be recognized by the IPA, without involving himself personally in the negotiations. In January 1954, the report of the Commission of Enquiry was hostile due to "inadequacy of training", claiming in its final conclusion that:

> We were unanimously against the Lagache group forming an affiliated Society of the IPA for the following reasons: a) in practical terms the Lagache Group cannot give appropriate training to the large number of students they have registered, since Dr Lagache and Dr Lacan are the only training analysts; b) more importantly, the training methods of the Lagache Group have deviated too far from the procedures of the component Societies and appear unacceptable.

From the various documents sent to them during the Summer and Autumn regarding the situation in Paris, it was known to members of the Executive that Dr Lacan had shortened the duration of an analytic session, sometimes to 15 or 20, sometimes to 25 or 30 minutes. In a private conversation, Dr Lacan had stated that he used such procedures in the framework of "une nouvelle technique", in his own words, to provoke "une rupture des resistances".[4]

June 1954 saw the inauguration of the Institut de Psychanalyse de Paris under the direction of Sacha Nacht. Ernest Jones came to bring the badge of approval of the IPA, but this was largely ignored by the French ministerial authorities.

In July 1955, during the Nineteenth International Congress in Geneva—since the life of the SFP would henceforth find itself studied during the two-year intervals separating the Congresses—a new refusal faced their request for recognition. In November, in Vienna, Jacques Lacan issued a new rallying cry, which was to become famous: "The return to Freud". The latter was indeed the forgotten man of French writers, who paraphrased more than they studied,

---

[4] A paper written by Adam Limentani, "The History of the Association Française de Psychanalyse", makes reference to some unpublished documents in the Archives of the IPA that I have not consulted.

read, or translated. It was one of the great merits of Jacques Lacan that
he demonstrated this erasure of the original Freudian text, despite the
fact that his own language began little by little to replace it.

Meanwhile, enquiries and negotiations continued. Theoretical
and clinical papers appeared from one side or the other, in the traditional *Revue Française de Psychanalyse* or in its new competitor, *La
Psychanalyse*, or, again, in such collections as "La Bibliothèque de
Psychanalyse et de Psychologie clinique" produced under the direction of Daniel Lagache with the publisher PUF, or that which Sacha
Nacht inaugurated with the same editor under the title of "La
Psychanalyse d'Aujourd'hui". After all, was it not essential to prove
to the French public as well as to the judges of the IPA that one was
providing the best training, the most serious atmosphere in which to
work?

Sacha Nacht having been elected Vice-President of the IPA at the
twentieth International Congress, which took place in Paris in 1957, it
became necessary to wait until 1959 before the Société Française de
Psychanalyse presented a new request for affiliation. Despite the request of the then Secretary of the IPA, Pearl King, information on the
SFP's activities arrived too late, and the decision was only taken by
the Executive Committee three weeks before the Twenty-First Congress in Copenhagen to reject the application once again, and to nomi-
nate a new Investigating Committee, including Paula Heimann, P.
van der Leeuw, Ilse Hellman, and Pierre Turquet, Wilhelm Solms
being added later. At the beginning of this chapter I cited the general
impression of the Secretary of the new Committee, Pierre Turquet,
following meetings with the French psychoanalysts in June 1960. In
the report he produced, Jacques Lacan was labelled "enfant terrible".
This was less sharp than Jeanne Lampl de Groot's written remark
in 1953, "*er ist brillant, intelligent, aber verrückt!*"[5] Meanwhile, all the
attacks continued to concentrate on his practice as training analyst.
That was the obstacle to recognition of the Society, while that of
Daniel Lagache and Juliette Favez-Boutonier posed no major problems.

Some of the analysts who had been students at the time of the 1953
split but who had since climbed the echelons of the hierarchy wished

---

[5] "He is brilliant, intelligent, but mad." Unpublished letter to Ruth Eissler, 20
January 1954 (Archives of the IPA)

to attempt the impossible: to negotiate the reintegration of the SFP into the heart of the IPA, and to include Lacan's training therein.[6] They hoped that he would make concessions on his methods and even on his manner with colleagues, where he did not spare his sarcasm. This was a vain hope, as Lacan would not budge an inch from his position, convinced as he was that the importance of his theoretical contributions could not be underestimated for long by the international psychoanalytic community. In other respects, there was no doubt that he relished his marginal position. He knew himself to be a thorn in the flesh and enjoyed playing skilfully with the aura that this gave him.

Among the negotiators of the new generation, three names stand out. That this union was known as "the troika" shows how much the atmosphere of the "cold war" was reflected in these skirmishes with the powerful association and its American majority.

The most prominent was Serge Leclaire, in turn Secretary and then President of the SFP; he was one of Lacan's analysands and resolved to remain loyal to him. Another was François Perrier, who, after a training analysis with Maurice Bouvet of the SPP, had done a short second analysis with Lacan. His was a curious, non-conformist mind, and his institutional career was to lead him to abandon Lacan in 1969 to found, together with Piera Aulagnier and Jean-Paul Valabrega, Le Quatrième Groupe OPLF. The third, Wladimir Granoff, had not known Lacan's couch but was intellectually seduced by his training. He was considered an astute politician and was among those who tipped the balance of events two years later.

For the moment, in 1961, it was above all the visits of the Investigating Committee that occupied centre stage: cross examinations on the length of analytical sessions, and on their frequency. In August 1961, during the Twenty-Second International Congress in Edinburgh, the Société Française de Psychanalyse withdrew its request for direct affiliation and accepted the status of a Study Group of the IPA. Pearl King wrote to Daniel Lagache on 29 September: "The Central Executive agreed to grant to the Société Française de Psychanalyse the status of Study Group of the International Psychoanalytic Association under the direct sponsorship of the Central Executive through the medium of a special Committee." This was a new form of spon-

---

[6] Elsewhere, the term "Trojan Horse" was invoked.

sorship, and she added: "I draw your attention, however, to the fact that it was agreed to accord your Group the status of Study Group of the IPA on the condition that you conform to certain Requirements. These Requirements are expressed in 19 points. . . ." To these were added at the last moment—when the French negotiators claimed they were already on the plane home—an unequivocal twentieth: "13a. *That Dr Dolto and Dr Lacan be progressively withdrawn from the training programme, no further candidates being sent to them for either training analyses or supervision of cases.*"

This was followed in 1962 by much hesitation: Serge Leclaire agreed to cross Françoise Dolto off the list, to her great indignation, but what of Lacan? How would he take it? He wished to hear nothing, mirroring the equally rigid position of the IPA.

It seemed vital to do nothing for the moment, while, on the part of the Psychoanalytical Society of Paris, Serge Lebovici finally convinced Sacha Nacht to leave the post of Director of the Psychoanalytic Institute that he had occupied for nine years. In September Marie Bonaparte died. Meanwhile, in France a series of radio broadcasts by Marthe Robert devoted to the history of psychoanalysis successfully propagated the image of the "psychoanalytical revolution".

In January 1963, the Board of the Société Française de Psychanalyse decided that for reasons of political order no measures of exclusion could be considered. Pierre Turquet had, however, produced another report pointing out the passivity of a large number of members of the Society and the stagnation of the Lacan problem. He came to a meeting in Paris, which was widely reported in an explosive account by François Perrier. The hour of decision was approaching.

Just before the Twenty-Third International Congress in Stockholm, a *"motion des motionnaires"* was put forward following a General Meeting of the Société Française de Psychanalyse on 11 July in which, once again, in spite of interminable discussion no clear position emerged. The motion proposed holding to the agreements made in Edinburgh, but also that Lacan should continue his teaching. The signatories were Piera Aulagnier (who soon retired from the group), Jean-Louis Lang, Jean Laplanche, Jean-Bertrand Pontalis, Victor Smirnoff, and Daniel Widlöcher. For the first time these analysands of Lacan thus appeared to be much more actively supporting the efforts of their seniors to reintegrate their Society within the IPA.

On 31 July the status of the previously endangered Study Group was confirmed in Stockholm, and Wladimir Granoff found himself elected "member at large". But an ultimatum followed: notification to Lacan's analysands that they must change their training analysts by the following 31 December if they wished to have their training recognized by the IPA.

Two and a half months later, on 13 October, a *"motion d'ordre"* was proposed by the Commission d'Études and Lacan's supporters lost. The motion stipulated that "From this day, Dr Jacques Lacan will no longer appear on the list of analysts entitled to perform training analyses or supervision" and was signed by Juliette Favez-Boutonier, Daniel Lagache, Wladimir Granoff and Georges Favez. The Rubicon had been crossed by a fraction of the Society.

After the Autumn Meeting and a rather stormy General Assembly, the Board of the SFP, the majority in favour of Lacan, decided on 11 November not to apply this decision. However, a new General Assembly would have to enact that decision. It would be in place on 19 November, when the previous Board would find itself disenfranchized. The President, Serge Leclaire, the vice-president, Françoise Dolto, and the Scientific Secretary, François Perrier, resigned immediately. The crisis was out in the open.

On the following day, Jacques Lacan solemnly announced that the Seminar on "Le nom du père" to be given that day, would be his last.

The following month, one of his pupils, Jean Clavreul, founded "A Group for the Study of Psychoanalysis"; the intention was to regroup those who did not accept the exclusion of Lacan (the Excommunication, as they called it) nor the composition of the new Board that clearly supported the IPA, under the Presidency of Juliette Favez-Boutonier and with the help of Daniel Lagache. The Société Française de Psychanalyse was now divided into two hostile blocks.

The beginning of 1964 was marked by the resurrection of Jacques Lacan's Seminars. They now took place in the École Normale Supérieure, since Jean Delay had felt it undesirable to continue holding them under the auspices of the Hôpital Ste-Anne. The theme of the new Seminar was "The Four Fundamental Concepts of Psychoanalysis", and this change of venue was of major importance for psychoanalysis in France, since it marked an orientation in Lacan's thinking, which was becoming more and more detached from clinical work. This meeting with the young "normaliens", including Jacques-Alain Miller, would determine the ultimate orientation of this thinking and of the Lacanian movement.

In May, the International Psychoanalytical Association recognized a new "Groupe d'Études Françaises", which was announced on 9 June. It was clear that the SFP would disappear and be replaced by another institution. Twelve days later, Jacques Lacan announced— "still alone, as I always have been in my relation to the psychoanalytic cause"—the creation of an "École Française de Psychanalyse", soon to be renamed "École Freudienne de Paris".

On 11 January 1965, the now defunct Société Française de Psychanalyse was dissolved and its property distributed between the newly created Association Psychanalytique de France (APF) and the Lacanian EFP.

Some months later, during the Business Meeting of the Twenty-Fourth International Congress in Amsterdam, and with William Gillespie's powerful support, the APF was elected as a component Society of the IPA. The second French split was complete.

The French psychoanalytic landscape was now composed of three institutions: the SPP, which was to become identified with orthodoxy and a tendency to conservatism; and, allied rather coldly with the aforementioned, but wishing to appear more liberal, more intellectual, less medical, in any case nearer to academic disciplines, and also detested by the Lacanians, the Association Psychanalytique de France; and, finally, the EFP, which owed its prodigious expansion— together with its new splits, such as that which led to the Quatrième Groupe—to Jacques Lacan, and which lasted until its final dissolution by Jacques Lacan, then himself on the brink of death.

* * *

I no longer need to emphasize that this description is drawn with too little detail to be completely accurate and that it cannot do justice to all that happened and was produced in the psychoanalytical field in France during this period, even without considering the political aspects. It is only intended to offer some reflections on the theme of "some splits in the history of the psychoanalytic movement" to an international audience, and to suggest some elements for further discussion.

Indeed, it seems that the schisms that we have looked at can be studied from multiple aspects from which I propose to select three relevant elements—*affective rupture, separation–dissidence,* and *ideological schism*—and to utilize the events recalled to illustrate them. A subtle mixture of variable proportions characterizes each split and gives us better evidence to understand their histories, and likewise to avoid confusing pseudo-psychoanalytical explanations.

Concerning *affective rupture,* one may classify the circumstances and consequences of the breaking of interpersonal relationships that occur in every such schism. Collegial and transferential allegiances are broken, previously repressed negative emotions explode, or conversely, filial submission to a Master is pushed to the extreme. Here one must find a place to trace, through time, those psychoanalytical genealogies that it is essential to take into consideration when studying the history of psychoanalysis and that allow us to understand certain mysterious or paradoxical reactions and to reconstruct the formation of a particular audience. For instance, I have suggested this clue in relation to the analysands of René Laforgue who, before the 1953 split, tightened their allegiances with the politically ruined image of their analyst and assured the SFP of a certain kind of analysand on account of their religious connections, which were essentially Catholic. The theories of Jacques Lacan, fundamentally Catholic in nature, resonated with most of them, in preference to those proposed by certain Jewish members of the SPP—a phenomenon that was just perceptible before 1953 but not actually obvious on account of the opposition of the Church to Freud's materialistic atheism. This opposition ended later, when Lacanian theories, linked with serious linguistic ideas, appeared more "scientific" to theologians as well as Marxists, who began to use Lacanian couches.

We must also review the sudden and violent end of the friendship that had appeared to link Sacha Nacht and Jacques Lacan. Could this friendship really have been deep and sincere? One may well doubt this, if one considers how few were the months that sufficed to convert it into a lasting hatred and contempt that was to last on both sides for thirty years. No doubt the unconscious ties that had existed since before the war between these two analysands of Rudolf Loewenstein can be questioned. Let us recall the scorn poured by Jacques Lacan on the American partisans of the ego psychology so supported by his old analyst, as well the late conversion of Sacha Nacht during his last meeting with Rudolph Loewenstein to the notion of an "aconflictual ego", which so astonished the participants at the Congrès des Psychanalystes de Langues Romanes in 1967. Nor should we forget the existence of the third analysand of Loewenstein, Daniel Lagache, whom we have previously noted as relatively young and less emo-

tionally implicated or apt to show his feelings, although his psychoanalytic work on jealousy certainly fails to hide those personal roots
that allow us better to understand his role in the history of the two
splits.

But it was not only the leaders who were emotionally involved,
and the effects of rupture showed themselves even at the level of
members and students, who were concerned about which orientation
to choose. Some stopped their analyses, some their supervision. Many
transference relationships were traumatically broken, with little hope
that they could be worked through in the future. Often remarked
upon, the "familial" aspect of psychoanalytical institutions became
more evident, and from the time of the International Congress in
London in 1953 the image of "divorce" was used, by Anna Freud in
particular. One can see how open the wounds remain even today in
France, and how difficult, if not impossible, it is to organize any
confrontation between the witnesses to the schisms about the events
of their past.

The factor that differentiates psychoanalytic schisms from any
others, whether political or religious, is the breaking of transference.
The shadow of the curative element is always present, with its deep
emotional and specific investments. In certain cases or at certain
phases of the analytic process, one must not generalize, the intensity
of the transference neurosis can, if it coincides with various external
events, transform the secessionist or conservative position of an analyst in his patient's eyes into an intolerable or fragmenting acting out.
Similarly, certain administrative requirements can be felt to be intrusive: can one imagine the feelings in all their transferential depths of
the analysands of Jacques Lacan during the long years of investiga-
tions, interviews, cross-examinations, and the attitudes to be taken in
public about him and his technique?

Many excessive reactions, paranoid or paranoiac attitudes, and
depressive reactions probably find their fixation point in all of this,
which was at the limit of what was analysable.

The phenomena of *separation–dissidence* have a particular hold on
the life of institutions and as such are found at the root of new administrative structures. They are integral to what is called the "psychoanalytic movement" and its history. Impassioned feelings appear
only as an undercurrent, judicial arguments seem to prevail. Nonetheless this domain bears the scars of bitter battles for power, and
thus carries intense narcissistic implications. This situation was

clearly in the foreground of the history of the schisms of 1953 and 1963, as well as during the long years between them.

The events described are characterized by the manifest concentration of the interested parties on the problems of analytic training. Was it not indeed maintained that psychoanalytic societies were created for just this—as if the discussion of ideas, practice, or the testing of new proposals were only of secondary importance?

Training analysis was at the centre of many heated disputes and was even called "pure" analysis by Jacques Lacan. "Controls", which would become "supervisions", and the tests for admission to the title "psychoanalyst" occupied many minds and filled dozens of pages of reports. Everyone proposed his or her own ideas for "the training most suitable for an analyst", to quote Freud (1927a, p. 252),[7] and selection and qualification procedures rivalled each other in subtlety. It is well known that this major preoccupation and its institutional consequences did not disappear in 1965, either in the traditional societies, where "statute reform" became the hobby-horse for internal opposition to each group, or at the École Freudienne, where the institution of "the pass" was the determining factor in the split that originated the "Quatrième Groupe OPLF" created in 1969 by Piera Aulagnier, François Perrier, and Jean-Paul Valabrega.

The "schism–dissidence" effect would also have the consequence of condemning Jacques Lacan in 1964 to assuming the position of head of his School—something he had avoided for the preceding ten years. He would come to know not only the grandeur, but also the tribulations of power games that were not only symbolic or imaginary, but would be exercised in a reality that drains both people and things.

The same period saw the rise in power of the International Psychoanalytical Association, in which Pearl King took an important part. The weight of its decisions on the standards of training analysis and supervision, the power of its "Site Visit Committees" and "Sponsoring Committees", effectively found an anchoring point in the novelty of the first schism of 1953. It should be noted that in the context of a characteristic anti-American stance among members of the French

---

[7] Cf. also the collection of articles, in French, on the history of psychoanalytic training in France, in *Revue Internationale de l'Histoire de Psychanalyse*, 2 (1989): 293–417.

left, the demands put upon Jacques Lacan by the IPA conferred upon him the aura of a revolutionary (particularly during the disturbances of May 1968) or at least a resistance fighter, with the prestige of a modern-day Robin Hood battling against Yankee Imperialism.

Nonetheless, it is ironic that the goal of the first separatists, the foundation of a "Free Institute", led to a reinforcement in the power of the Central Executive.

* * *

Underlying the other two, both *affective rupture* and *separation–dissidence*, are those phenomena that can be considered as belonging to the order of *ideological schism*: this was unlike most of the other splits that had previously torn the psychoanalytical movement apart. Because of the attempts made by the SFP at reintegration with the IPA, quarrels over teaching methods somewhat overshadowed the fractures that occurred at the level of psychoanalytical theory and practice.

Questions about new or apparently different developments made since Jacques Lacan had paved the way, the "debates" in the scholastic sense that should have followed his speech in Rome, questions about the coherence of Lacanian with Freudian theories, together with their evolution after 1939, were on the whole avoided.

With some rare exceptions, all those on the side of the IPA distanced themselves from any mention of Lacan, as if they believed that this erasure would suffice to make the man and his theories disappear. One need only open the books published by one side or the other to see how univocal they are, allusions to the work of the other side being possible only in the form of mockery. Equally, reading the minutes of the debates in the General Assemblies of the SFP one can see frequent comments concerning the absence of scientific meetings between the pupils of Lacan and the other members of the Société, each isolated in their own group and finding little of importance to say to their neighbour.

Following the pattern of the Rome Congress in 1953, during which participants from the two Societies spoke in succession without actually meeting, the Colloquium de Bonneval on "The Unconscious" showed that a contradictory and deep debate was impossible. In their contest for the "true Freud", which took centre stage, the other side could only be designated as usurper.

The expression of psychoanalytic ideas was at the same time exalted and restricted: exalted because it is so often easier to write attacking one's adversary and consciously to direct aggressive forces against a rival experienced as being in the outside world (examples from publications of both sides demonstrate this point); equally, restricted, however, since going round in circles within one's own theory and refusing to argue with the "contemptible" other side condemns one either to worn-out and mortifying repetition or to an overvaluation of originality, whatever the cost. A certain fetishization, either of analytical theory or of the spokesperson for the theory, goes hand in hand with this denial, so that the confrontation of theories loses all scientific basis and is transformed either into condemnation or overestimation, akin to the reactions of dogmatism or religious intolerance.

While there were still bridges and some more or less secret communications by means of such persons as André Green and Conrad Stein, each school separately asked themselves these questions: What does it mean to be a psychoanalyst? What circumstances allow for an analyst's development? What are the implications of a standardized training? How can a community justifiably recognize that which is transmitted not only by bookish theory, as in the academic tradition, but also by the impalpable "psychoanalytic process", which cannot be taught or known (except not always, and this is the whole problem) in any other way than during the course of a personal analysis? How, in his turn, does another individual become skilful in sharing this with his or her own patients and, later, pupils? These are questions that had never preoccupied Adler, Jung, Rank, or even Freud on the way to their discoveries, though Freud himself had some preoccupation with them while writing *The Question of Lay Analysis* (1926e), and he had also been concerned about the "wild" element among his followers.

These things are possible, provided that the transferential links developed do not imprison the protagonists in the kind of idealized relationship emphasized by so many writers as alienating in character. The essential reasons invoked by the IPA for rejecting Jacques Lacan were the absence of the analysis of the negative transference, together with the accent on seduction and the length of sessions.

Also, they are possible provided that a fragile group identity does not become established—one that is tightly turned in upon itself and that claims theoretical and clinical perfection, thus creating a paranoid block that will prevent the establishment of any relationship with the rest of the world other than on a persecutory model. Such a group will explode into a thousand pieces, should the idealized identificatory link that maintains the illusion of cohesion and coherence happen to break. When Freud died, this did not happen, but Lacan's dissolution of the École Freudienne and his own death a year later resulted in something like an explosion into many little groups.

But these phenomena are common to fields other than psychoanalysis, such as in political and religious groups and at the level of nations, though it must be emphasized that for psychoanalysts, the investment in theoretical and clinical ideas is linked specifically with the personal analysis and carries therefore a particular intensity that requires re-examination at the deepest level of the personality when serious rifts occur.

* * *

It will be realized that the three categories that I have proposed are only the preliminary spadework for those who will one day write the history of the schisms in France and their consequences for the evolution of the psychoanalytic movement and even of psychoanalysis itself, since the importance of the work and teaching of Jacques Lacan have created irreversible modifications in the theoretical as well as the practical aspects of psychoanalysis. Without doubt it is too soon to write such a history, and time must pass before the wounds begin to heal. Future generations will be able to look at what has come down to them from the traumas of their predecessors with a new eye and turn themselves to the analysis of the "identification fantasies" (Mijolla, 1987; cf. also Mijolla, 1981) that characterize their psychoanalytic genealogies in order to develop a different way of reconstructing the facts and interpreting their deep-seated motivations.

This future work will, however, not be possible unless the repression and denial that mask and distort the events of that troubled time are beaten down at the present moment. If we work patiently and consistently towards the confrontation of contradictory arguments and on those documents that bear witness to them, if we can come to make each side recognize the existence of the other, then there will be no need to resort to intellectual terrorism instead of public debate, and there can be an interdisciplinary recollection of the facts and their interpretation.

Dark zones will always exist, and the most private unconscious motives of the principal players will remain forever hidden, as they were so often to the actors themselves. But did the recognition of the "navel" of the dream prevent Freud from accomplishing his interpretive research?

A history of psychoanalysis that is less like a work of propaganda will no doubt come one day, and we must do all we can to promote its arrival without falling victim to the illusion of an ecumenical paradise. For, as long as mankind can think, there will be new theories, and thus new splits, with their procession of emotional reactions, hunger for power, and ideological certainties. That, too, is a sign of life.

Summary

The 1953 split originated from diverging concepts in French psychoanalysis, its uses and communication. Mostly as a result of sociopolitical and political circumstances after the end of the Second World War, it crystallized ideological currents that had existed since the introduction of Freudian ideas to France despite its incarnation in three men with strong personalities—Sacha Nacht, Daniel Lagache, and Jacques Lacan.

These origins gave the split both its emotional impact and its effect on the history of the French psychoanalytical movement. The events that convulsed the landscape of the French psychoanalytical movement for ten years were the creation of the Institut de Psychanalyse by the Société Psychanalytique de Paris, the creation of the Société Française de Psychanalyse, the conflicts and agreement made to obtain the recognition of the latter by the International Psychoanalytical Association, and the growing influence of the thought and teaching of Jacques Lacan, culminating in the development after 1964 of the Association Psychanalytique de France and of the École Freudienne de Paris. This was also a period of theoretical inventiveness and political vicissitudes, but we could only touch on this here.

CHAPTER TWO

The passion of history confronted with the failure of psychoanalytic historical thinking

André Green (Paris)

In one of her recent papers, Pearl King (1996) expresses both dis-appointment about the present state of affairs in psychoanalytic technique in the British Society and concern about the future. "We have lost the high ground that we once held. We are also in danger of losing Freud!" The starting point of her comments is the widespread technique of the here-and-now, which in her eyes—just as in mine—leads to an impoverishment of psychoanalytic thinking. It is not my intention to interfere in what might be called a domestic quarrel—what I can say is that it is not only in the British Society that one can deplore the loss of the high ground once held by representatives of psychoanalysis. Nor is the danger of losing Freud limited to our British colleagues.

But why should we have to worry about that? Many will observe that in other disciplines there is no concern about "losing" an ances-tor. It could be a sign of health to be freed from the weight of the past as the discipline shows signs of growth. No one can agree today with a long-standing reference to the intimate link between Freud—and his family—and psychoanalysis. If that argument could have been raised while Freud was alive against those who separated themselves from him—in fact from his fundamental hypotheses—and claimed still to be called psychoanalysts, it no longer holds, as Freud is no longer here to tell us what has the right to be included in the discipline he founded and what contradicts the principles on which it was built. But do we really need to be told? Are we not grown-up enough to make up our own minds? To rely on his writings would unhappily suggest that we are using them the same way as the Scriptures. So if we still want to quote Freud or any other psychoanalytic thinker, it is not a way of testing our faithfulness or our betrayal of his work but one of examining the ideas and concepts that are behind it in order to give our opinion about where we think the truth lies. The problem we meet here is that one can claim to possess the keys to truth and prove that others are wrong. Scientific validation does not fit the matter under discussion. The only advisable thing is to sustain one's position by giving a detailed account of the hypotheses on which the basic concepts rest and to explain their necessity theoretically and clinically, to enlighten the material studied. It is my belief that notwithstanding his own prejudices, limitations, and restricted clinical experience, Freud's hypotheses are closer to what I believe to be true, not only compared to the Kleinian views discussed by Pearl King but also to other contemporary movements in psychoanalysis, including ego psychologists, self psychologists, Lacanians, intersubjectivists, and so on.

* * *

Pearl King has become justly renowned for her work in the field of the history of psychoanalytical institutions. I consider the *Freud–Klein Controversies, 1941–1945*, which she edited with Riccardo Steiner (King & Steiner, 1991), to be, without doubt, the most important work ever achieved in the history of psychoanalysis. In this book we find collected all the aspects of the life of a psychoanalytical society during a period that was itself historically loaded: administrative and organizational matters alongside scientific discussions, considerations of training, exposure of their technique by the main teachers and theoretical leaders of the period—all those aspects of the life of a psychoanalytical society are accounted for. The personal, emotional aspects are also not forgotten. One may be tempted to evoke ironically the theologians of Byzantium discussing the sex of the angels while the invaders are at the gate of the city. Sometimes one has to remind those forgetful colleagues heated by their debates that there is a blitz outside!

Pearl King has gathered and ordered the material with all the respect due to the documents because she obviously has a passion for history. Though she is working on documents, these "memory traces" are not only objective. Agreeing with the generally accepted opinion that history is always the history of the present, the history constructed from the point of view of the present, we read these pages looking to our past as we stand anchored in the present. One should be tempted to draw a clear-cut line between the history of psychoanalysis established through the evidence of documents, well dated in the archives, having suffered neither censorship nor deformation, and the history of the analysand about which nothing is certain: memories are confused with fantasies, amnesia is responsible for a picture full of holes, in black or white necessarily submitted to interpretation and lacking validated chronological order. Even if there were a possibility of a good recording regarding the events, one would still not be able to grasp the causal mechanisms that interrelate the different themes. In fact, if all these reservations incline us to modesty, we should not idealize the task of the historian and the innocence of historical evidence. Reading the Controversies, the psychoanalyst completes the information he is given via other sources of acquaintance in the actors of the event—their whole biography before and after the period dealt with, the knowledge he acquires from their work before and after 1941–1945, their relationships with each other, and even sometimes unverified rumours that cannot be stated in the present, having to wait until the passing of a sufficient length of time uncovers what happened backstage. That allows us to read between the lines and to detect even what is unsaid in this voluminous book, in a way similar to what we infer about the psychic processes beyond what the patients say. The unsaid is supposed to complete what is missing in the text or what has not been spelled out by the different participants; moreover, today we are able to see how the unsaid structures in depth the outspoken statements.

Alongside the unsaid of the protagonists of the historical drama (nothing is missing in the plot of the Controversies, including the tragic aspect of the hatred of a daughter towards her celebrated mother, who has won, in compensation, so many other adoptive daughters), no traces can be found of what we know cannot be totally unveiled and exposed in the printed matter, just as with sexually hidden relationships. We also have to take into account not only the

influence on the reader of the unsaid, but also his unthought processes, because behind the chronology of the facts during these four
years we sense how much and how many times processes come into
play that are not identified because they are not part of the work of
the historian but, rather, belong to the psychoanalyst who because
of the circumstances is asked to keep his mouth shut. Here he is not
allowed to interpret. But as we are dealing with psychoanalytical
history, even if we can obey the strategy of silence, we can't stop
thinking and fantasizing. So the difference between the attitude of the
historian and that of a psychoanalyst is, in these circumstances, less
acute than one may think, because our psychoanalytic identity cannot
be eliminated when we write the history of psychoanalysis. We shall
have to consider this specific problem and the question of what has
become of historical thinking in psychoanalysis. These remarks are
meant to show Pearl King's great passion for history and the way she
links them with her acknowledgement of the failure of psychoanalytic
thinking.[1]

* * *

The historical method cannot do without concerns for exactness and
objectivity. No one will pretend that it can dispense with these exi-
gencies. While on the one hand we can compare the *Controversies* to a
historical work because of the editors' scrupulousness in relating the
events, on the other, because these historical events will be seen (read)
with different eyes if one is a historian or a psychoanalyst, our comparison is not entirely well founded. In the latter case, the psychoanalyst will not only compare what happened in London between 1941
and 1945 to other critical periods in the history of psychoanalysis in
Vienna, Zurich, or Paris; he will "project" on the facts his own experience and thinking about the structuring of events in an individual, as
psychoanalysis has taught him to do.

With this remark, we come back to Pearl King's paper of 1996. But
whatever agreement or disagreement I may find with the author's

---

[1] It is no wonder that Pearl King could get along in her work with a labelled
Kleinian, Riccardo Steiner, who is inhabited by a comparable passion for the
history of ideas. It is interesting that working together in harmony did not change
their basic theoretical options. Neither converted the other to their point of view; to
share a belief in the importance of history was enough.

statements, I will recall our common experience of working together in a European group of psychoanalysts, which included different members of the British Society belonging to the various subgroups that are known to be part of that analytical institution. Pearl King writes excellently: "The analytic relationship, and what happens within it, is both within Time and beyond Time. It is also out of time." Knowing her for many years, I want to say that it is not her habit to abuse capital letters when mentioning questions of theory. And she is also not the kind of colleague who expresses herself in paradoxes and metaphors. Perhaps, having reached her present age, she feels more inclined to give a free hand to a trend that she had to control in the past. One does not expect an archivist to write like this!

As for myself, I can only be happy with the statement as it brings us closer than ever. What we have seen above is that, whenever writing on the history of psychoanalysis, something of the analytic relationship remains at the back of the text related to time and also beyond time and even out of time. Because, when the matter is psychoanalysis, an orthodox point of view—that is, a style that would strictly adhere to the principles of history—is just not possible. One aspect of the history of psychoanalysis tries basically to retrace the relationships between persons whose professional activity is to evaluate the mutual effects of conscious and unconscious processes. This psychoanalytic history is itself creating its own field within the general field of history, without the possibility of avoiding a consideration of unconscious factors. Pearl King has been driven to such formulations about psychoanalysis because—as she rightly observed—in the here-and-now technique transference is equated with a relationship. What is wrong with that? History has disappeared from the experience. The relationship is entirely seen as actual experience. If the past is, in fact, not denied, it is considered to be entirely projected—that is, transmitted in totality from the earliest past—in what happens in the communication between analysand and analyst at each moment of the session. Pearl King deplores all that is forgotten with this new reductionism, listing seven items that take part in her view of the patient's past history. The problem is now twofold: the deliberate blindness and deafness of the analyst to the patient's past goes hand in hand with the deliberate ignorance of our psychoanalytic past—our heritage. If we have no heritage, we have no genitors, we have no ancestors—how could we have successors? We are self-made or made through an actual relationship by spontaneous generation.

The historian King went back to the Controversies to find a quotation for the psychoanalyst King to blame Melanie Klein. What in fact she found is a beautiful description of transference full of thoughts related to considerations of time, contradicting the actual views of some Kleinians. So one can only note that the present tendency about time in psychoanalysis raises a more complicated problem that has to be analysed.

- The here-and-now technique, as Pearl King shows, is widely applied by many of the Kleinian group, some of the Independents, and even some contemporary Freudians.

- One can also relate this confusion of transference to a relationship with other "relational" perspectives: if Fairbairn's influence has been rather limited, the present followers of intersubjectivity and all those who emphasize the "interactional" dimension of the analytic relationship as expressed in the transference are spreading.

- Thinking of the recent past, the Lacanian movement in France has progressively turned away from the historical dimension in psychoanalysis in favour of a synchronically oriented conception borrowed from the structuralistic movement in other fields, just as, in the case of Melanie Klein, the followers of Lacan went far beyond what he indicated as a possible orientation. In fact, Lacan criticized essentially the oversimplification of the current conception of time determined by the genetic perspective.

- Even for those who remained attached to the importance of time, Freud's views were oversimplified. His complex theory of time was progressively reduced to the so-called "genetic point of view" that Hartmann added (with the structural one) to the three classical points of view of Freud's metapsychology. Freud's conception of "Constructions in Analysis" (1937d) was replaced by the concern with reconstructions. The validity of psychoanalytic reconstruction was to be found in child and infant observation.

- In the present status of the psychoanalytic movement, a new tendency put forward by the leader of infant research has the goal of testing psychoanalytical hypotheses—in fact, in building a new psychoanalytical theory, scientifically grounded through the use of objective method. Criticisms about Freud's metapsychology have led to a wide movement of rejection.

So we can answer Pearl King, who asks: "What happened to psychoanalysis in the British Society?" with another question: "What happened to psychoanalysis throughout almost all the world on the topic of history ?" To this extension of the question, I dare to answer: *"a failure of psychoanalytical historical thinking"*.

In mixing up the transference with a relationship, as some analysts do, we can see that the confusion lies in the fact that *the end product is taken for the product itself*—therefore the illusion. Working on the process of transference while there is no elaboration of what is transference is self-evident and goes without saying. Comparably, but in the opposite direction, when Bowlby wanted to build a new psychoanalytic theory that would be more scientific on the basis of attachment theory, *he confounded the starting observable point of view with the process described in the psychoanalytic theory of development*. It seems that what is unbearable is that the process could have sources that escape our thinking and involve aspects that cannot be observed. Bion would surely say that analysts have lost their *negative capability*.

To equate relationship and transference, one needs to explain what is transferred. This calls for several answers: "What is the material that lends itself to the operation by which it is transferred?" "What are the fields in which the above material circulated?" "How do they differ?" "By what means is the material displaced from one field to another?" "Under what pressure?" "What is the relationship of the material that is moved on to what is already present in psychic activity?" Moreover: "What is the relationship of the less available material to consciousness, more or less deeply hidden, to memory conscious and unconscious, and what is its relationship to the past?" Finally: "If it is so, through what effect does the material unavailable to consciousness change its former condition and take another appearance, invading more or less easily, more or less violently, the field of consciousness?" "How does it address the analyst?" "Why him?"

Freud and Pearl King take the trouble to answer all these questions. The here-and-now partisans will probably respond that these matters are already settled and that our general agreement needs no further comments. *This is what I am not at all sure about*.

It is not enough to express a general dissent about drive theory and to give one's preference for object relations theory. One has to be aware that all the questions raised cannot be answered by object relations theory, nor by any other, except by drive theory and by it alone.

If the here-and-now has been preferred to the classical technique, it was with an affirmation that did not even need to explain why we should be abandoning the classical technique, except that the latter was supposed to divert the patient from the actual present relationship. No alternative theory of the relation between past and present was presented. One objection, at least, should be considered, analysed, and answered: the possible effect of suggestion in the transference. What happens if the patient is not given the opportunity of breathing in his psychic space in moving from what is "here" (in the session) to what is "there" (outside the session: over there and related to once upon a time), alternating moments of deep immersion in the transference and moments of retreat. To say that these are only resistances is to express the wish to maintain the patient in a state close to hypnosis, refusing him the possibility of considering what happens to him from different angles. To transfer is to convey, to remove, to hand over *from* person or place *to* another. Winnicott, describing the transitional object, says that it is the *journey* from the internal world to reality. The fact that it is named transitional gives it its specificity; it no longer belongs to its location of departure though it has not yet reached its point of arrival. It is not improbable to think that the route is sprinkled by moves to and fro, between past and present, in and out.

If we have to go back to Freud's conception of time, we realize that much of what it includes has fallen into oblivion. One can notice that up till now there is not one single work in the psychoanalytic literature that will try to give a full account of it. Time is the most neglected concept of Freudian theory in contemporary psychoanalysis. I have personally counted at least ten items that are directly related to it. Freud himself never tried to assemble them for an articulated exposition. It is out of the question to develop all the implications of such a conception or even to comment on them, but only to list what belongs to that category of the past that has disappeared in some techniques.

1. The development of libido.
2. The bi-directional (progressive and regressive) characteristic of some processes in the dream work, which generalizes the role of (topographic) regression.
3. Repression (with its consequence for infantile amnesia).
4. Deferred action [*Nachträglichkeit*].

5.   The timelessness of the unconscious.

6.   Primal fantasies as organizers of psychic experiences.

7.   Repetition as a substitute for remembering (repetition compulsion).

8.   Forces of destiny (as a function of the superego).

9.   Psychic features as expressions of non-memorable events (hallucinations considered as equivalent to reminiscences of very early traumas).

10. Historical truth mixing an indiscernible return of truth though deformed and not recognizable as to its links with the past.

The list is probably not exhaustive. I am sure a thorough study may find others. Some of these aspects can easily be agreed upon because any psychoanalyst will meet them while practising psychoanalysis. Some others fell into oblivion (deferred action), though they also are clinically evident and need no prior theoretical agreement. They only require a bit of sophistication in the analyst's thinking and a reminder of its importance. Rereading the case of the Wolf Man will make it as plain as the nose on your face. Others need to be in agreement with Freud's hypotheses, as in the case of the debatable phylogenetic origins of primal fantasies. But it is not necessary to admit the phylogenetic origin Freud assigned to them in order to accept their organizing function. Others also may receive alternative explanations to understand how they are related to the past.

One will observe that this list of items is extremely difficult to articulate in a unified conception. Also, it is not so simple to handle and to think about when one accounts for psychoanalytic experience. Finally, Freud's conception of time includes a certain number of hypotheses. When we try to sort out the events related during a transference process, we realize that our understanding of the case is not really enlightened by the chronological order in which they happen. Even Freud succumbed to the temptation to think that a clarification may result from that orderliness. But he did so, for instance, in the Wolf Man's case because he was confronted with a very difficult problem: the dating of the primal scene. We should remember that, at the same time, he asked himself what the nature of the event was: a real and full experience the patient witnessed as a child? When? At 18 months? At X years + 18 months? Or was it a fantasy built on a trivial observation (coitus between animals), which triggered early impressions, suggesting a reactivation of memory traces in that new context? We have already noticed that it is in this same text that Freud gives full consideration to this mechanism of afterwardness. In other terms, it is wrong to consider that the trauma is directly connected to an event; it is more probably due to its reappearance in a new context that adds some supplement to its meaning that was not present in earlier evocations and uncovers, by association, other meanings in it, as if its connections with other unconscious fantasies increase its traumatic potential.

This favours a *network conception* of key organizers reverberating, more than a direct, linear causality. It is evident that Freud's conceptions of time compel us to give up our traditional views borrowed from philosophy, which apply to our most deeply anchored concepts that are necessary to our conscious thinking, to which the awareness of time is associated. *All the alternatives to Freud's open and non-unified conception of time have only changed the contents that are related to this experience and kept the mode of thinking of secondary processes of traditional theory.* The here-and-now technique has, in addition, reduced the time of the experience to the indicative present, using only two of the three persons of conjugation: I and you. Moreover, as Pearl King observes, the question that has to be raised from this point of view has become: "What is the patient *doing* to you now?" Could that be just a way of speaking? I am afraid that this commonly adopted expression indicates *that the model of action has replaced Freud's model of representation*, which is implicit in Pearl King's formulation: "Who do you think you are in the transference?" Even in the contemporary alternatives to Freud's concept of time, as in intersubjectivity, we find the same reference to action—in the form of interaction. It is not an oversimplification at the expense of thinking to elaborate a less complicated conception of time. This is a new consequence of the pragmatic model used in linguistics and psychology. Now we understand Pearl King's statement that the analytic relationship is both within Time and beyond Time, and even out of Time. Beyond Time is a reference to the timelessness of the unconscious, just as out of Time can be related to repetition compulsion.

If one can be satisfied only with the oversimplification—which is in fact less an explanation than an acknowledgement of a failure to think—we have to find the reasons for that change. Pearl King mentions a 1942 paper by Marjorie Brierley asking the question: "Is a theory of mental development in terms of infantile object relationship compatible with a theory in terms of instinct vicissitudes?" Contrary to her forerunner, who gave an affirmative response, she concludes that the two theories have not proved compatible, the theory of object relationship having replaced drive theory. To come back again to Melanie Klein, one has to note that she was not entirely responsible for that substitution. In her work she continues to make use of the term "instinct", though it is true that it occupies a smaller part in her later work than at the beginning. Still, it is mainly during the development of the Kleinian movement that instinct theory was progressively superseded by object relations.

* * *

No psychoanalyst will pretend that the past of the patient does not play a major role in the clinical picture that has made him wish to change his situation and seek for help. The actual questions then becomes: "Under what form does the past appear in the clinical picture?" "What is the meaning of the various expressions of the past in the clinical material?" "How should we handle them in the transference?" And, finally: "What kind of interpretations are necessary to overcome the burden of the past on the patient?"

"Under what form does the past of the patient appear in the clinical picture?" All over Freud's work, he has wondered about the relationship of memory to psychic activity, which includes disguised forms of memories. One thing is certain: the relationship between conscious memories and the past is only the visible part of the iceberg. We have to remind ourselves of the existence of screen memories, which mix up memories of different periods of the past reorganized for the circumstance in a new creation. We can think of the comparison between this reshaping of different pieces and the secondary revision of the dream, which proceeds to a similar superficial unification. The relationship between fantasies and memories sometimes does not allow a clear-cut distinction. Dreams can carry unconscious memories, and, to end with, acting out may be a way of remembering. Needless to say, the historical dimension of transference, with its repetition of the past which comes to life again in the analytic situation, is the most important one, even if transference also includes other aspects. There is also room in it for what is new, what has never

happened before. Therefore it is impossible to include all these different sorts of expression of the past in the so-called here-and-now strategy, because this overlooks the patient's working through about his
time processes and towards his personal past.

*"What is the meaning of the various expressions of the past in the clinical
material?"*   These various expressions are translations of the relationship of the ego's patient to the traces of his past according to
their location in consciousness and/or their relationship to his unconscious. In this last instance we will have to distinguish between
unconscious representations and unconscious affects, with their corresponding characteristics: repression, condensation, displacement,
unbound energy, deformation of contents, according to psychic reality, and so on. Sometimes the past will express itself through a
stronger disguise because of its belonging to the id: repetition compulsion, hallucinatory features, actings out, somatic symptoms. It is
obvious that these various expressions are linked to more or less early
fixations, more or less regressed states, more or less resistance to
insight. To blur the differences in a here-and-now understanding
means to confuse deliberately all structural levels in a levelling-down
way, on the pretext of wanting to reach the earliest. This is an illusion
that does not consider the possibility of the influence of the later
stages of evolution in the material, all of them being considered as
defences that can be neglected in order to focus our attention on the
more "primitive". This does not pay justice to the architecture of the
psychic apparatus.

"How should we handle them in the transference?"   It follows from the
preceding remarks that the different expressions of the past are linked
to different degrees of resistance. The question is whether the analyst's task is to ignore resistance and use interpretations as weapons
to hit the so-called "deepest" layers of the patient's mind, which are
also supposed to represent the oldest relationships, or to proceed
from level to level, from surface to depth, to have a chance to modify
the patient's freedom and help the ego of the patient to master the
most rebellious features of his mind. It has already been argued that it
was a naive belief to think that the older and deeper layers of the
mind can appear as such, intact, without being reorganized during
their passage from depth to surface by other less old and more superficial layers. The role of the pre-conscious is here predominant as a

zone of exchanges and negotiations between the unconscious and the conscious. One must also remember that it is not a one-way trip, once and for all, but a kind of journey through different countries, including several customs passages where clandestine travellers try many times to cross the border and are rejected once they have been identified, until they succeed in getting into the country where they wish to go without being arrested. Moreover, when the analyst has to face a negative therapeutic reaction with strong masochistic tendencies, will he/she favour a wrestling match with the patient? If in all cases we have to endure this painful type of object relationship, what will be the attitude of the analyst? Will it be wise to accept the patient's closure in the here-and-now, as it is the patient's wish to deny that his present reactions are repetitions of a past relationship? Is it not preferable to establish the actual relationship in the diversity of different registers, leaning on various levels of awareness, dealing with various periods of his history as constructed by the transference?

"What kind of interpretations are necessary to overcome the burden of the past on the patient?"   There is a common agreement in certain circles that interpretations should only be transference interpretations in the same view of the here-and-now. Exclusive transference interpretations have many disadvantages.

- They favour the analyst's impingement on the patient, repeating a traumatic object relationship and reinforcing the defences of the patient against it, instead of enabling the analyst to analyse them.

- They restrict the freedom of thought of the patient, who has the feeling that he has to comply with the analyst's view of the situation.

- They appear to be a return of suggestion in the transference, as if the analyst is inviting the patient to look at the productions of his own mind with the same glasses as those of the analyst. This, unfortunately, resembles the behaviour of some mothers of psychotic patients, which, in the best outcomes, generate false selves. In training, false analytic selves happen also to exist, unfortunately.

- They prevent the progressive integrations of the patient's insight through the experience *outside the cure*, in the absence of the analyst's pressure.

- They help the patient to consider his own material from different "vertices" or, more simply, angles.

In the end, all these disadvantages combine to reduce the complexity of the mind, the analysand being trained by the analyst to consider his own productions in only one way—that is, in thinking.

Do these remarks undervalue the role of the object, in practice and in theory? Not in our view. The object, during development, is the greater integrator of time experience for the child. It helps the child to build his own time, necessarily split between his subjective time and the objectively perceived one, according to the distinction proposed by Winnicott. But this influence of the object cannot be substituted for the role of the drives without which it is impossible to conceive what is the dynamic source and the motor of psychic development. Instead of opposing drive to object, one should in fact accept their dual polarity and intercourse. Neither model—drive theory or object relations theory—is satisfactory. The answer seems to consider *the couple of drive and object exchanges* as giving birth to psychic activity. We cannot give a detailed description of the fecundity of this hypothesis within these space limitations. The aim of this paper was mainly to question the exactness and usefulness of the widely accepted here-and-now technique and to restore psychoanalytic historical thinking.

* * *

How to conclude? Freud's teaching—which has not to be considered as the teaching of the Law, but which we still have to question, *because it is not certain that we have grasped all its implications up to now*—reflects the development during his forty years of work and the evolution of his thoughts about time. It amply demonstrates that we cannot be satisfied with a simplification of the conception of time processes in psychoanalytic theory and practice. These processes may be more difficult to think about, to understand, to use in clinical practice, and to handle in the countertransference. But, as Freud says, "there is no help for it". The real choice is between taking the easy way of schematization, applying recipes for the conduct of the analysis and making our listening and interpretations uniform, or to accept the difficulties of hypercomplexity, the uncertainties of our understanding, the trial and error of our interpretations, and the hazards of the psychoanalytic adventure. After all, this is what Bion referred to in recommending, after Keats, *negative capability*.

CHAPTER THREE

The young R. D. Laing: a personal memoir and some hypotheses

James Hood (London)

A n earlier version of this contribution was presented to the 1952 Club, of which Pearl King, Charles Rycroft, Armstrong Harris, and Masud Khan were founder members. In the discussion, Pearl said that she always had a soft spot for "Ronnie", whom she had taught during his psychoanalytic training with the British Society from 1956 to 1960. She reported that Laing, whose candidature for election to associate membership aroused controversy, never missed any of her seminars (personal communication).

My chapter is part of a larger project, a work-in-progress that may culminate in a book. I submit it in warm appreciation of Pearl's continuing contribution through the Archives Committee, and elsewhere, to the history of the British Psychoanalytical Society.

I am writing a memoir of Laing while my memory is still fresh enough to do so. I do this because I reckon Laing is likely to be important enough in a future scheme of things to stimulate scholars and others to want to know what he was like when young. This is especially so as I regard Ronald Laing one of the three most talented

---

A first version of this chapter was presented at the 1952 Club, May 1996.

and probably the most intelligent and entertaining of all the men I have ever met and come to know well in my lifetime.

The title suggested for my memoir proper is "Dividing R. D. Laing and Friends: An Inquisitive Recall". I mention this because I am particularly keen to discuss the significance for Laing of the accidental death in January 1959 of the person whom he had always regarded as his best friend—Douglas Hutchison. Douglas was killed while climbing in Scotland with a party of which I was a member. At the time Ronald appeared devastated, so torn with grief and disbelief that he was, as far as I can recall, unable to make any contact with me at the funeral.

When Laing himself died of natural causes in August 1989, I wrote an obituary notice for *The Independent* newspaper. An extract from this serves as introduction to what I have written.

> The R. D. Laing whom I knew well, and sometimes intimately, in his best years, as medical student and mountaineer, was a generous friend and a private rather than a public person. We were contemporaries at Glasgow University, and afterwards as psychoanalysts in training in London. Our ways did not diverge until the mid-1960s, when Laing was living in Kingsley Hall in East London, the first home opened by the Philadelphia Association, while his first marriage was falling apart. It was, I think, one of the more foolish aspects of this enterprise that staff members were expected to devote themselves entirely to it, with the consequence that their wives and children were in effect abandoned.
>
> To his medical peer group in Glasgow Laing showed himself to be an extraordinarily gifted musician, scholar and discussant. He formed a Socratic Group. He introduced us to psychoanalysis. In a population still heavily influenced by puritan values, and by highly respectable civic expectations, his behavioural example and the range of his mind were exhilarating. The serious core to his thinking, and his originality, were already evident when he qualified in medicine in 1951. When I knew Laing in London in 1959, he still had a strong sense of his Glasgow connection, and gave full credit to his mentors there, especially to Professor T. Ferguson Rodger. He told me that it was Rodger's example that made him determined to make good use of the copious clinical material and notes that he had accumulated in psychiatric practice before he was thirty. In the intervening years he had worked with tremendous energy and an inspiring vision on behalf of incarcerated mentally ill people.

That Laing lost his cool in North America and in my opinion never fully overcame the public versus private identity crisis of his mid-thirties should not be allowed to detract from the importance of his contribution to society, and to literature.

How my life overlapped with Laing's

R. D. Laing was 34 when *The Divided Self,* which is widely regarded as his best book, was published in 1961.

Laing had qualified, or was on the point of qualifying, as a psychoanalyst. His training analyst was Charles Rycroft, his supervisors Marion Milner and Donald Winnicott. Laing had begun private practice and was still working in research under the auspices of the Tavistock Institute, but he was shortly to achieve fame as co-founder of the Kingsley Hall experiment. I had left Glasgow in 1959 to begin my psychoanalytical training in London, and, once I had set up house with my wife Catriona and our two small children early in 1960, we got together with Ronald and his wife Anne, whom he had married in 1952.

Until this point our medical and post-graduate training had followed similar lines, with this difference—namely, that whereas Ronald went straight into psychiatry when he was called up for two years' National Service in the Royal Army Medical Corps in 1951 and then continued in his chosen speciality, I had spent five years in general practice, including Army Service, before opting for psychiatry. In Glasgow, where we both worked as junior psychiatrists, there was already a well-established interest in psychoanalytic ideas and practice, mediated by Professor Isaac Sclare, Dr Angus MacNiven, Dr James Halliday, and Dr Fred Stone, among others. Dr Tom Freeman, a psychoanalyst who supervised us as trainees, was an NHS consultant, dividing his time between the Landsdowne Clinic of Psychotherapy (founded in 1936), which he directed, and Glasgow Royal Mental Hospital. Fergus Rodger, who was building up the new University Department of Psychological Medicine, was a former colleague of Dr J. D. Sutherland in Scotland. With Bowlby, Bion, and others, as is well known, they had played a major part in the development of selection methods and in rehabilitation during the Second World War. Rodger was sympathetic to psychoanalysis. Laing and I, with Douglas Hutchison and David Sherret, were in fact part of the Scottish

Diaspora—that steady trickle or stream of Scots psychiatrists who came to London to undergo psychoanalytical training throughout the late 1940s, the 1950s, and the early 1960s.

I give this brief outline in order to avoid the confusion that could arise as my narrative, moving to and fro across a span of twenty years, is not strictly chronological.

First impressions

Ronald accompanied Donald Hutchison to a mountaineering club meeting at Glen Nevis Youth Hostel, near Fort William, in December 1946. In a photograph in my possession taken on the freezing summit of Sgurr a Mhaim, Laing, like most of us, is wearing a knitted Balaclava cap or helmet (supplied by my father's knitwear firm?). His is pulled down to cover his face, a small aperture exposing only his eyes and nose.

As a third-year medical student, beginning work in wards and outpatient clinics, I had joined the university mountaineering club (known as GUM Club) in November 1946. Laing and the other club member medics who were becoming my friends were in the year behind mine, reading Anatomy and Physiology.

A group photograph taken on 25 January 1947 shows a clean-shaven, slightly chubby-faced Laing with a thick mop of black hair. Is he sporting a wig? He is wearing climbing britches, cotton jacket, and bow-tie and carries a bowler hat and cane. Charlie Chaplin? Another newspaper photograph of the same period shows Laing, similarly attired (but wearing his bowler hat), with a group of "mountaineers" leading a goat supposedly captured on Mount Everest. Like others present, all members of GUM Club or associates, he is playing his part in the culminating events of the Rag or Charities week. Just prior to the creation of the National Health Service, thirty thousand pounds is collected, or extorted, from a more-or-less willing Glasgow population in the course of five or six days. On the Saturday most of the student population of about seven thousand is let loose upon the city streets. Tramcars are held up, raiding gangs invade offices and factories—in these days there were factories—groups of girls are held to ransom, a hilariously good time is had by all—or most—participants. I tend to remember Ronald in these early appearances as an actor, but especially as some combination of Groucho and Chico Marx. He was an outrageously outspoken, mischievous, and funny man, and he played piano like an angel.

In the Men's Student Union coffee-room after lunch Ronald was frequently to be found with a crowd of admiring listeners around him. He would usually start with Mozart or Chopin, and we would be impressed by his elegant classical renderings; but it was his jazz Blues and Boogie-Woogie playing that had us enthralled. Ronald apparently improvised and/or played by ear or from memory; I never saw him use sheet music.

As he played jazz, he would hum, tap his feet, sing snatches of song, and put on an act, swaying from side to side, rolling his eyes so as to show the white of them, and throwing his head back in exuberant gestures. Images of the great mainly black musicians such as Teddy Wilson, Fats Waller, and Jelly Roll Morton, popular among those of us who listened to late-night record programmes, came readily to mind. Mutual appreciation of music became a point of contact between us, and much later it was Ronald who introduced me to Dizzy Gillespie's New WAVE!! (Jazz Bossa Nova) disc 1963. It was a pointed gesture from Ronald because we were no longer close, and I think he was trying to make amends to me for his withdrawal and for the fact that his extramarital "careless love"—one of the songs on the disc—was meanwhile breaking up his first marriage to Anne Laing, whom both my wife Catriona and I myself liked very much. The coincidence of this title's appearance on the disc would have amused Ronald, because he had a coy side to him. Perhaps he felt that as one of his loyal friends over many years, I ought to understand that he had a mistress. I didn't at the time.

Laing's speaking voice, with his rich educated Glasgow accent, showed a remarkable range of pitch and timbre, bringing to mind highly esteemed preachers of the Protestant faith whom I had heard, and sometimes admired, in my early to mid adolescence. The trick was to emphasize the high notes, perhaps as a means of keeping a restive, mainly young audience wide awake.

Ronald Laing's everyday self-presentation was modest, and he was neither shy nor unduly loquacious. He was always willing to listen to what the other person had to say. When engaged with a person or subject that interested him, he became animated, persistently thoughtful, and probing.

In argument, in which he excelled, he had a habit of looking intently, from various angles, not always eye to eye—as if, like a boxer, he were looking for his opponent's weak spots. Sometimes in conversation he would look away altogether, as if to find time and space in which to gather up his thoughts and perhaps also to save himself from embarrassment as he separated himself out from the other person with whom he had been in intimate empathic contact. When roused to feeling, he could give vent to the most passionate utterances. He was capable of being much more articulate and linguistically inventive than the average Glasgow medical student and was, I believe, markedly superior in this respect even to the best of them.

R.D.L. drunk or R.D.L. sober

Ronald told us that he had been drinking—certainly drinking by his account more heavily than any of the GUM Club Set—from the age of 18 onwards. I was reading *Materia medica/pharmacology* and seeing gravely ill men with cirrhosis of the liver in the wards. In conversation, we assumed that at this rate Ronald could be a confirmed alcoholic by 30 and even dead by his forties. But there was no argument or disagreement. Ronald went his own way, and if we were somewhat reluctant to enter the Glasgow pub scene, Ronald found congenial drinking company outside the University. Some of us, Mike Scott and Norman Todd for example, were emulous, but none of us could match Ronald in his capacity to imbibe alcohol and remain in full command of his mental faculties. Perhaps habituation played a part, but we already suspected that he had an exceptionally powerful and commanding intelligence, and that this helped.

An example: London, May 1958

I had come south at Douglas Hutchison's invitation to see for myself about psychoanalytic training and to meet him, Ronald, and other staff in the Tavistock Clinic setting. Joe Schorstein, Ronald's friend and mentor, was staying in the Cumberland Hotel, Marble Arch. The four of us went for an evening meal in Ronald's car, to Knightsbridge, and ended up very merry, having had a good deal to drink. Leaving the restaurant by way of Hyde Park Corner, Joe Schorstein, being only slightly more sober than the rest of us, offered to drive as far as his hotel. As we were rounding Marble Arch, we were stopped by motor-cycle policemen. Ronald immediately jumped out of the car and took charge, explaining to the police how his distinguished guest from Scotland etc. was unfamiliar with London traffic conditions, lane discipline—and so on. Douglas and I cowered in the back seat. It was a small car; we were still rather in awe of the Metropolitan police and amazed at Ronald's bravado. In a minute or two we were waved on, to explode into relieved laughter, having half expected to see one or more of us spending a night in the police cells.

The GUM Club Set

The groups that congregated at various Youth Hostels and other climbing bases in the North and West Highlands of Scotland in the mid to late 1940s often included R. D. Laing. His most constant com-panion then, and also later, until his death in a mountaineering acci-dent in 1959, was Douglas Hutchison. Other climbing members of Laing's set at university were Mike Scott and Norman Todd, medical student contemporaries. Soon to join in were Bill Donaldson, a math-ematician, Robin T., an engineering student, and Stanley Stewart, studying law.

Mountaineering Club meets provided a venue to which Laing could bring his friends from outside the University. A familiar pattern was that keen mountaineers would set off for the Highlands by bus on a Friday evening. On the Saturday Ronald would arrive as a passen-ger on Johnny Duffy's motorbike, or, following a successful hitchhik-ing trip, with one or more of his public house familiars. Duffy was one, Joe Keegan another, and Donaldson, I know, liked to join them. I think it amused Ronald to see his working-class friends played off against what he felt was the (puritanical) bourgeoisie element, but more usually harmony prevailed and strong, only sometimes discord-ant voices were added to the customary evening singsong. It was refreshing, too, to hear their renderings of traditional bothie ballads. Ronald probably knew many of these already because his father, like Robert Burns's, was a native of the north-east lowlands of Scotland, which was the main source of the best of the bothie ballads, for example "The Ball of Kirriemuir".

Douglas Hutchison

Douglas, known as Hutch, was, like Ronald, the only son of lower-middle-class parents and a product of one of the best Greater Glasgow Schools, Paisley Grammar. Lightly built, of average height, with above-average good looks, he was strong, agile, and extremely well balanced in his physical make-up. He was soon to become an outstanding mountaineer. He had a modest, engaging personality: trustworthy, thoughtful, and prudent, he would carefully study the available options on a climbing expedition and then come up with the ideal, challenging solution. In this respect he was a born leader—enthusiastic, but not to the point of foolhardiness, inspiring, thoroughly reliable, but never dull. I was very fond of him, and he became one of my three or four best friends at University and afterwards. In 1948 we made the first of several climbing trips to the Alps together, visited Annecy at Marcelle Vincent's invitation, and saw Paris for the first time.

Douglas liked to keep himself at a peak of physical condition and consequently tended to eschew alcoholic beverages. He was less prurient and more innocent than Laing, and I think his cool head exerted a restraining influence on Ronald's, which Ronald appreciated. Certainly he was and remained, as long as he lived, Ronald's soulmate and primary male confidant.

The Glasgow Men's Student Union

In this connection my diaries record fellow year members David Dick and Hugh McBryde alluding somewhat pedantically and publicly to the morals of the Socratic Club leader, Ronald Laing. Was it his intemperance that they were referring to? I do not know, and I said nothing. David, a professed Christian, was a friend of mine, and besides, I was already party to the intriguing information that Ronald was experienced in the realm of relationships—in the modern usage of this term—well before he came up to University.

He had told us that he had seduced (or been seduced by) one of his music teachers when he was 16 years old. This always seemed to me to be quite possible, because he was so enormously charming and, at least musically, talented, besides being intensely curious about other people's sexual endowments. Early heterosexual relations would fit in, both with my observation then that Ronald seemed, somehow, always to have a man's head on boyish shoulders, and later, with his subsequent sexual behaviour.

At the same time, I think that part of the attraction of his working-class mates to Ronald was, perhaps, that they, and certainly Johnny Duffy, were setting a reassuring example in this sphere, which was more challenging, and obvious, than that of the GUM Club Set. Johnny Duffy was certainly an indefatigable womanizer.

Carousing together

On Friday 10 December 1949, the day on which I learned that I had passed my medical Finals, I dined out with Douglas Hutchison, Norman Todd, Ronald Laing, and David Sherret. All five of us were to become psychiatrists, though we didn't know it at the time. The company was excellent, "the mirth and fun grew fast and furious" (Robert Burns, *Tam O'Shanter*). We went on afterwards to a Veterinary College dance.

"A man's a man for a' that, for a' that, and a' that"

"The mirth and fun grew fast and furious"

"Perhaps it may turn out a sang
  Perhaps a sermon"

[All Robert Burns]

My considered opinion is that lowland Scots historical traditions were an all-important source of Laing's intense emotionality and defiantly individual stance among his elders and his English-speaking and North American public. He spoke and sang in the Anglo Scots and vernacular language and traditions, which found their paramount expression in the poetry and in the original and collected songs of Robert Burns. In a childhood and adolescent milieu characterized by strongly moral Presbyterian religion, Burns's celebratory alcoholic indulgence, anger at man's inhumanity to man, ambivalent conflicted attitude to women, preference for mocking satirical or bawdy humour, and hatred of prissy genteel and "holier than thou" attitudes were exemplary. Growing up in the southwest of Scotland, we were taught from an early age—say, 6 or 7—Scots not English history and to admire Burns along with William Wallace, Robert the Bruce, and Mary Queen of Scots. This is just an example to emphasize my point. And Burns, not so long dead in the popular imagination, was and is continually celebrated as the great Scots hero.

The substance and evolution of Laing's writing: a partial account

Laing's writing evolved in such a way that *The Divided Self* (1961a) was and remains distinguished from all his other books with regard to the following:

1. The clinical illustrations on which Laing's argument are founded resulted from his own observations and notes. These demonstrate his outstanding capacities in interviewing—that is to say, his clinical skill, empathy, insightful understanding, and judgement.

2. Laing's argument throughout is sustained and gains force from these illustrations.

3. Individuals, lay or professional, empathize with the persons or patients described by Laing, so that, given a voice, as it were by Laing, they speak for themselves. Laing did not invent them, but his intervention had given meaning to their utterances.

The model is medical, psychiatric, or psychotherapeutic: like sociological works, it describes and denotes.

The clinical observations took place and the writing was done in Glasgow. At the time of writing, Laing was still essentially unknown to a wider public. He was also working in a familiar and supportive human context. This included the two persons whom Laing regarded as his chief mentors—the "astonishing" Joseph Schorstein, scholar and brain surgeon, and the extraordinary scholar, sage, and psychotherapist, Karl Abenheimer. Also, Douglas Hutchison was around.

I consider that the publication of *The Divided Self* marked an important turning point in British psychiatry and especially social and psychiatric nursing care. It did so largely because Laing was able to collate, digest, synthesize, and crystallize ideas that were already current or latent in continental Europe and North America. Laing's originality lay in his power to complete the task and in his capacity to present the ideas that had by then become his, with clinical illustrations, in such a way that a very large number of people were persuaded, and continue to be persuaded, that he was right.

I will quickly pass over Laing's second book, *Self and Others*, published in 1961 and his next, *Sanity, Madness and the Family* (1988), co-authored by Aaron Esterson, who did most of the interviewing. The planned sequel on "normal" families never appeared, giving the scientific psychiatric establishment, followed by many of the more orthodox psychiatrists in the United Kingdom, an opportunity to debunk Laing, using the limited evidence of *The Politics of Experience and the Bird of Paradise* (1967). Laing's best-selling book along with *The Divided Self*—it had already sold 400,000 copies by 1971—comes into quite a different category. The medical model is completely overthrown. Not conceived as a book but in effect a compilation of speeches and articles, it is literature nevertheless—that is to say, its language "evokes and values, strategically using its inbuilt ambiguities not to give a neutral denotation of the exact universe but to persuade men into a fictive or verbally creative universe" (Malcolm Bradbury). A well-known example: "If I could turn you on, if I could drive you out of your wretched mind, if I could tell you, I would let you know." Another: "The fibrillating heartland of senescent capitalism." Alan Tyson uses the word "dithy-rambic" (from dithyramb, an ancient Greek hymn sung in honour of Dionysus), meaning rapturous, wild, and boisterous, to sum up the prevailing mood of the book.

At the time of writing, 1964, Laing was, as his son Adrian puts it, "exploding on to the popular scene". The style of the book is rhetorical, the language that of hyperbole, mythomania, poetry, and polemic. Malcolm Bowie's phrase, "The glorious human impulse to make fictions", comes to mind.

The book is highly inventive, occasionally very amusing—if one can understand the bawdy Glasgow humour and, very much, Ronald. It is seriously constructed to persuade—and it worked. Laing became the guru of the hour and (among a very substantial population both in Britain and in North America) almost of the decade. A climate of opinion came into being that was closely identified with the writing and person of R. D. Laing.

The change in Laing's output, behaviour, and public standing over five or six years was dramatic. He had substantially left behind his more conventionally rooted colleagues and almost fully engaged in the "pop" and post-modern cultural scene of the late 1960s.

Observations of Ronald at work

In the early 1960s I was a member of one of the working parties that met regularly at Laing's West Hampstead house on Sunday afternoons. Other members were David Sherret, Aaron Esterson, and David Cooper. The work in progress was the next book, to be published under the title of *Reason and Violence* (1964), a study of Sartre. Ronald always had coffee, usually cold coffee, by his side. He kept a jug on the piano. He and David Cooper were the leading spirits of this enterprise. Esterson was argumentative. Usually Ronald kept his cool very well; he was like cold steel, but not a well-tempered steel. I couldn't always keep up with the pace. Sometimes I felt uncomfortable because of the high tension and what seemed to me to be excessive mentation. It struck me that if there were such a thing as mental masturbation, this was it. There were definite sexual undertones; we were reading Sartre on Genet at the time.

On one memorable occasion, just for fun, but also to point up the women's menial function, Anne Laing and my wife Catriona dressed up in waitress's caps and aprons to bring the afternoon tea and biscuits. Sherret and I were very amused. Ronald didn't even notice the act being put on by his wife and her friend. By this time *The Divided Self* had been published, but to little acclaim, and as I now know, it was not selling well. The R.D.L. I perceived then was visibly and in his predominant mood very different from the Ronald whose company I had enjoyed with Douglas Hutchison during my visits to London prior to 1959, when I moved south from Glasgow. Then he had been relaxed, cheerful, appropriately sensitive or celebratory, and in full command of his personal resources.

The unquiet grave: Douglas Hutchison

Rephrasing and adding to what I have already said: Douglas was less prurient and more innocent than Laing, and there was a sense of quiet refinement about him that Laing lacked. Stan Stewart wrote after his death: "The great thing about Douglas was his sympathetic nature and his radiation of gentleness and understanding." I also wrote in another context: "bold, imaginative, amusing, not given to useless small talk, yet capable of many a yell of joy, Hutchison was as a companion life-affirming." I agree with Adrian Laing's view that when Douglas died, "something died in Ronald".[1]

To give live substance to my account of Douglas, I am now going to quote an extract from a letter from him to me, dated 5, 6, 7 May 1950 (freshly delivered in Douglas's own hand). I was by this time House-Surgeon in Dumfries.

> Postmarked 6 May 1950
> Glasgow S.W.2

Dear Jimmy,

As I write this letter there is still alcohol in my blood. I have just been out dining and drinking with Stan, Ronald, and Robin and for some unknown reason I feel impelled to write to you. Perhaps it is because just an hour or so ago problems of human love and affection were whirling around in my mind—perhaps so. There was some hard hitting tonight. I told Robin he was charming but useless and Ronald warned me to watch out or I would be hitting people below the belt, on the solar plexus as he put it. I myself had been subjected to a black magic rite (as I lay on the floor) from Ronald and Stan and then they too were each subjected to all the brutality and frankness which we could muster. Apparently, I must seduce a fair maiden soon or be completely fallen in Ronald's estimation. It was on this theme that we harped against Stan but Stan can always hit back with powerful wit. As this was going on my drunken thoughts kept turning to the problem of what really holds us together—who are my friends—what is the love between us?

But it was really fun tonight, we were in the S.M.C. Club room and there were high lights; poetry, song and drink. I gave birth to a child (Stan) after much pain of childbirth and Robin and Ronald wanted to drown it in the Clyde as a useless syphilitic brat . . .

To return to my account of Ronald at work in the early 1960s: in summary, I was now seeing him in a state best described as barely controlled frenzy. My hypothesis is that Ronald Laing was damaged

---

[1] Adrian researched, interviewed, and corresponded very widely while writing the first major biography of his father (A. C. Laing, 1994).

by the sudden death of his best male friend and in an important sense never recovered from this loss.

To the evidence of my own observations can be added the following:

1. Letter from Ronald to Marcelle Vincent dated 24.1.60, following the death of Albert Camus. "Why do so many people go on living? . . . The long delay in publishing is driving me up the wall . . . I am filled with panic at how I spend my time from 6.30am to 10.30pm . . . What else is there to do."

2. Private written statement by Ronald. "In Douglas's death I have lost my brother." During the year following Douglas's death, Ronald suffered a mysterious severe illness from which he nearly died. (Source: A. C. Laing, 1994.)

3. Laing admired Cyril Connolly. Bill Donaldson told me that he gave Ronald a copy of Connolly's 1945 *The Unquiet Grave* when the second edition came out and was widely available in 1949. Confirmed by personal communication, 1997. (Source: A. C. Laing, 1994.)

4. On Ronald's friendship with Douglas, the passage that follows makes a fitting comment:

    "You and I moved by a sunset or some emotion such as love for each other are the most real thing I know. Feeling, rather than thought or knowledge, is the test of reality; thoughts are real when we feel them, knowledge the same." [Source: Cyril Connolly/Noel Blakiston letters]

As Michael Radcliffe wrote in his *Times* Review, "Senses out-numbered intellect by five to one. Critical intelligence was crucial, but feeling came first" (18 December 1975).

Finally, my summing up of Laing

A Scotsman with a streak of genius in him, a potentially great psychiatrist who became an inspirational writer, a wizard with words, Laing's artistic achievement as a whole remains problematic. But in his range, and output, and forcibleness he stands comparison with

Hugh McDiarmid, the outstanding Scots poet of the twentieth century. An extraordinarily empathic therapist, it could be said of him as he met an appreciative public that he had a calling that he served rather than a career that he worked at.

In his best years and good times, he played with words as well as with music and clearly enjoyed himself. He had a great "Alive, Alive Oh" Spirit.

CHAPTER FOUR

"Et in Archivio . . . [a] Pearl": a personal appreciation of Pearl King's work as a historian and archivist of psychoanalysis

Riccardo Steiner (London)

"Oh, hello dear . . . oh, yes . . . I will wait for you and Jenny tomorrow . . . What? Do you think it's going to be very hot? . . . Oh, it does not matter. . . . I will sit in the back of the car and everything will be OK. . . . I will wait for you both tomorrow . . . Bye bye for now, dear."

So try to imagine one early morning towards the end of July a couple of years ago, Jennifer Johns and I going to Child's Hill, Lyndale Avenue, to pick Pearl King up. But it was not just an excursion to the country. Pearl had offered to come with us to see how and whether it would be possible to collect and obtain the Archival material that Mark Paterson and the Sigmund Freud Copyrights had told us they wanted to put at our disposal. It was the small but complete Archive belonging to the heirs of Angela Harris. Angela Harris had helped the late James Strachey in his revision of the *Standard Edition* and had, in some ways, continued his work. The material seemed to be important, but what had stimulated Pearl into coming with us was the possibility, in some way or other, of acquiring this material for the Archives of the British Psychoanalytical Society, which Pearl, over the previous fifteen years, had practically created from nothing.

I do not want to dwell too long on the adventures of the trip, but in the end we reached that small and extraordinary village by the sea called Wivenhoe, near Colchester. Wivenhoe seems to condense what is most mysteriously English, at least for a foreigner like me, and one could also say that its setting appears to have been invented, on purpose, to act as a sort of backdrop to highlight those characteristics that I think are also so quintessentially Pearl's: the understated, noble elegance of many of the houses that at first can rather puzzle the visitor as they appear to be so unpretentious. But their mysterious and intriguing features need to be discovered, and if one walks along the village's small and narrow streets, one soon realizes that they reveal a very long history. It is not by chance that Wivenhoe has often been chosen as the setting of many of the historical films of a certain Great Britain. And then there is the magic of that little harbour. Not so much for the seagulls that sit on the pediments of what were once very elegant, and are now rather shabby, houses or for the gulls' piercing cries as they fly around in circles overhead; something that the person who arrives here for the first time by sea, as I did, will never forget. What the harbour reveals is one of the strangest of scenes because the vista changes continuously: ships, usually merchant ships, that at first appear to be travelling at a distance, suddenly seem to become enormous, and one feels almost able to touch them. And then, a few hours later, as if by magic, they become much smaller and distant. All the purely physical happenings that are part of nature suddenly seem to have a magical aura about them, and it is as if one were observing through a kaleidoscope the movements in the harbour, the ebbing and flowing of the tide, the lapping of the water as it meets the mouth of the small river that surrounds Wivenhoe, in total fascination.

It is as if one were watching *in vivo* a scene from Alice in Wonderland or the multiform realism of one of Fellini's films (please forgive me this cultural reference, which is not strictly British). But it is something that I have often felt when speaking and working with Pearl. Beneath her apparently modest way of being and the simplicity with which she faces problems, she disguises, in reality, an ability to use at its best a tradition that constitutes the backbone of a British culture that is based on common sense, in the literal sense of the word, and on pragmatic empiricism, but which, at the same time, has something that, if not magical, is certainly mysterious and difficult to put into words, particularly for a foreigner. And anyone who has passed a few hours in Pearl's famous garden will, I think, feel this, because she is able suddenly to call your attention to magnify a detail of a flower, or a plant that she particularly cares for, so that one almost feels that something magical has happened in that moment. Then things settle down again when one looks at the garden as a whole. And this is actually what she often does, particularly when she is faced with organizational or administrative tasks that appear to be unsoluble. Suddenly, in picking up a detail, in enlarging it, and in working at it she finds the best solution available, and things go back to their proper proportions, like the ships passing through the harbour towards the sea at Wivenhoe. "We should think about it, leave it with me for a while, dear", she often says with that mental and psychological attitude so typical of the "insular" sense of time of the British, which, at the same time, also reveals her enormous flexibility and her remarkable ability to change her point of view whenever necessary, always to find the positive even in the most negative of persons—something that at times has puzzled me. These are all virtues and qualities that, in the almost fifty years of her professional life, have made Pearl, in her own way, one of the key figures of both the scientific and the institutional life of the British Psychoanalytical Society, but not just of the British Society. Indeed, we had the chance to see her at work and use her skills even during our visit to Wivenhoe.

Now, imagine our arrival, the exchange of greetings at Mark Paterson's office, our lunch in one of those typical pubs near the sea where Mark and his Archivist, Tom, had invited us to, and, of course, imagine Pearl very carefully choosing her vegetarian meal.

And for those who know Mark Paterson, the lunch would not have been such without plentiful libations. It was in the early afternoon, after Mark had invited us to his home for a cup of tea or for another glass of Scotch when, all of a sudden, Pearl, with her inevitable pitch, said to us: "Now let's get down to work." And for the next three hours, all the time standing and not saying anything about her problems or how tired she might be Pearl helped us to read, select, and then start to photocopy the Archive. As time was running out and there was still a lot of photocopying to be done, to help speed matters up I offered to make a personal contribution towards the cost of employing someone to finish the job later. But Pearl paid all the photocopying expenses out of her own pocket, without waiting for the Institute of Psycho-Analysis to advance her the money, because what mattered most was the material, the letters of that Archive, as they could have been very important for the revision of the *Standard Edition.* It was only when we were in the car on the way back to London that, looking at her, I asked how she felt. To which she replied: "I am all right now, dear . . . You see, I feel a bit tired because in a few weeks they should operate on my eyes. I had to force myself to look at all those documents . . . But I am all right. I like listening to the music played by the radio cassette", and she dozed off for a while.

These are the small details, the human traits, of Pearl's personality, and I wanted to begin with them and to tell you about them so as to stress that if we did not take them into consideration, it would be impossible for us to understand the incredible amount of work that she has done in collecting and cataloguing the many documents pertaining to the British Psychoanalytical Society, such as the Controversial Discussions, for instance. Nor would it be possible for us fully to appreciate the organization and the effort that has gone into setting up the Archives of our Society, created by Pearl almost thirteen years ago and, more often than not, personally financed by Pearl. To all those persons who work in the field of the history of psychoanalysis, all this work has made Pearl a real "pearl".

A great French sociologist, Halbwachs, whom we have suddenly and very recently rediscovered, in a time in which even those without memory seem to be interested in the problems of historical memory, has quite aptly said that there is a dichotomy between those who still remember because they have witnessed or have been part of events and those who, after the event has taken place, work as traditional historians and try to reconstruct the past by making use of archives, documents, and all sorts of other material. With her work in the field of the history of psychoanalysis and her knowledge of the psychoanalytical establishment, Pearl, to my mind, occupies a place that is quite unrivalled. Indeed, if one excepts Freud and some of his first more creative pupils, such as Ferenczi and Abraham, one could say that Pearl has met or can remember nearly all those persons who mattered and who were still part of the heroic period of psychoanalysis. Some of you should ask her to describe her meeting with Lacan at a dinner-dance at the Ritz, for example. From this point of view Pearl is a member of what Halbwachs has called the living collective memory—that is, the memory of those who were witness to, or who took part in some event or happening. And in her work in the Archives,

Pearl could also be considered to be one of the few authentic historians of psychoanalysis as far as archival expertise is concerned. It is on
the quality and the significance of her work as a historian that I would
like to expend a few more words.

I have already mentioned how much we owe her, even on a
personal level, for what she has accomplished in the Archives of the
British Society, now so admired and envied by everybody, as they
also constitute a potential teaching model for those who would like to
follow what Pearl has achieved. On the financial side, Pearl has even
bought most of the computers; on the organizational front, for years
she led a group of colleagues who embarked on the formidable task of
putting onto computer files the enormous amount of material. It is as
if her involvement in this work replicates and condenses the work she
did in her pre-analytical days. One should not forget that in the
period that immediately followed the Second World War, Pearl wrote
some of the most important papers on psychology applied to industry
and organizations. These papers were published in *Human Relations,*
one of the most respected periodicals of the Tavistock Institute.

But now I need to turn to different issues and concentrate on the
philosophy, as people here in England say, or on the strategy that she
adopted in creating and organizing the Archives, and in fostering the
research that has produced such important results.

I speak, of course, out of personal experience, and therefore please
do not take my words as the only, or the definitive truth about Pearl.
I began working with her nearly 15 years ago. Prior to that, she had
been one of the supervisors for my membership course. It was at that
time that we became friends, because once, during a supervision,
while listening to my vicissitudes and interests, she at a certain point
said to me: "My dear, try not to misunderstand me, but I think that
Institutions can ruin people like you. . . . " No doubt she was right,
particularly when I consider the difficulties I had encountered in my
pre-analytical days when trying to deal with the type of power that is
so ingrained and so routine within so many political and academic
institutions and the difficulties I also experienced in settling into the
British psychoanalytical institution. But Pearl's spontaneous remark
made me feel that I had found one of the few English allies who
understood my way of thinking and working.

Here I do not have the time to go into the details of how we started
to work together on the Archives. Because of my knowledge of German and my cultural background and expertise, I had been asked by

the Publications Committee, at that time chaired by Malcolm Pines, to study the controversies of Strachey's translation. At that time, Bettelheim, but above all Ornston, and others in America, had again begun to criticize Strachey's translation of Freud, and it was obvious to me that the problems did not lie solely with the translation as such. From the documents I discovered in the Archives of the Society, it became quite clear that the translation of Freud's work had been one of the cores, if not the core, of the cultural hegemonic strategy of the British Society via which—whether consciously or, at times, particularly at the beginning, possibly unconsciously—had succeeded in creating an extremely powerful common language for psychoanalysis, which, for decades, brought prestige and financial rewards to the Society. But in order better to understand what had happened, I needed further documentation to really study some of the aspects of the administrational and institutional life of the Society in the 1920s, 1930s, and later.

People began to get rather worried, or even suspicious, and quite understandably so. How could one allow a person like me to consult documents that were rather delicate and complicated? Furthermore, due to my notorious non-political ability I had already found myself in a certain amount of hot water with some of our American colleagues, who had become too demanding and imperative. Pearl came to my rescue and, at the same time, tried to guide me into the *"ingens silva"* of the documents of the Society. Sometimes in the evening, when she happened to be free, we would pass hours, either in the reference library or in some other place, looking into documents. And it was on those occasions that I really learned a bit about her way of working. For instance, I discovered that for years and years, assisted by her secretary, she had selected and catalogued all the documents concerning the vicissitudes of the Controversial Discussions—something I was interested in because, in the early 1980s, I had written a brief paper for a congress held in Italy on the epistemological basis of psychoanalysis and had chosen the Controversies to try to show what a so-called fact, or some new view, implies in our field, and how many personal, political, and institutional variables one always has to take into consideration. But Pearl also told me that she had collected, and was still collecting, all the documents concerning the institutional and educational history of our Society—an immense task for one single person—with a view to writing its history one day. Files and files of documents, all chronologically ordered and systematically organized, are indeed available at Pearl's home.

It was here that I met someone who, quite instinctively, was a natural historian, whose foremost interest lay in the preliminary operation: the collection of data and documents, the creation of an Archive without which any historico-social reconstruction and interpretation would have been impossible. So, as I said, during those evenings was born this odd, bizarre, small, and eccentric confraternity: of a continental and "eternal wanderer" like me—still full of the beans and the tensions that came with my difficult background, prone to interpret and link psychoanalysis to any possible context, imprinted with all the theoretical interests and difficulties of a generation that, culturally speaking, had grown out of the bubbling cultural and political melting pot of the European and Italian milieus of the late 1950s and early 1960s that had found its peak in the anti-institutional battles of 1968 (although I was considered a moderate by my colleagues on the Continent)—and of someone like Pearl King, whose background might have had curious similarities with mine inasmuch as she too had spent her early days wandering around the world, but whose knowledge of organizations and institutions was formidable. Do not forget that in the late 1930s Pearl had also been a fervent Communist, very much involved in politics. But she was nevertheless on the whole able to water down my enthusiasm through the magical use of her empirical and pragmatic skills and by telling me about her memories.

What struck me was that every time I found something interesting in the documents, Pearl would look at it, and suddenly the living memory would begin working: the context of the document in relation to the whole, how it linked up to other facts, or to the people connected with those events, and so on; all these details would pour out from Pearl's prodigious memory. It was as if Pearl was in possession of the internal keys to those committees and their history, and the histories of the personalities involved. The most moving aspect of all this—which, I have to confess, would at times distract me from my work—was Pearl's ability to add to those documents all sorts of personal anecdotes, and to reconstruct the entire genealogy of those same documents, with names, dates, events, and so on. Many of you will have seen her at work when with her small, gentle hand she scratches her forehead for a second, or perhaps just touches it, while pronouncing a typical British sentence such as *"What's his name?"*—immediately to come out with a whole series of dates, events, names of people, and so on, all related to what she is searching for or speaking about.

There is something in all her work which, *mutatis mutandis* and, of course, keeping things in perspective, can remind one of a particular historiographical tradition, such as that of the great researchers of the seventeenth and eighteenth centuries in England, Germany, France, and Italy; of the friars Maurini; of a certain Leibniz; of the great Italian Archivist and Historian Muratori; or of the great British biographers of the eighteenth century. Those were the people who, by managing to bypass the manipulations and the personal interests of the Catholic Church and of the various kings, began to collect and to revise documents and facts and to create the modern collections of documents and the modern Archives, without which any historiographical or more sophisticated interpretative historiographical attempt would have been impossible. They were all empirically orientated minds, and they avoided any immediate interpretation of the data they were in the process of collecting because they believed that unless they had gathered all the evidence possible, to write history would have been impossible. And not only the Gods in Heaven know how important this is for the history of psychoanalysis, particularly when one thinks of what has happened in the short life of our discipline.

But I would not want you to think that Pearl's merits and achievements are merely confined to her dedicated labours of collecting and ordering the documents pertaining to the history of the British Society. If you look at the book on the Controversial Discussions, you will easily see how intelligent and perceptive, and of what fundamental interpretative importance, is the work she has done (with the help of her extremely precious secretary) in collecting all that material that in some way or other relates to the Controversies. Of course, had we had more time and more help, certainly the Controversial Discussions would have been better edited and documented. Yet her work has allowed us all to understand how necessary and important it is, even in our profession, to consider all the possible variables, be they personal, institutional, educational, administrative, or even sociopolitical or cultural, if we want to try to comprehend what lies behind what we call scientific discussions or disagreements. Pearl's achievements in this field have been unique, and I know that, particularly abroad, historians of science, sociologists, and other people whose work does not have a direct relationship with psychoanalysis have been fascinated by the possibility of studying psychoanalysis in this broader context.

I would now like to tell those of you who were not there of one of the most typical and moving, not to say most amusing, moments of Pearl King's career as Archivist and Historian, and a member of what Halbwachs has called the collective memory. It was on the occasion when, more than 10 years ago now, Pearl was invited to speak at the first International Congress held in Paris by the International Association for the History of Psychoanalysis and organized by de Mijolla, one of her fans. Pearl read a paper on the importance of the contribution of British psychoanalysts during the Second World War. It was an extremely illuminating paper because, as a result of the enormous wealth of data presented by Pearl, it was possible, for the first time, to understand so many things, including the role that British psychoanalysts had played in helping restructure and revitalize the Army after what had happened at Dunkirk. But you should have been there to see and to hear Pearl, who stood on the podium dressed in a red hat that was not only marvellously eccentric but also very appropriate for the occasion, and who read her paper with a quality of voice that was very similar in tone to Churchill's or Montgomery's when reading the War Bulletins. And in this voice she proceeded to describe the work that had been done by the people at the Tavistock, and by others, to help reselect those pilots still suitable for the RAF. Pearl succeeded in making all the 400 people gathered in that room explode with laughter and applause when, at a certain point, she began a sentence, which now, among her friends, epitomizes her persona, by saying: "Mind you, we still had not won the war, but the pilots of the Royal Air Force were starting to bomb Germany again with great success . . ."

But what does all that mean, someone may object? What does this have to do with psychoanalysis, with clinical psychoanalysis as we understand it here in England? Aren't you being rather eccentric, the four or five of you here in England who are interested in the history of psychoanalysis, to use any understatement you wish? There is no doubt that particularly over the last fifteen years this type of question and these sorts of criticisms, have been asked and have been made and, indeed, much worse things have been said about some of us by those who want to label or demonize us because of our particular interest in this field—although there is no doubt that, from a certain point of view, some of the more moderate criticisms can be understood, even if not justified.

Of course, the skeletons in the cupboard that worry some psychoanalysts, no matter where they live or work, are not to be found solely in the Freud Archives. As far as our Archives are concerned, one need only remember the problems that arose as a result of the reports that Rickman wrote on German analysts immediately after the War, following his visit to Germany to establish whether there were any analysts suitable for the IPA. Yet with great tactical flexibility and sensibility Pearl and Adam Limentani made these documents available to a group of young German analysts before they attended the Hamburg Congress of 1986. Therefore, what looks like pure academic eccentricity that needs to be watched with great suspicion is, in reality, not so.

Behind Pearl's passion for the history of psychoanalysis lies a very precise way of understanding and envisaging the relationship between the past and the present in our discipline—something that also has deep educational and clinical implications. There is the wish not to lose contact with a certain past, with the most brilliant and most heroic moments in the history of psychoanalysis, which, when all is said and done, Freud and his first pupils helped to create. None of this can either be ignored or wiped out, unless we want psychoanalysis to cease to exist. A certain use of the here-and-now—which is not a purely technical device and does have behind it a whole theoretical apparatus and, consequently, ideological implications—tends today, in this country and everywhere, both inside and outside the consulting-room, to wipe out this past or to ridicule any attempt at reconstructing it, while, at the same time, it denounces the non-clinical or the non-scientific value of this endeavour. In my view, this attitude, because it denies the role that is played by the past, if pushed to an extreme, could actually lead to a rather behaviouristic model of the time–space dimension of psychoanalysis. One need only to consider empirical psychoanalysis today, the extreme scientistic filiation of the here-and-now device, where any effort to reconstruct the past is looked upon as a quixotic attempt to fight windmills.

Yet it is the winds of time that we have to constantly remember, and it is against oblivion that we have to fight. Indeed, even if we make use of the sophisticated tools of research that are now available even in our field, it is only by looking at our discipline from a historical perspective that we can understand its complexities and save it from becoming an omnipotent, dead technology. It is only by looking at it in its historical context that we can learn to adopt a less omniscient or a less moralistic attitude in the way we approach things. I refer here to that kind of moralism defined by Bion as moralism without a moral.

Therefore, with her work in the field of the history of psychoanalysis, Pearl brings to our attention the curious and uncanny paradox of a discipline that was born out of the attempt to use the complex temporal stratification inherent both in German Romantic philosophy and in a Spencerian and Darwinian type of evolutionism, and the attempt to apply them to the understanding of our unconscious and conscious life. Today, however, we seem to have a overall fear of looking back into the past and a particular dread of looking into our discipline's own. This, in my view, leads to a fugue into the present or to a naive, manic, scientistic celebration both of progress and of the future, which is just as dangerous as a fugue or a retreat into the past—as history in every field of research has shown us. Indeed, the dangers in this attitude are that one risks losing contact with some of the core elements that contributed towards the creation of psychoanalysis. And the importance of these core elements is not linked solely to the notion of psychic space that is today repeated *ad nauseam*, but also to psychic time. It is no coincidence that André Green should remind us how complex and still not properly studied and, therefore, misunderstood, is the notion of time in Freud's work.

There is just one last thing I would like to mention before I conclude, and because I have worked so closely with Pearl, there may be some bias in what I am about to say. What has always struck me and at times moved me about working with her is her tolerance: her tolerance towards my points of view, my idiosyncrasies, my way of thinking, even though sometimes our opinions differ. If she had not been so tolerant, the work we did together in the Archives and the editing of the Controversial Discussions would not have been possible.

What I think can be said is that even her tolerant ways can be understood through a historical approach, because they form part of the great cultural heritage of the late European Enlightenment, born in England in the seventeenth and eighteenth centuries as a result of the religious wars, which created some of the basic principles of modem liberal and radical democracy. In observing her natural curiosity, her wish to make sense of the experiences of others, even though they may differ from hers, and the passion and the fervour with which she argues against psychoanalytical monolinguism, I have often been reminded of the words of a man who, in some respects, was one of the greatest thinkers of the French Enlightenment: Helvetius, today almost forgotten, but whose works were familiar to both Mao and Freud (Freud indirectly through the work of Lange). In his *Traité de l'esprit* at one point Helvetius polemically declared that "Every nation, convinced that it is the sole possessor of wisdom, takes all others for fools and nearly resembles the inhabitants of the Marian Islands who, being persuaded that theirs was the only language in the Universe, concluded from there that all other men know not how to speak."

But this same tradition, whose roots are in the English Enlightenment, can be found in the constant references that Pearl makes to Jones's valedictory speech, read by him to the British Society at the end of the Second World War, on his retirement from office. Pearl has often referred to this speech in our conversations, particularly where Jones emphasized the necessity to foresee the future of the British Psychoanalytical Society—something that could only be inspired by the capacity and the willingness to accept and develop different points of view. Pearl has these very qualities: the ability to look at the complex reality of psychoanalysis, a keen interest in the "other" or the "others" as other and others for the very reason that they are different from us, the ability to see the need to understand the multiple reasons that have made us what we are, that have given us our specific personal, cultural, and institutional identity—all attributes that I believe should also form the basis for all our research in the field of psychoanalysis. A way to celebrate Pearl's eightieth birthday would be to try to continue her research for the future by continuing to make use of her living memory, and by taking the opportunity to work on the material on the history of the British Psychoanalytical Society, which, with such unending patience and dedication, she has collected and catalogued and looked after at her home. Indeed, to fight for the history of psychoanalysis, as Pearl has shown us, is to fight for its survival and its future development.

CHAPTER FIVE

The evolution of organizational and training procedures in psychoanalytical associations: a brief account of the unique British contribution

Ron Baker (London)

In her Ernest Jones Centenary address to the British Psychoanalytical Society, given in 1979, Pearl King noted that, when he founded the British Psychoanalytical Society on 20 February 1919, Jones had learned the lesson gained from the problems encountered in the original London Psychoanalytical Society some years earlier. At this early stage of psychoanalytic history, the new Society now decided that all new members must be proposed by someone who knew them and nominated by the Council before being balloted by Members. They were invited to attend the Society, first as visitors, and only later, in their first year of Associate Membership, were they asked to read a paper. Yes, in those days there was no formal training—nor, for that matter, was there any informal training. Associate Members were re-elected annually, with the result that there was something of a "turnover" of membership, since those who did not "take" to psychoanalysis were unceremoniously dropped. Nonetheless, a gifted and talented group of enthusiastic psychoanalysts gathered around Jones to assist in the establishment of psychoanalysis in this country.

Jones was already aware that the survival of psychoanalysis required more than a group of reliable enthusiasts, and so he was quick to develop publishing facilities, premises, and a library with a view to launching a clinic and a training organization later. *The International Journal of Psycho-Analysis* was founded by him in 1920, and some of Freud's works, translated into English, were published therein and later in the International Psychoanalytic Library.

In 1924 Jones and Rickman formed the Institute of Psychoanalysis, an organization separate from the scientific ethos of psychoanalysis, dedicated to publishing activities, the formation of a clinic, and the development of educational facilities. This was the financial and administrative arm, which would service and supplement the work of the Society and take over the financial and administrative responsibility for its assets. This structure, including its Board of Directors, remains to the present day.

The London Clinic of Psychoanalysis was officially opened in September 1926. In the same year the elements of a training organization were in place, prior to which short personal analysis and minimal supervision were the limit of the educational requirement. However, by 1928, under the firm leadership of Jones, the British Society as we now know it had emerged.

One of Jones's enduring achievements in those early years was to tackle the perennial problem of criticism of psychoanalysis. In pursuit of this, he succeeded in persuading the British Medical Association to set up a Committee to investigate psychoanalysis. He and Edward Glover prepared evidence for the committee and answered their questions and criticisms, as a result of which the official national body for the medical profession recognized the distinction between psychoanalysts and pseudo-analysts, and so psychoanalysis gained respectability and acceptance by the medical profession. The proceedings of this episode are recorded in the *Handbook of the British Psychoanalytical Society*.

Ernest Jones's considerable scientific contribution is beyond the scope of this chapter. However, it was in the scientific realm that Jones's organizational and administrative talents became manifest in relation to the manifold divergences in psychoanalytic theory between the British and Viennese Societies following the early delineation of Melanie Klein's approach from the late 1920s onwards. Having regard for this, Jones and Robert Waelder initially arranged exchange lectures, but it is apparent that these did not contribute to resolution of the conflicts. At the same time sharp opposition to Melanie Klein's theories surfaced in the British Society, notably from Edward Glover and Melanie Klein's daughter, Melitta Schmideberg.

With the advent of the Second World War, local differences were suspended, and at this time Jones, who was also President of the IPA, used his influence to enable Freud and many other analysts to escape from Vienna. These colleagues were welcomed and offered membership of the British Society. The earlier differences between Vienna and London now began to be played out at close quarters, with the scientific atmosphere in the Society becoming increasingly acrimonious. Jones was now thrown into the position of having to muster his considerable skills to move the situation towards compromise.

Between February and June 1942 the problems were addressed in five Extraordinary Business Meetings, which by all accounts were handled with consummate even-handedness by Jones. The two main outcomes of this were groundbreaking:

1.   The Controversial Discussions. These are now recorded in book form (*The Freud–Klein Controversies, 1941–45*), courtesy of the outstanding conjoint editorship of Pearl King and Riccardo Steiner (1991), who lovingly devoted themselves to the task of publishing this historical document. It is now required reading throughout the world.

2.   The decision to form a committee to investigate questions relating to tenure of office and the holding of multiple official positions in the Society.

As a result of the latter, the Society's rules changed in 1944, so that a President could remain in office for no more than three years. Once the new rules were in place, Jones resigned, and Sylvia Payne was elected President. Jones became Honorary President, having led and successfully nurtured the Society for 25 years from its inception. In 1946, looking back over 40 years in psychoanalysis, Jones noted two major changes that in his view would have astounded the early analysts. These are (a) the respectability and general acceptance of psychoanalysis and (b) the theoretical divergences that already existed within psychoanalysis.

There is little doubt that Jones's capacity to tolerate clinical and administrative divergences and controversies was remarkable, and history might well prove that this represents his unique gift to the British Society and psychoanalysis. Jones knew that too close a uniformity of orientation in theory, technique, and practice could stand in the way of psychoanalysis flourishing as a science and that it would then run the risk of degenerating into a fundamentalist theology. The fact that in the British Society we are three groups under one roof is ample witness to this great legacy, and it has fortified successive generations of psychoanalysts to carry on this noble tradition of scientific debate.

Returning to the Controversial Discussions, it is difficult to do justice to this complex period of our history in one short chapter. Nonetheless, in order to transmit something of the heat and passion of the wartime climate of our society, it is worthy of note that the issues that were addressed included the question of whether Klein's theories were compatible with psychoanalysis as formulated by Freud and if not, whether these theories should be taught to students. Moreover, in relation to the selection of training analysts, the possibility of the exclusion of Melanie Klein and her followers from training was also debated. Having regard for these issues, it was agreed that four papers embracing Klein's contributions would become the focus of intense scientific study. These debates were at the heart of the Controversial Discussions.

At the same time, the then Training Committee were in deep consideration as to the effects the Controversies were having on candidates. A propos of this, Strachey, in a working paper summarizing the issues, posed the question as to whether or not psychoanalysis was a closed system, with no room for growth and development, or was it to be viewed as Freud had done when he described it essentially as an empirical science, "It keeps close to the facts in its field of study, seeks to solve immediate problems of observation, gropes its way forward with the help of experience, is always incomplete and always ready to correct or modify its theories" (Freud, 1923a [1922], p. 253). In response to this, each member of the Training Committee was invited to write a memorandum mapping what they regarded as central points in their technique, but again there were wide differences between them.

Finally, a majority report delineating the principles governing training activities and criteria for selecting training analysts and the Training Committee was submitted to and approved by a Business Meeting. Anna Freud and Edward Glover had already disagreed with this and resigned from the Committee in February 1944. Soon after this Glover also resigned from the Society.

Sylvia Payne became President in July 1944, and a new Training Committee, which did not include Anna Freud, was elected. Payne met the pervasive unhappiness in the Society by beginning a dialogue with Anna Freud to ascertain the conditions under which Miss Freud and her colleagues could take part in the training. Resulting from this, in June 1946 it was agreed in principle to create two parallel courses: Course A, which would have teachers drawn from all groups, and Course B, which would teach psychoanalysis on the lines supported by Anna Freud and her colleagues. In November 1946 the ad hoc Committee charged with working out the details reached the following agreement:

1.   There should be one Training Committee responsible for all matters regarding the selection, training, and qualification of students.

2.   Students could opt to take Course A or Course B.

3.   Lectures and seminars other than those on technique would be common to all students.

4.   Students would attend clinical and technical seminars taken by analysts of their own course or group. They could attend as guests those taken by members of the other Course.

5.   The first Supervisor must be from the Student's own group, the second from a non-Kleinian member of Course A—the Middle Group.

6.   In the third year all students would attend clinical seminars run by teachers from Course A and Course B.

Parallel with this arrangement was the "gentlemen's agreement"—namely that there should be representatives of all three groups on the main committees of the Society: Council, Training Committee, and other policy-making bodies. This very creative compromise has enabled the three groups to continue to work together for the good of our Society.

Pearl King began her training in psychoanalysis in the immediate post- Controversial Discussions era. It might be said that she was a child of this creative compromise between embattled parents—parents who struggled sensibly, even ingeniously, to stay together despite their differences, putting the good and the future of their society first. And as a child of that generation, so to speak, she became a formidable champion of the importance of discussion and compromise between warring factions. It must also be added that her well-known opposition to appeasement, which she experienced when she was still a very young woman in relation to Chamberlain's failure to tackle Hitler's destructive expansionism firmly, added another important dimension to her capacity to ride out the difficulties and work out healthy solutions, whatever the odds. No, Pearl was never one to surrender, nor would she ever sell her soul to save the hour. Make no mistake—the 1950s saw the continued polarization of theoretical positions, with students and some members becoming increasingly intolerant of the divisions. Much work had to be done to protect and build on the fragile gains, and Pearl King was both perfectly qualified and well positioned to play a central role in this development.

In 1961 a second ad hoc Committee recommended that while clinical seminars should remain separate, a basic lecture course should be devised for all students. During the first two years only Freud's writings would be covered, other contributions being deferred until the third year. The revised curriculum was drawn up by analysts from the three groups, and common lecture courses for Course A and Course B were settled. The lectures were launched in 1967 and were given by working parties consisting of analysts from all three groups.

Although the outcome of this change was not as satisfactory as was initially expected, it did spawn an increasing capacity for the analysts manning these working parties to learn from and communicate constructively with one another. In 1968, the Council agreed with Adam Limentani's suggestion that a major review of the aims and objects of the Society's training activities was warranted, following which the Council set up an Interim Training Committee to explore what was wrong and to submit proposals for change. Among other advances, this major shift put paid to the unsatisfactory previous practice of appointing a Training Committee in the often heated political climate of the Society's AGM.

Under Limentani's Chairmanship, with Pearl King as Hon. Secretary, the Interim Training Committee set up six working parties to explore these problems. As a result the Education Committee has now evolved into an Executive consisting of a Chairperson, Secretary, and Clinic Director, together with the Chairs of six sub-committees: Student Progress, Training Staff, Admissions, Curriculum, Child Psychoanalysis, and Membership. This Committee is responsible to the Council for formulating and agreeing educational policy and for coordinating the activities of the various executive committees. The Chairperson is an ex-officio member of the Council. Its design, which has now been adopted throughout the world, has paved the way for mutual trust and respect to replace suspicion and jealousy in respect of the Society's educational activities.

Time does not allow me to describe how each of these committees operates and how the changes have affected the training of students, postgraduates, and applicants for training analyst and supervisor status; these are matters about which readers are probably cognizant. Let me simply use Pearl King's own words, those with which she concluded her paper on the subject of education of a psychoanalyst (1980):

> the problems faced by the British Society are by no means unique.
> . . . What may be unusual is the way the problems were worked on and contained within . . . [our Society], and then finally integrated within a new type of organization that gave space and time for each point of view to be expressed and for the results to be watched and assessed by others. . . . But it must be remembered that for such an experiment to work there must be at least some key individuals in each group who, whilst disagreeing theoretically, are prepared to work together to help maintain the Institution and to promote psychoanalysis in their locality.

In her tribute (1995) to Adam Limentani on the occasion of his commemorative meeting, Pearl King, with characteristic generosity, credited Limentani with this particular success. However, without the energy, devotion, and passionate commitment of Pearl King, who served on three of the six working parties, I doubt whether it would have come to fruition in the way that it has. Many of us have reason to believe that the final structure of the Education Committee and its sub-committees is the brainchild of Pearl King, and we owe her our heartfelt thanks for this enormous contribution to the organization of Education in our Society.

There is a striking parallel between the ways in which Ernest Jones established the ground rules and procedures that gave birth to our Society and Institute as we know it and the immense contribution of Pearl King to the rationalization of our Education and Training process as it functions today. The common ground shared by Jones and King is one of conviction—namely that an overarching unity and over-compliant sharing of identity in relation to theory, technique, and the practice would inevitably damage psychoanalysis as a science, and it would then degenerate into a theology. For instance, in relation to fundamental matters of theory and practice, Jones (1925) stated, "My plea would be essentially for moderation and balance, rejecting nothing that experience has shown to be useful, while ever expectant of further increases in our knowledge and power." This viewpoint is very much influenced by the British Empirical tradition to which Jones was committed and to which Pearl King has been a determined champion.

Finally, I turn to Pearl King's contributions to organization and training in the international context. Pearl was Secretary of the International Psychoanalytical Association during William Gillespie's Presidency from 1957 to 1961. I don't think she will take exception to my revealing that in 1957 she was a mere two score years less one and charged with, among other complex matters, the awesome responsibility of bringing order to a confused and multiple nomenclature in the particular area of the IPA's constitution and bye-laws. This began during her time as Secretary and continued through the subsequent Presidency of Maxwell Gitelson, during which, between 1961 and 1963, Pearl King was intimately concerned with and a prime contributor to a draft of the IPA Constitution and Bye-Laws, which had been subject to many revisions, the most recently updated version of which was placed before the IPA Business Meeting at the International Congress in Stockholm in 1963.

In a historical address, Pearl King (1964) presented the rationale and thinking behind these statutes with breathtaking clarification. In particular, there were two main focuses that required elaboration and consideration. These were as follows:

1. That new officers of the IPA were assuming positions and responsibilities without having had direct access to the oral traditions of the Association. Many of the procedures were based on precedent and oral tradition, and it was therefore important that policies and procedures were extrapolated from this tradition and formulated in a written form.

2. That the expansion of psychoanalysis was giving rise to pressures from sponsoring societies, study groups, and so on, who required guidance as to the procedures and standards acceptable to the Association.

The role of the British Society in the revision of these statutes is indeed striking. The original Committee included William Gillespie,

Sylvia Payne, Elliott Jaques, and Pearl King, with Anna Freud and Willi Hoffer serving from a later date. Their brief was not to write "the rules" but to "create a phase-adequate social structure"—a structure that Pearl King felicitously describes as being "as important to an Institution as an ego structure was to an individual". The committee thus undertook a careful historical study of the preferred modes of functioning of the IPA, examining in fine detail the minutes of past meetings, the history of the American Psychoanalytic Association, and the copious correspondence that led to the formulation of the statutes needing revision. Further additional information was gleaned from direct correspondence and interviews with long-standing IPA members.

This preparatory study was followed by an examination of the threefold functions of the IPA, namely the scientific communication between analysts, the promotion of psychoanalysis, and the authorization and recognition of training and qualification of analysts by local psychoanalytical societies. The constitutions of other international bodies were studied, which proved useful in relation to the first two functions but not so in relation to training and qualification issues. In this respect the Association was found to be unique. It was also found to be unique with regard to the fact that it is ruled by the principle of group responsibility for the selection, control, training, and qualification of psychoanalysts.

The design of the constitution under consideration had therefore to take account of the unusual structure of the IPA with its parallel roles of local organizations and individuals within the association. The two factors of, on the one hand, individual membership being contingent on membership of a local association and, on the other, different responsibilities, standards, training programmes, and qualification procedures in the various local organizations can immediately be seen to be potentially problematical. Nevertheless, the control of the IPA was seen to remain in the hands of individual members taking part in the Business Meeting of the IPA, which, incidentally, is held only on alternate years at the time of the International Congress. The Committee therefore concluded that the recommended social structure was right for the Association at this time but recognized that "there may come a time when the control might be delegated to representatives of component groups". This remarkable statement, of course, anticipates the House of Delegates—a structure that has been in place only during recent years, but one that has gained in strength to the point that it has achieved a position that some regard as being close to Executive status. The Constitution broke new ground for the IPA because its content had never previously been brought together in a single legal document.

There were two specific innovations:

1. The Statutes explicitly recognized the difference between Regional Associations and Component Societies. This held particular relevance in relation to the American Psychoanalytic Association. The situation at the time was one whereby the APA had achieved a degree of organization and responsibility in relation to standards that no other component society had reached. The APA had been awarded the status of Regional Association in recognition of this achievement. The appointment of Regional Secretaries was a direct outcome of this innovation.

2. The second innovation was the introduction of the idea of Associated Organizations. This applied to groups who had lost their status within the organization and whose authority to train candidates had been withdrawn. It was agreed under this statute that individual members would be able to retain their membership of the Association.

In addition the statutes included two methods of sponsoring new groups: on the one hand, sponsorship of a Study Group by a Component Society and, on the other, groups sponsored by committees appointed by the Council of the IPA. These flexible arrangements were aimed at facilitating the growth of psychoanalysis.

Members were thus placed in the interesting position at Business Meetings of having the dual task of seeing the Statutes from their own national viewpoint and at the same time trying to understand how these Statutes would affect analysts from other countries. Above all, they had to learn ways of working together in mutual understanding, the Statutes representing a new and creative way forward. Pearl King's thinking behind this was based on her firm belief that if the association could evolve an appropriate social structure, morale would improve and this, in turn, would lead to raised standards and a lessening in the growth of dissident groups.

When Pearl King presented these statutes at the IPA Business meeting, she received deserved acclamation. In the discussion that followed one main focus of special importance was debated, namely the method by means of which the new Constitution could be amended once it had been adopted. The APA had raised the question of a mail ballot, and a very wide-ranging discussion on this topic ensued. It is indeed interesting today to observe the resistance that was common in the 1960s to the mail ballot innovation. Part of that resistance was located in the fact that the entire authority for the conduct of the affairs of the IPA was invested in the biennial Business Meeting, and this was based on the rather absurd assumption that those who were truly interested would surely make certain to attend and to vote. The arguments against a mail ballot really do seem antiquated and even bizarre today—for example: "lots of us throw our non-personal mail in the basket without reading it", and so on. The pressure for the postal vote was mainly in relation to proposed changes in the Constitution, and the decision to implement it was regrettably deferred in favour of the much more important and historical voting for the adoption of the new Constitution itself. Not surprisingly, this was passed by a general positive consensus with only a single negative vote.

Those of us who have had the pleasure of seeing Pearl King at International and Regional Conferences will not fail to have noticed the extent of her recognition by analysts from other countries, who invariably greet her with delight and affection. This is because they are aware of what she did for international psychoanalysis in her creation of the Constitution and Statutes of the IPA, and for this she is much revered, much valued, and much loved, no less so in our own Society, for whom her local contribution is also historic.

On 14 July 1998, Robert Tyson, the [then] present IPA Secretary General, wrote a congratulatory letter to Pearl King on the occasion of her 80th birthday. In this he referred to her "exemplary work" as Secretary of the IPA. He lamented the fact that "we lack a good and accurate history of the IPA" and noted that only "fragmentary" references to it occur in certain works, such as those of Ernest Jones and Peter Gay. He pointed to current discussions on matters of historical record and asked Pearl King whether she could help, especially in relation to the formulation of the Constitution.

Pearl was predictably quick to reply, guiding Bob in the direction (among other matters) of the historical data that I have shared with you today, which is published in the Proceedings of the Business Meeting of the Stockholm Congress. But Pearl adds: "To make sense of it, I want to write up some background to it. . . . So when I have written up my version of events I hope to be able to read them to [William Gillespie]" (presumably for his view of these events).

Bob's reply is as follows: "The clarity of your thought and the relevance of your responsiveness make me wish you were on Council right now! Just to take one point—your observation that there are other central issues in addition to the non-medical one, issues not considered in Bob Wallerstein's (1998) (recent) piece." (He is referring here to Wallerstein's important paper in the *IJPA* entitled, "The IPA and the American Psychoanalytic Association: A Perspective on the Regional Association Agreement.")

He continues: "I am delighted that you are interested in writing [this] up. In the absence of an accurate and reliable history, current events have an opportunistic way of exploiting the vacuum. . . . There is some irony in finding myself in the position to educate the American. There is some pleasure in finding in you an ally." One week later Pearl wrote a three-page, closely typed letter to Bob, under five headings:

1. The problem of finding and preserving early records of the IPA.
2. The effects of the background history of the pre-war disagreements between the APA and the Executive of the IPA.
3. The Business Meeting of the Paris Congress 1957.
4. The Central Executive Meeting of the Copenhagen Congress 1959.
5. The Working Party to consider Statutes and to make recommendations for revisions and clarifications.

Alas, space does not allow me the opportunity to elaborate. This is but an *hors-d'oeuvre*. We all have something to look forward to. Pearl is at work, and, as with what she has given us in the past, she will be no less generous this time. We are in for a most unusual historical treat.

It was a great honour for me to serve the Society as Secretary during Pearl's all-too-short Presidency—and, incidentally, she was our first non-medical President. It is again a much cherished honour for me to be invited to participate in this tribute to Pearl King for her wide-ranging contributions to psychoanalysis.

CHAPTER SIX

Psychoanalysis—London or British?

Eric Rayner & Dilys Daws (London)

Both of us have good reason to appreciate Pearl King. One of us [D.D.] is a child psychotherapist who was in analysis with her when training, the other [E.R.], a psychoanalyst, has worked closely with her administratively for years. Both of us authors have spent our working lives in London, but with family roots in the North we have a prejudice that this is where the real human species live. Then, having failed to move back there, we have spent a good deal of our married life pacing each other to help psychoanalytic work in the regions. It seemed most fitting that this should be our contribution to a book for Pearl, partly because she has directly done so much for psychoanalysis throughout Britain, as well as the rest of the world. But, more generally and importantly, she easily looks out from a single viewpoint to wider vistas. This facility of hers to think from context to context has fostered a love of open-mindedness in many of us, not least about London and beyond.

This essay compares the problems and achievements of our two professions in those regions. We will start with the psychoanalysts.

In 1913 Ernest Jones founded the London Psycho-Analytical Society. It soon fell into a Freudian–Jungian schism. Jones solved the problem by dissolving the London Society and starting another in

1919, which he called the British Psychoanalytical Society. There is no doubt that this Society has been a world leader in carrying forward Freud's tradition and creatively developing from it. But, nearly eighty years later, it is even still questionable whether it is yet a British Society or just a London one.

Some simple statistics (taken from the *International Journal of Psycho-Analysis*, and from the Society's roster) mixed with some personal narratives show something of what has happened. By 1926 the Society was well established, with 59 members and associates, 14 of whom lived and worked in Britain outside London (24% of the total); only 1 lived and worked abroad. In 1935, there were 64 members, 11 of whom (17%) were outside London and 3 were in other countries. In 1946 there were 97 members with 12 (12%) outside London and 13 abroad. At this time there nearly was a training in Manchester: Michael Balint was there, and D.D.'s father, then a GP in Huddersfield, seriously intended to train under him.

Not long after this, at least one person was noticing something amiss. In 1949 John Rickman, in his Presidential address to the Society, said: "There is another topic of general concern which is often mentioned but never seriously discussed. This is that it is certainly not satisfactory if we consider the needs of patients that the great majority of our members who are resident in the United Kingdom should be in London. It is commonly said that nothing can be done about the geographical question: but it is more true to say that the matter has not been considered." But Rickman died too soon to do anything about the problem. In 1954 there were 128 members, with 17 (13%) outside London and 18 abroad. By 1965 there were 280 members, with only 14 (5%) in the regions and 55 abroad.

From the early 1970s onwards several London analysts, knowing of the scarcity in the regions, have for years routinely travelled to help with supervision, teaching, and therapy, especially in the Midlands. They are little recognized, or helped, by the Society, but they are much appreciated by their students and patients.

In 1982, one of us [E.R.] was Vice-president of the Psychoanalytical Society; and one evening Alex Pollock, its Hon. Secretary, and he made a list of all the main functions of the Society and then estimated which of these were working well and which were not. Working "Outside London" glared out as one of the worst. They told Pearl King, the President then, and the three introduced a packet of constitutional changes to the Society's Council. One change addressed psychoanalysis outside London. All three have been much involved in it since. It was several years before the first step, which was to begin the yearly "Outside London" Cambridge colloquium, organized for several years by Alex Pollock. Even so, not much change was visible. In 1985 there were 396 members of the Society, with only 20 (5%) outside London and 71 abroad. Later Jon Sklar took over the Colloquium, and in the mid-1990s this gave birth to a full Regional Development Committee of the Psychoanalytical Society.

In the late 1980s Paul O'Farrell from Edinburgh asked the Colloquium to think about a psychoanalytic training in Scotland. From this Anne-Marie Sandler, then Vice-president and later President of the Society, made the most important step so far. She initiated negotiations to gain the co-operation of the Scottish Institute of Human Relations; and, more successfully, to set up an emergency training course called the Sponsored Scheme. Started in 1989, this was due to end recruitment in December 1998 but has been extended. It selects recognized psychotherapists a long way from London and provides a "top-up" training for them to qualify as Associate Members of the Society. Anne-Marie Sandler chaired the committee, running this in the first years, followed by E.R. The scheme has often been criticized in London for "lowering standards", but as its students, and later Associates, have come to be known better by London members and students, they have begun to be trusted and respected. By Spring 2001 the Sponsored Training had produced 13 new Associates in Scotland, Northern Ireland, and Northumbria and should produce 7 more before it ends.

At the time of writing in 2001, the Society has 441 members, 38 of whom (9%) live and work in the regions (those retired are not included), with 86 abroad. This does not show much progress; but without those qualified under the Sponsored Scheme, the Society would have sunk even further: from 24% in 1926 living and working in the regions outside London to an abysmal 5% ... where, incidentally, about 80% of the population of Britain lives!

How has psychoanalytical child psychotherapy progressed by comparison? It was not until soon after the end of the Second World War that formal psychoanalytically based child psychotherapy trainings were started at the Anna Freud Centre and at the Tavistock Clinic in London. This was followed later by a Jungian child training, also in London. About a decade ago the British Association of Psychotherapy started another psychoanalytically based child therapy training in London; and some, largely with Tavistock origins, were started in Birmingham and Scotland. By 2000 the Association of Child Psychotherapists (ACP) had 403 members, 75 of whom (19%) were living and working outside London; 70 were in other countries. You will note that the total number of child therapists is now about the same as that of psychoanalysts; however, they have nearly three times the number outside London, as well as two training schools there. There are cogent reasons for this difference from the analysts, which will emerge later.

Wondering how our regional colleagues in the two organizations had been faring, we wrote asking them to send us impressions of their professional lives. We modelled ourselves on the social biographer, Tony Parker (1985), and in no way upon formal research. However, we think our account is a fair one. We wrote to more or less all the psychoanalysts and child psychotherapists (CPTs) in the regions and to some who travelled there. Somewhat fewer than half replied. We were frankly moved by them; they all deserve printing, but there is no space here. We can only skimpily quote them to illustrate key issues that emerged to us. The writers' names are not used, as some did not wish to be identified; but many were happy to be, and it will be clear from place names who these are. We will first report on the psychoanalysts, then on the child psychotherapists. To set the stage, nearly all of a letter from one of our veterans:

"I went to Glasgow in 1952, after I qualified . . . Fairbairn was very pessimistic about prospects for analysis in Scotland. I worked as a general psychiatrist and had patients in analysis at home. In 1958 I was appointed medical director of a clinic in Glasgow. This was an out-patient clinic—a mini Tavistock—which had been founded in 1935 to treat neuroses . . . I was able to get two consultant posts established. Two young analysts . . . who had just finished their training took up these posts. I had begun to establish an analytic group in Scotland.

I approached the Council of the [British Psycho-Analytical] Society in 1962 or 63 for support, but there was little interest. No one ever thought of coming up to Glasgow or inviting us down for discussions. I believe this had a bad effect on the younger members and it certainly had on me. I decided to try and obtain a post in Glasgow which would establish our position more firmly but I was rejected. I reacted very strongly . . . and decided to leave

Glasgow which I did in 1965. Then in 1968 I came to Belfast where I had qualified in medicine. Here I ploughed a lonely furrow, but I was fortunate in that I had a close connection with the Hampstead Clinic. I was in London every month until 1989. For several summers I went, with my family, to Walberswick where I had analysis for periods of 6 weeks and again in London when I was visiting.

I had analytical patients at home and worked in the mental hospital. Shortly before I retired at the end of 1984, "James" [who later trained and qualified under the Sponsored Scheme] came to see me wanting analysis. That was followed by . . . the others. It was an entirely spontaneous development. I had lost the pioneering spirit, or should I say left it behind in Glasgow so I had not tried to establish or develop anything. It was the enthusiasm of the group that carried it on. From 1989 we had people over from the Society . . . I am grateful to you and all those from London who have come over."

Now let us look briefly at some issues that recur in the letters. We will illustrate each issue by brief quotations from several letters. Some of those quoted came to London to train and then returned home; others "emigrated" from London.

No one says they fundamentally regret moving out of London. For instance: "I moved from London in 1989, and although I miss London in many ways I have never regretted making the move" . . . "I was made very welcome" . . . "Moving here has enormously improved the quality of our lives."

Some found setting up in practice to be easy and enjoyable:

"I decided to retire from the NHS in 1986. . . . Time for change. . . . A chance encounter with an old friend led to conversations about a project she and others had started in 1976 . . . a group practice to offer psychotherapy and to put on courses and workshops. . . . The decision to move was not one I felt needed discussion with anyone in the Society: I was going with the intention of working flexibly. I did not see myself as a psychoanalytic missionary, though the fact of my training with the Society was a big plus from the point of view of those I was joining. The decade has been a fulfilling experience. . . . There is increasing competition for educational events from the University and other organisations; more and more therapists are training. Speaking generally, I have experienced good professional support and friendship from colleagues . . . and hope I have been able to contribute to them."

But others were much more troubled. For instance:

"I think I failed to connect as a colleague with the psychotherapists here by turning some things down when I first arrived. Obviously it is important to get known and I am now being asked to give talks and agreeing to do so. There seems to be a fine line between allowing yourself and your training to be trashed and being arrogant. I think it is difficult to get known in a new place without having an NHS job."

In fact, perhaps the most striking impression from these letters is of a dynamic tension between loyalty to psychoanalysis as based in London and loyalty to local professional colleagues, often psychotherapists. Some of the "emigrants" seem glad to be gone from London. For example:

"When I moved north . . . I was feeling somewhat disillusioned with the 'religious' quality which appeared to be inseparable from psychoanalysis. It seemed to me to be exemplified by the 'apostolic succession' which ensured that the pure psychoanalytic truths were confined to London since only in London could one obtain a 'real' analysis. I did my best to encourage my colleagues and my trainees to take seriously everything that their patients told them, and not to wall themselves off. I am now involved with a school of psychotherapy . . . if we both avoid jargon it is perfectly possible to communicate. This seems more important to me than to perceive ourselves as missionaries to the natives of the heathen North!"

Here is another report with a similar message:

"I could reassure anyone toying with the idea of moving that it is a delight to get away from the arrogance, dogmatism, narrowness and pressure to conform to some party/group/dynastic line, predominant in some parts of the Society at least. It is much more possible to think in a original and independent way when one has been able to move away from 'home'. Of course, the price that has to be paid is that in the minds of the précieuses and apparatchiks one may be seen as heretical or "not a serious analyst". The intellectual snobbery and disdainfulness of some of the leaders of the

Society has meant that interest in the development of psychoanalysis outside London has been too little, too late, and too restricted with too rigid and narrow ideas of how the help should be given. The Society has lost the initiative and the vacuum has been filled by psychoanalytic psychotherapy training organised by people sometimes less well trained than one would have wished."

Here is another analyst—of long standing—perhaps more devoted to those in London, but more pained by the experience:

"As to my feelings as to what the Institute [of Psycho-Analysis] did or did not do for me and my work here. . . . Far from being helped by the Society, my situation as an analyst outside of London was, of course, forgotten and ignored from 1968 on and I sometimes even experienced the feeling of being disapproved of for daring to be in the situation without express permission. Nevertheless I kept the flag flying as best I could here. I felt stabilized by the fascination of the work with individual patients and it was generally a joy to work with some of my colleagues here, but it would have been of inestimable value to have felt there was some psychoanalytically qualified person to appeal to for an outside view."

On the other hand, there are those whose professional heart is still close to London. For example:

"London will always be the centre towards which we look, but bricks and mortar bearing the Society's name in other parts of the country would suggest confidence in the resilience of the seed of psychoanalysis."

Here is another:

"I have hesitated with this letter because it sounds very complaining. A local child psychotherapist and I are friendly but I have no contact with any training she organises. I have linked up with two other psychotherapists to some extent. I found myself driven crazy by the way in which they conducted things. I have had very little to do with the two local consultant psychotherapists. I realise I must overcome my reluctance to do things in my free time if I want to link up with fellow professionals. I find it difficult being a psychoanalyst outside London, largely because it is a lonely job anyway, and even more when without colleagues. I have found it very important to keep my ties with London."

Here is someone similar but now finding some professional value in being out of London:

"When my children were little I did not feel isolated but now I have become very aware of missing my London colleagues. I travel but this does not entirely compensate for more frequent contact. Here I seem to be more of a transference figure and only one of two analysts in a sea of psychotherapists. However the fact of being away from the Institute has in many ways helped me to become aware of my own thoughts and views and helped me to be more creative in some ways. It has felt a healthy thing to be thrown on my own resources. I am grateful the Institute is now showing interest in spreading psychoanalysis beyond London."

Here is another one—trenchantly critical of local psychotherapists:

"I qualified in the late 60s. I thought a Consultant Psychotherapy post would offer an ideally secure base from which to begin build-ing a psychoanalytic practice. Colleagues advised me of a post which was entirely devoted to psychotherapy and attached to the main teaching hospital and University. I was indeed courted for the post. My wife and I spent sleepless nights considering the move with its question of professional isolation. In the end I ap-plied and was appointed. My psychotherapy colleagues were not very sympathetic to psychoanalysis and made life difficult for me in a number of ways. They were very unaccommodating about the flexibility of working hours I needed to attend to my private practice. This, to my delight expanded very quickly soon six pa-tients in five times a week. My psychotherapy colleagues and myself founded an Institute of Psychotherapy and later to their credit mounted an introductory course Various of my offers to teach were rejected on the grounds that the region contained all the resources necessary. I fought to have this policy changed. I was seriously tempted to get out and return to London. I over-heard myself (and other analysts) referred to by a senior colleague as "our pet analysts". I tried to remain in reasonable social contact with my colleagues. Within the local psychotherapy institute there has been a desire for further training and this is where my efforts began to turn. We established a working party and many analysts and child therapists from London have been generous with their time, support and encouragement."

Finally here are two summaries by older members who have reached a certain philosophical resolution in bringing psychoanalysis and psychotherapy together in the regions. Here is the first:

"I have come to realise that this final part of my professional life has been the most productive and satisfying. It was a lonely business without a great deal of progress, until I found you people at the first Cambridge Colloquium, 'outside London' meeting. Having left the support of the Psycho-Analytical Society without a firm enough grip on my professional skills, I was all too aware that I was out of my depth in venturing alone into the jungle even though it was to my native land. A link had to be forged with the Society in London and the gap was wide. The country's social and economic division was reflected psychoanalytically which was that the preserve of the rich, cultured and privileged was in London. The first effort was the Commission driven by Anne-Marie Sandler's energy and the 'Topping Up' (Sponsoring Committee) arrangements along with an increasing number of senior colleagues who allied themselves to the distant regional groups."

Here is another older member:

"Psychoanalysis here has a long and chequered history. We have probably had more analysts here than anywhere else in the provinces. The main disappointment was we never managed to get training off the ground. Only one person trained from here and it was very hard going. Otherwise we have encouraged likely people to move to London. We have contributed a lot to other trainings especially the BAP and child psychotherapy. There is quite a group of BAP here, but as far as I know there are only two child therapists.

"I can't speak for others but I have supervised a considerable number of people doing other trainings. I have done this with some uneasiness since I do not always trust their training institutions. But most of these people showed a genuine interest in psychodynamic work, both theoretical and clinical. Choice of London training from here is limited by the practicalities. I think we have had a considerable impact. We have had some help from London senior analysts were always ready to come. These stimulated a lot of interest. I could always have filled my practice with referrals from London.

"I was made very welcome but this also had a lot to do with the aura of the Tavistock I brought, so I have been used as a psychoanalytically orientated consultant to organisations. I sometimes think I run a one-woman Tavi here."

Turning now to the replies of Child Psychotherapists (CPTs) who received the same letter as the analysts, we will be addressing the same issues. For instance, D.D. remembers sitting at an ACP officers meeting in London in the 1970s and, noting that three of the four had been born in the North, she wondered: "Why isn't the meeting in Yorkshire?" Perhaps this was the moment that the Child Psycho-therapy Trust was born. We will see in a moment that this Trust is a major agent for CPTs in the regions.

It will soon be clear that the endemic tensions for CPTs and ana-lysts are different. One CPT who has worked in London and in three different regions says the following about going into new posts there: "The major difference between being in or out of London is being in or out of an atmosphere where the inner world is taken seriously." However, he ends his letter with expressing no wish to return to London and passionately arguing how important it is for CPTs to move out. Several express their uneasiness about the dominance of London. Only one expressed any wish to return: "Eleven years later I find myself longing to return and worrying about being so far away from colleagues and structures . . . which can understand what psy-chotherapy means." Many of the writers, unlike the psychoanalysts, had not had to move to London to train. This is largely due to two most important decisions made about twenty years ago by the Tavistock child psychotherapists, led by the then senior tutor, Martha Harris. The first was to reorganize their whole CPT training course so that students in the regions could commute. Lectures and seminars were concentrated on one day of the week, and the minimum number of times a week for their analyses was reduced to three. The second was the decision to extend teaching to subjects where allied profes-sionals could take part—such as the widely valued infant observation as part of the Psychoanalytic Observational Courses. About ten years ago D.D. was one of the founders of The Child Psychotherapy Trust, which works as a direct partner of the ACP. Being primarily educa-tive, particularly of politicians, in Westminster and locally, and of managers, its aims include encouraging the creation of NHS posts. Following this trainee posts, paid for by the local NHS Trusts, and training costs paid by the Regions were negotiated by the ACP. It has been quite surprising how receptive many influential people have been.

Even so, it was clearly often not easy to get started in the regions. For instance:

"There were certainly times during the first 18 months, when I felt despondent. . . . Psychotherapy and psychoanalysis were not widely known in the area, even amongst allied professions."

But in most cases interest grew—for instance:

". . . I was then asked to teach various courses for the WFA and . . . the Counselling Service. Initially I said yes to all teaching requests. It was a lot of work and the pay was a pittance. Very gradually I began to pick up a little more work . . . there is a strong need for psychotherapy in the area, and I now have a very full private practice."

Most found their feet working in clinics and colleges:

"I found my 'home' with the Clinical Psychology Department in the Hospital. . . . I was involved with training MSc students. I taught Child Development at the University. I was well used."

Here is a similar report:

"It was several years before my presence was fully registered, but with this . . . there were requests for supervision and direct refer-rals requesting child psychotherapy. . . . I have found that making an initial effort to get involved in teaching and consultation . . . always eventually improved the general 'climate'."

Here is another:

". . . I began to organize lectures locally. The response to this has been very positive."

As one reads the letters, it begins to emerge that the social dynamic for the CPTs outside London is markedly different from that for the psychoanalysts. For the latter there was often tension with the local adult psychotherapists, to which the analyst responded either by join-ing them and tending to dissociate from London or by standing aloof locally and remaining "loyal" to London. This must largely have been due to the analysts feeling that they must remain detached from local organizations in case a patient is present. The CPTs, on the other hand, without this restriction, appear to have naturally joined the local therapists and counsellors. In fact it becomes plain that their ethos centres on working in teams. Their colleagues are then "different but equal". Perhaps it is because of this that they were able to report that they did not centrally encounter local resistance to psychoanalysis—rather, the opposite.

Here are examples:

"Psychoanalysis and psychotherapy have provided a creative base . . . in the county where I worked."

Another from Yorkshire says:

". . . psychoanalysis is not any more only something I have learned . . . it is my way of being and of addressing reality and the mystery of it. This also comes I think from the fact that over the years I have entered a dialogue with many other professionals, in other forms of therapies, and this has enriched my experience. . . ."

After 30 years' experience in three different regions, one CPT concludes:

". . . Maybe I have been exceptionally fortunate in the places and conditions in which I have worked, but I have not encountered anything like the barriers to practice and understanding that I have heard others complaining of. Rather, what I have generally felt was an appreciation, sometimes exaggerated, of my child analytic training."

Another says:

"There continues to be a receptive climate for psychotherapy and psychoanalysis in Liverpool and the Mersey region due largely to the vision of Prof. Tony Cox and Prof. Jonathan Hill, the current professor of Child Psychiatry."

From Nottingham comes:

"For brevity I will simply list . . . collaboration with the Tavistock Clinic . . . two members of staff visit monthly . . . collaboration with Birmingham, with the Leeds child development course, with the Adult Psychotherapy Department in Nottingham . . . and across the region with medical and non-medical staff."

Another report from the Midlands says:

"Now there are child psychotherapists with input into various hospitals and clinics in Birmingham, Walsall, Solihull, Stafford, Worcester."

And another reports:

"My experience is that there is a real *hunger* for psychoanalytic thinking in the Midlands. This seems to be particularly acute in Community Health teams; they tell us that they have been wanting 'this type of thinking' for years but didn't know where to find it."

A CPT from Gloucester thinks:

"If there is a team ethos that values emotions and the imagination . . . then there is a sense of being supported and the stresses of the work of helping troubled children and families is contained by the group."

And from Sheffield comes:

"The University . . . has established a 'Centre for Psychotherapy Studies' which is taking an increasingly explicit approach to teaching and training."

However, there definitely are still troubles for CPTs in the regions—but they come from a different quarter: often, but not always, from NHS and local authority managers. For example:

". . . In what now appears to have been an attempt to sabotage the service, the cost as posed to GPs was a staggering £129 per patient/hour . . . most GPs felt they were robbed and chose to decide, with tremendous backing from the Health Authority, to no longer invest in psychoanalytic psychotherapy."

From another region, in the North, comes this report:

"However, despite numerous meetings and discussions with all the purchasers and providers it remained impossible to further the cause of new . . . posts. This was, I believe, due to the implacable opposition of senior child. . . . psychiatrists . . . This position remains to this day."

A report from the West Country says:

"We work in a business minded, objective, culture, where there is little concern for internal worlds which cannot be measured and quantified. Interest in a psychodynamic approach has declined as 'quick cures' are sought."

Turning to another aspect, there are repeated sarcastic comments from CPTs in the regions, as some psychoanalysts had noted, about the narrow arrogance of the "London" attitude. For instance:

". . . we are very affected by the concentration of analysis in London."

Or:

"In London, I come across ignorance of the geography of the North West . . . paralleled by a lack of interest in getting to know more about the cultural influences that prevail. . . ."

Here is a similar comment:

". . . several people associated Birmingham with some third world country and most believed it to be 'somewhere in the North', i.e. North of Watford. I encountered folk who could not imagine that there would be enough hospitals and clinics for students . . . having decided it was such a backwater as to only warrant one hospital!"

On the other hand, one institution in London receives little but praise and gratitude for its help to the regions. This is the Tavistock Clinic . . . unlike the Psychoanalytical Society (at least until recently). We noted that this came about after much reworking of ideas and organization by the Tavi years ago.

With this in mind, we conclude with excerpts from a description of one man's journeys between London and a northern region spreading analytic ideas.

"*Reminiscences on Travelling to Liverpool.* The west coast route is old and rackety. Even with Virgin's newly painted coaches it is still old and rackety. In 1989/90 I was running an infant observation seminar at the Tavistock. . . . I was asked, would I like to do some teaching in Liverpool? Next day I said I would. . . . Some months later after going to lecture several times managers from Health and Social services came to see if they would be interested in 'purchasing' places on courses I might be asked to run . . . this was scary, a new kind of experience for me, there was some hostility but also interest. I started three 20-session teaching groups with about 12 in each group. The work with residential social workers highlighted the tremendous need for support . . . it always felt fresh and serious. . . . Nearly all the Senior registrar Child Psychiatry programme joined the theory and work discussion groups and many did the infant observation course . . . this was encouraged by Prof. Jonathan Hill. What an opportunity to influence professional development. Around 1993 another child psychotherapist moved to the Wirral and another came up weekly from London. The work of getting Liverpool established as a satellite centre to the joint Tavi/UEL MA course involved an enormous amount of work by people in London and Liverpool. In July 1996 I had to finish teaching due to illness. But most luckily my job was completed, a bit prematurely perhaps . . . the bridge was built . . . enough child psychotherapists from Liverpool to run the MA and develop teaching. When I went back in 1997 . . . the moment I opened the carriage door at [Liverpool] Lime Street it felt as though I had never been away, and all day I struggled with the wish to be part of it all in the old way . . . how on earth did this conception bear so much fruit in such a short time? I think it is a story about relationships between a few individuals some of whom held positions of considerable power and influence. . . . This story does not exclude mistrust, fear, rivalry and envy, but on balance the more envious feelings were contained in a remarkable way and great generosity was and is given. I do think that it is this conflict of feelings between people in various crucial roles that is at the heart of why projects thrive or fail. It was an extraordinarily complex equation that led to the burgeoning of Child Psychotherapy in Liverpool and Merseyside. People had been trying for years in Manchester but things hadn't gelled. I think most essential . . . was Prof. Hill's enthusiastic, balanced and trusting support and the support of the department generally. He certainly does not idealize psychoanalysis but he also, I think, recognises there is something creative, valuable and deeply investigative about the observational method that lies at the centre of psychoanalysis. . . . As with the growth of an infant . . . an educational environment is a fragile and emotional process; it is a passionate thing."

Another Merseyside CPT says of this great effort: "An ordinary man doing an extraordinary job."

It can be said with truth that the child psychotherapists have achieved marvels in the regions. Certainly it appears that overall they have established themselves more successfully than have the psychoanalysts. This might simply be that the analysts are more self-effacing in their reports. But the statistically much higher growth rate of CPTs in the regions and their enthusiasm argue against this. It is more likely that psychoanalysts have a much harder task. For a century now, they have gained their core identity by working basically alone with patients. So they have set out from London in that way, and are then often seen as aloof. This itself may create resistance to psychoanalytic ideas. The solution would then be, not to forsake the solitude of their clinical work, for it is utterly essential; but at other times to take pains finding a truthful equality with other professionals. They can then be mutually informative without expecting other locals to become total converts to psychoanalysis.

The success of a few brave psychoanalysts in being prime movers starting high-quality psychotherapy training schools in Scotland, Newcastle, Belfast, and Birmingham suggests that the sociability of psychoanalysts really can bear fruit. The next step, perhaps even now emerging from mere dreaming, thanks in part particularly to Pearl, will be psychoanalytic training to back up these therapies in the regions.

Acknowledgements

This chapter has been made out of many contributions sent in to us from psychoanalysts and child psychotherapists living and working outside the London area. It could not have been done without their generous help. The child psychotherapists were Tom Adams, Robin Balbernie, Lynn Barnett, Paul Barrows, Mary Boston, Sue Brough, Simon Cregeen, Lynda Ellis, David Hardie, Nina Harris, Debbie Hindle, Leslie Ironside, Martin Lyon, David Millar, Turid Nyhamar, Eileen Orford, Miranda Passey, Janet Philps, Chris Reeves, Marta Smith, and Linda Winkley. The psychoanalysts were Kate Barrows, Bill Brough, Sidney Carlish, John Churcher, Iain Dresser, Richard Ekins, Michael Fitzgerald, Tom Freeman, Pip Garvey, Hyla Holden, Isobel Hunter Brown, Graham Ingham, Chris Lucas, Ron Markillie, Isabel Menzies Lyth, Michael Mercer, Brian O'Neill, Vera Pettitt, Stephen Small, and Jim Templeton.

CHAPTER SEVEN

The Holocaust, its aftermath, and the problem of the superego

Bernard Barnett (London)

In this chapter I explore the mechanized and prolonged extreme cruelty associated with the term "Holocaust". I also consider how far Freud's account of the system superego and later analytic contributions can throw light on what is arguably the most horrific event of the twentieth century. Lastly, I describe some case material to illustrate the long-term effects of the Holocaust on superego functioning in a second-generation survivor.

As is well known, in his work carried out over many years, Freud progressively differentiated an unconscious part of the mind—the "ego ideal", which was concerned with setting standards, ideals, rules, regulations, and laws. He described the ideal as originating with the parents and becoming gradually modified by the influence of siblings, relatives, peers, teachers, and others. In his account he laid great stress on the influence of traditional and cultural values being handed down from generation to generation. He also recognized love, concern, and respect as benign aspects of this development.

Implicit in this idea of an ego ideal was a self-observing, self-evaluative, and self-critical aspect of the mind termed the *Über-Ich*, which was translated as the "superego". This part of the mind then watched over "the self" and judged it critically. As an unconscious aspect of the mind, the superego derived its "energy" from instinctual life and acted as a dynamic force continuously operating on the conscious mind. The conscious aspect of the superego (and the ego) imply the idea of "agency" (an aspect of self that can act dynamically) and a sense of, or the awareness of, "conscience". This mental process may be summed up in the simple statement: "I feel a desire to do something but then I feel that I should not do it" (Freud, 1923b, p. 12).

In one of his final formulations, Freud arrived at a concept of a superego system. This combined the three functions "of self-observation, of conscience and of the ideal". Other features of this complex dynamic system were a sense of guilt, the capacity for concern for other people, remorse, ethical standards, and so on (Freud, 1933a, p. 129).

I want to draw attention to a few more of Freud's observations on the system superego as they are relevant to my discussion of the Holocaust and its aftermath. The first is that a child's superego "is constructed not on the model of his parents but of his parents' superego"—a statement that clearly lays stress on the developmental aspect of the system.

Freud described the superego tendency to turn inwards and attack the self, and thus provide an outlet for a person's aggressive tendencies. It is also well known that, in considering the situation in which superego aggression is turned outwards rather than inwards, other mechanisms, such as splitting and projection, come into operation. This gives rise to the problem of what causes the aggressive superego to move in one direction or the other.

In one further comment pertinent to my theme, Freud, in discussing the development of conscience, said: "God has done an uneven and careless piece of work, for a large majority of men have brought along with them only a modest amount of it or scarcely enough to be worth mentioning" (Freud, 1933a, p. 61).

The Holocaust
and the Nazi superego

In what follows, I use the term "Holocaust" to refer to the highly organized implementation of the murder, torture, starvation, and so on, of many millions of men, women, and children—mainly Jews, but including gypsies, mentally handicapped persons, homosexuals, Russian and Polish prisoners of war, and other "undesirables" comprised of many nationalities. This mass killing and other brutalities initiated by the Nazi leaders were carried out by a large number of specially trained Nazis, the German army, and others. It illustrates a degree and quality of cruelty that is super-ordinary in scale, organization, and implementation. In this discussion I also assume that a historical event of this dimension will not yield easily to psychoanalytic or any other explanation, and I am aware of a danger of cheapening and degrading it by reductive and simplistic argument, psychoanalytic or otherwise.

However, I shall nevertheless briefly consider how it came to be that the usual human constraints on the practice of cruelty—that is, the individual's sense of guilt, the capacity for concern, conscience, moral responsibility, and so on—could be so underdeveloped, or so damaged, as to be virtually absent in the initiators and perpetrators of unspeakable torture and mass murder.

In his paper, "Group Psychology and the Analysis of the Ego", Freud describes how the ego ideal was of central importance to the process by which an individual came to submit to the will of a leader by substituting *his* ego ideal for that of the leader. He says that an individual may come to be ruled by "those attitudes of the group mind which exhibit themselves in such forms as racial characteristics, class prejudices, public opinion, etc." (Freud, 1921c).

More recently, Jeannine Chasseguet-Smirgel (1975) has described how certain individuals tend to maintain a strategy for initiating and preserving their narcissistic illusions by means of the new authority of the group, and by this means attempt a union of ego and ideal in which the individual superego is merged.

It is, of course, well known that the Nazi cult emphasized the worship of the all-powerful mother goddess ("Blut und Boden", i.e. "blood and earth"). Chasseguet-Smirgel describes how the Nazi ideology, in proposing a return to nature and to early Germanic mythology, contained "an aspiration to merge with the mother and by this means to develop the illusion of omnipotence". She suggests that a leader such as Hitler activated "the primitive wish for the union of ego and ideal ... [and is] the promoter of illusion ... makes it shiver before men's dazzled eyes ... [and is one] who will bring it to fruition".

We have only to recall the effects of Goebbels' role as the master illusionist to appreciate the force of this argument. However, in her stress on the maternal, Chasseguet-Smirgel perhaps underestimates Hitler's status as a father figure and the Führer mentality of the Nazi take-over.

An example of putting aside superego considerations in favour of the Nazi ego ideal, which emphasizes the significance of German blood, is provided by the notorious leader of the SS, Heinrich Himmler, who once said:

> We must be honest, decent, loyal and comradely to members of our own blood, but to nobody else . . . [If] 10,000 Russian females fall down from exhaustion digging an anti-tank ditch . . . that interests me only in so far as the anti-tank ditch for Germany is finished.

However, an ideal such as this, which aimed to promote the German war effort above all other considerations, cannot account for the other "war" that was waged against the Jews, which was often blindly pursued against the interest of winning the war against the Allies. To consider this phenomenon further, it is necessary to give more detailed consideration to the large-scale, extreme, maniacal cruelty with which this war was waged.

This problem can be considered in terms of retaliation and revenge. For the Nazis and those who carried out their orders, the Jews as scapegoats came to personify both weakness and power. The weakness was projected upon them, and their power identified with. Victor and vanquished were then linked by a bond of mutual hatred. In outlining this argument, Anthony Storr says: "Ordinary people have hidden paranoid tendencies and a proclivity for brutality. . . . It is a mistake to believe that ordinary men are not capable of extremes of cruelty" (Storr, 1968).

A recent account of how usual considerations of conscience can be set aside is found in Daniel Goldhagen's book, *Hitler's Willing Executioners: Ordinary Germans and the Holocaust* (1996). In this work, Goldhagen evaluates different explanations for the Nazi tendency brutally to maximize the cruelty and torture. In his discussion of horrific acts carried out by individuals, he differentiates cruelty perpetrated in the process of obeying orders from cruelty performed on individual initiative, which he calls "voluntaristic cruelty". He describes German cruelty as "nearly universal", "endemic", and "characterised by widespread German dedication and zeal". He suggests that, despite the extraordinary and horrific nature of the campaign of extermination and, therefore, what must have been, or perhaps should have been, an horrific experience for the perpetrators, "few were deterred from treating Jews in the customary German manner of those years". He also offers good evidence that with very few exceptions, and in spite of the opportunity to do so, the perpetrators notoriously failed to exit or express dissent. The author's repetition here of "German" is deliberate and, as his critics have observed, a weak aspect of his thesis, since although it seems evident that many Germans may at the time have had a "genocidal mind set", it is well known that terrible acts were also enthusiastically carried out by perpetrators from many other nationalities. However, the strength of his argument is implied in the word "ordinary", which speaks to the hidden Nazi within everybody.

In trying to account for the extreme cruelty of the perpetrators of the Holocaust, I would emphasize Freud's argument that the ego ideal and the superego are not rigid but, rather, changeable structures. It seems that the standards and capacity for self-judgement of the individual perpetrator, when under certain pressures, withered away and was replaced by the mystical Nazi version of "the collective will . . . the agent of a law of nature and of history". This new ego ideal stimulated the notion of a threat of contamination of the entire Nordic peoples. The malignity behind this idea of contamination is well summed up in the self-fulfilling slogan "Jews, lice, typhus!" (self-fulfilling since Jews were forced into situations where they developed typhus and became infectious). In conjunction with this perverse and poisonous "biological" doctrine, the idea of a "specific character structure" in the perpetrators has been suggested. It is known as *Kadavergehorsam*, which is usually translated as "blind obedience" (literally "obedience unto death") but can also mean to behave in a corpse-like, robotic manner—that is, without will, and therefore without conscience. The idea of *Kadavergehorsam* also clearly implies an extreme degree of personal splitting and dissociation. In the case of the Nazis, it is well illustrated in a statement by Albert Speer, Hitler's architect and Minister of armaments, in which, looking back on his past horrific misdeeds and absence of conscience, he states: "I was like a man following a trail of bloodstained footprints through the snow without realising someone has been injured" (Sereny, 1995).

The first generation of survivors
and the superego

Following this brief excursion into the Nazi mentality, I go on now to make a few observations about the superego and the victims—the so-called first generation of Holocaust survivors. The evidence suggests that, in general, a person in a concentration camp was often reduced to behaving like a starving animal. In some cases, such a situation led to a conflict powerful enough actually to fragment the superego. In the extreme, hostile environment of the camps, there was perhaps always present the unconscious idea that the death of one's neighbour satisfied the Nazis' lust for killing temporarily and thus prolonged one's own existence, even for just one more day. It seems that personal survival in this context often meant an ability to suspend temporarily all superego function, which then led to a regression to an early and primitive developmental stage. In some cases, the price paid for this overwhelming of the superego system and the perpetration of acts against the most firmly established taboos resulted after the war in a permanent psychotic state of depression in survivors (Krell & Sherman, 1997).

However, as exemplified in the Holocaust literature, even in the most horrendous conditions of the extermination camps there were interesting exceptions, which throw light on the complexity of the superego. For example, from a developmental viewpoint, a very interesting programme of research has been carried out by Kestenberg and Brenner (1996). In considering this work, we need to bear in mind the wide age range of the children in the camps, and in their research sample that would make any simple generalization about the children hazardous. Nevertheless, I think it can be fairly said that the findings are heart-rending and also heartening and even awe-inspiring. It is clear that the suffering of children of all ages was tremendous, and that unlike many adults, who became child-like, many of the children became "old before their time"—a feature that persisted in the survivors after the war. However, Kestenberg also reports that "children were more outspoken than grown-ups [and that] they joined the resistance and fed their families . . . [some] . . . even gained strength . . . [and] . . . a new zest for life". She has also been particularly interested in the effect of camp experience on the superego of the child, and I try to summarize her observations from this point of view. In the camp lives of the children, the horrific destruction of the ordinary standards, rules and regulations of child-rearing led to a fragmentation of the superego that had some persistent effects long after the war. One of these she describes as "a state of feeling bad that is conceptualised by the child survivor as being bad". She found that painful mental states and bodily disorders persisted in some child survivors. She also, however, sounds an optimistic note: "As former child survivors regained as adults a feeling of worth and could re-establish their old values and rebuild their superegos, their children were greatly helped in integrating their own. Parenthood raised the survivors' aspirations and helped them to heal the rift in the super-ego."

The following account is extracted from a report in *The Sunday Times* (4 May 1997) and also gives rise to optimism. The story concerns two survivors, Helmuth and Harry, both previously in Auschwitz, who were separated after the war and were then reunited in London after fifty years. In Auschwitz on 14 July 1944, a 13-year-old Jewish boy, Helmuth, standing in line and stripped naked and starving, was inspected and then waved to the left and condemned to die by Joseph Mengele. He then confronted Mengele and begged for his life. In his own testimony, he went up to Mengele, clicked his heels together, and tried to imitate the Hitler Youth. As he spoke perfect *Hochdeutsch*, Mengele assumed he was from Berlin and was clearly impressed, He offered him "his life" and in addition, a job as a messenger. Helmuth marched away, but was approached by Harry, who asked him to beg for *his* life. Helmuth did so, but Mengele lost his temper and said he would spare one only and got the boys to draw straws. Harry lost and urged Helmuth to make a third plea. This time Mengele, perhaps impressed by Helmuth's extreme bravery, perhaps for reasons of his own, agreed.

Helmuth, now aged 67 and looking back, wonders why he risked his life for a "stranger". He says, "Maybe I hypnotized Mengele. Maybe for one moment I made him think differently of the Jews. He must have had some respect for the 13-year-old who gambled his life to look after his friend."

The rest of the report is highly instructive and pertinent to my theme, since it demonstrates the vicissitudes, the ebb and flow of the superego system when striving to survive in an horrific environment of minimal life and sudden death. It is given briefly below as it enables us to follow the shifts, to and fro, of the ego ideal and the superego, the capacity for concern, guilt, and conscience.

For example, the boys were servants to the SS officers. In the daytime, they wore bright uniforms. In the night, they slept six to a bunk with the other Jewish prisoners. Harry's task was to raise and lower the banner "*Arbeit macht frei*". Helmuth, among other things, cleaned motorbikes. They experienced terrible things: Harry, for example, was constantly threatened with a gun. They heard terrible things, since operations were performed without anaesthetic and "the stench of smoke filled the air". Survival forced the boys to turn in on themselves, and an unavoidable and poignant split in the superego is exemplified in this comment by Helmuth: "In the evenings, I would break down and cry and think of my family . . . but at 3.30 in the morning I was cold and self-contained, as invincible as the officers. The people who had died overnight were dragged outside and you stepped over their bodies."

At other times both the boys gave scraps of food to the other prisoners. Helmuth also provided glass bottles to make bombs to blow up a gas chamber. The reporter notes that the story of Helmuth's heroism fulfilled the dying wish of his grandmother, who perished in the camp. In his account, Helmuth concludes: "For fifty years we kept it all inside us because nobody wanted to know. . . . I told friends and family the story but they thought I had made it up. Now I have found Harry the world can know it is true."

The second generation

I turn now from the child survivors to the second generation— children of survivors, who were born after the war—and consider their transposition into their parents' past. This phenomenon has been described by Kestenberg as "living in two separate epochs, the present and the past". Of the many significant issues relating to transposition, I shall concentrate on the "death imprints" that are embedded in the minds of the survivor parents, and that are unconsciously transmitted to the children of survivors. I shall try to relate some effects of this transposition to the malfunctioning of the superego system. (In this discussion, I am indebted to the work of Bergmann, 1982; Karpf, 1996; Kogan, 1995; Lifton, 1993; Pines, 1993a, 1993b; Wardi, 1992)

It has been reported frequently that one particularly cruel long-term effect of the transmission to the children of the parents' Holocaust experience is the hovering presence of death in the lives of the second generation. Dina Wardi, for example, has described how certain of the children in a survivor family may become "memorial candles" in homage to murdered relatives and, more generally, to the murdered millions.

Most recently, Anne Karpf has provided a vivid and detailed account of her experience of growing up in a survivor family. Her work has a special value because in it she monitors the changes in her "self system", including her superego, as a result of therapy and other life experience. I also consider it in some detail because it provides a useful comparison for my own and other clinical encounters with persons from the second generation (Kestenberg, 1993; Kogan, 1995).

Karpf describes various kinds of compulsive behaviour she carried out to keep a death threat at bay. She associates this fantasized idea of fighting the war all over again within herself with an intensive urge to repair. She describes a compulsive drive to achieve as her attempt to adjust to unconscious and conscious family demands. She says that she came to believe that without action—that is, "doing"— one would cease to "be". For her (as for her parents), achievement was equated with survival.

Karpf writes that she experienced her parents as fragile china that had been broken and then repaired, with herself as the "glue". If she separated from them, she sensed that they would break down, fall apart, or die. For many years, any kind or degree of separation was experienced by her with extreme pain and guilt, and she adds, tellingly, that this did not lessen with time. When some measure of separation was finally achieved, a part of her was still threatened by death-centred thoughts. Thus she tells us: "at the age of twenty-five and with the encouragement of my mother, I did leave home . . . but phoned home every day to check that they were still alive". In my own group work with second-generation groups, some, especially female members of the group, have related an almost identical story.

Thus, for Karpf, the idea of "becoming her own person" was an enormously complicated uphill task. She speaks of a false aspect of personality in which all she could manage was to "simulate" independence. The cruelty of this situation was sustained, because she was unable to imagine her survival without her parents, nor their survival without her presence. For her, as for her parents, separation and rupture were equivalent, and all endings became very dangerous, as she had no trust in reunion. She movingly describes the process of transmission and its roots as follows: "My parents . . . [had experienced] . . . sudden fractures . . . [and] . . . their experience had become my own. I'd soaked up their fear of loss. For all of us separation had become symbolically equivalent of death."

Karpf describes her identification with her mother as *"total"*. As I have suggested earlier, the identificatory processes, in the form of the internalization of parental values and standards, are central for the normal development of the ego ideal and the superego. Karpf's "total identification" suggests another distortion in the empathic and identificatory processes in the direction of overcompensation. She tells us that she would gladly have become one with her parents and suffered for them, but that she still could not have matched their suffering.

Kestenberg has described the process of transposition as a fantasy process of bringing the dead back to life. She writes that transposition is like descending into a time tunnel (living in two worlds at the same time) and having primitive fantasies about rescuing the Jews and restoring their lost children, parents, siblings, grandparents, and still others belonging to their parent's generation. She also draws attention to a split in the system superego in some patients who are manifestly "living in the past".

In her book, Karpf also poignantly describes a form of over-identification in the second generation in which the effects of the parental experience of cruelty have been directly transmitted into her body, and she provides harrowing accounts of her various life-long psychosomatic disorders (see also Kogan, 1995; Pines, 1993b).

Case material

I describe a second-generation patient of my own in the light of the discussion above.

Mr A impressed me as a bright young businessman. He sought help because of a lack of confidence in his relationships and because of a particular difficulty in separating from his parents. In this account I seek to illustrate only some striking features of the unconscious transmission of parental trauma on the patient's superego system as they were revealed in the course of therapy.

After about a year in analysis, Mr A told me of a incident told to
him by his mother, who had as a very young child been in a
concentration camp with her own mother (his grandmother). The
story was that a guard with a ferocious Alsatian dog had thrown a
half-eaten apple in front of the starving child, with the clear intention of setting the dog on her if she moved for the apple. My
patient's mother, in relating this, had conveyed the full emotional
force of the experience of torture, brutality, terror, and a pervasive
sense of utter helplessness. As we proceeded in the analysis and
he told me of current dilemmas in his own life, he sometimes
returned to this vivid and painful anecdote. In what follows, I try
to illustrate various features of his damaged superego and especially his unconscious transposition into his mother's past life and
his gradual bid for a personal space and autonomy during the
course of therapy.

Mr A seemed to me to demonstrate a compulsive need to keep his
mother safe in the present by attempting to "undo" the traumatic
effects of the past. In one session, he told me of how his mother
had generalized her past camp experience to her current life. He
said that she would often tell him that life was a matter of "dog
eats dog" and that "If you didn't get the other, they would get
you!" He told me that he found this difficult to cope with, particularly because part of him agreed with this point of view, and he
added fiercely that had I been in a camp, I would feel the same
way.

Now, although it was clear that another part of him had a more
balanced and more autonomous viewpoint, what struck me at this
time was how Mr A tended to perceive the outside world as
essentially cruel and hostile. I don't think it is helpful to label this
as "paranoid"; perhaps one can use the term "pseudo-paranoid",
bearing in mind his considerable degree of insight and his capacity to differentiate "self" from "other". In this same session, he
gave a rather vague and unclear account of how, on his way to the
session, a man had asked him for money and had made some
hostile remark to him. He had then reacted strongly and sworn at
the man, and this had put him in a very bad and fighting mood.
Now, whatever the reality aspects of this incident, this material
seemed to me to illustrate my patient's projection of the cruel,
persecutory internal world that he carried around with him,

which, at least in part, seemed to derive from his mother's past. It was as if he was transposed *into* a world of persecution, which belonged to his mother. He had developed a compulsive need to continue to fight a battle not his own and thus, in fantasy, to rescue his mother from her past (and his present) sense of help-lessness.

Some time later Mr A told me about eating problems in adolescence, when, it seems, he had experienced his school as being like a concentration camp. At the time, he said he had become anorexic. In one session he told me about his current feelings of guilt about things he "consumed". He described how he had realized that his mother had experienced starvation as a child but had survived, so that he felt now that *he* could not "consume", since consuming was an evil thing! I said that it was as though he also felt himself to be consumed by his mother's past. He agreed and went on to talk about his guilty feelings in allowing himself to experience even very simple pleasures in life. When I came to consider this material later, however, I understood it differently to mean that he had initiated the situation by unconsciously offering himself for his mother to eat up as a kind of compensation. I also came to see that something similar was going on in his relation-ship with me.

For Mr A, the unconscious, and sometimes quite conscious, pull towards merging with his parents and their past was very power-ful. It was also especially in evidence in relation to myself in any major break in the analysis. The full force of the cruelty of his internal situation is illustrated in a session a week before an Easter break in which in a rather upset state he began by telling me that he had again become distressed by his parents' attitude to life. His mother's philosophy was, he said, that you were on your own and had to fight your way through life assuming that everyone was the enemy. She thought *people were a pack of dogs* who had a choice of kill or be killed. His mother felt she was alone; she couldn't trust anyone because everyone was evil.

I suggested that he also felt distressed and betrayed by me, be-cause he felt I would abandon him. He responded that it had been my choice to stop for the break, and that this was not a good time for him. I noticed that his voice sounded choked. He told me that he felt like a snake trying to shed its skin, but he didn't think he could shed it. This was, he said, because he kept wondering how he could be happy when his mother had suffered *so* much. I said that he felt he could keep his mother happy only by being compliant, but he also thought this false and wanted to shed this part of himself. He said that the problem was his guilt—that he considered himself a Nazi collaborator, as bad as the people in the camp. He felt this part of him instructed him that he must never be gentle, or make apologies, or he would be a traitor and a betrayer of his mother. I said that he also seemed to locate this traitor from the past in me in the present. He responded that he felt he couldn't trust me because if he did, there would be a disaster, and it was time to end the session.

Discussion

I have tried to show how the process of transposition has a large fantasy element in that it seeks to bring the traumatic past, and especially the dead, back to life, so to speak: Kestenberg (1993) has described transposition as a process of descending into a time tunnel in which a person lives in two worlds at the same time. The child of a survivor has primitive fantasies about rescuing the survivor parents, the lost siblings, the grandparents, and still others belonging to their parents' generation and sometimes the whole Jewish race.

I have tried to illustrate a split in the system superego in the perpetrator and in some second generation survivors who are manifestly "living in the past". This fragmentation in the second generation has varied manifestations, one of which derives from a clash between a punitive superego and an undigested, parental ego ideal.

The material discussed above can be understood in terms of an overactive and fragmented superego connected to a severe distortion in the capacity for concern. This is in the direction of over-concern, which is a result of being enveloped in and reliving the parents' past. This problem hides an unconscious need for the second generation to carry heavy baggage in the form of a responsibility belonging to the "other"—in this case the parent or parents.

The second-generation survivors unconsciously expected to make up for the sufferings and deficits of the first generation. They have had to carry out a "mission" on behalf of the survivors, which led, in turn, to overcompensation and a distortion of their own sense of self. In line with the observations of others, I have tried to show how a child of survivors developed his own personal myth regarding a parent's survival and his own struggle with the mission and the rescue attempt.

My patient's over-involvement with his parents' life led to an interference with the autonomy of his superego and ego ideal. Put in another way, the pressure to return to the past was bought at the expense of the individual development of the self. A conflict thus arose between his superego and his parents' ego ideal, which may have given rise to a protracted, hostile bond between the two.

It seems that only an intrapsychic act of separation from this cruel fate could free this second-generation person and thus consolidate his sense of autonomy. The analytic contact sought to initiate and sustain this process and establish a new freedom from the shared bond of guilt.

CHAPTER EIGHT

Repetition and modification in the ageing process

Harold P. Blum (New York)

> All the world's a stage,
> And all the men and women merely players.
> They have their exits and their entrances,
> And one man in his time plays many parts,
> His acts being seven ages. At first the infant,
> Mewling and puking in the nurse's arms.
> Then the whining school-boy . . .
> . . .
> . . . Last scene of all,
> That ends this strange eventful history,
> Is second childishness and mere oblivion . . .
>
> William Shakespeare, *As You Like It, II,* vii, 139

In the first half-century of psychoanalysis, it was not considered appropriate to analyse a patient past the middle years. Freud (1905a), paradoxically, wrote at the age of 48: "The age of patients has this much importance in determining their fitness for psychoanalytic treatment . . . near or above the age of fifty the elasticity of the mental processes . . . is as a rule lacking—old people are no longer educable" (p. 264). The pathways to change were considered closed and the personality not only consolidated but much less flexible, if not rigidified; heightened narcissism and narcissistic investment in one's own lifestyle and adaptation, a lack of motivation for change, and diminished opportunity for effecting appropriate change in the external world were all considered to be major factors that would impede psychoanalysis for this age group. In addition, the classical period of psychoanalysis emphasized the formative years of childhood, the infantile neurosis, and the more-or-less permanent imprint on the personality left by early experience, especially traumatic childhood experience. The personality was formed through adolescence, and little attention was paid to changes in later life. In those formative years of psychoanalysis, the adult neurosis was considered to be a homologue of an infantile neurosis. The infantile conflicts would ostensibly be recapitulated in the transference neurosis and resolved through analysis. Though analysts themselves often continued to work into very advanced years, the problems of the geriatric analyst or elderly, impaired patient were hardly considered. Freud had made observations about the effects of ageing and the differences of ageing between men and women, but he had not systematically discussed the effect of the later phases of life on the personality. Unconscious conflict and trauma were timeless in their persistence and influence, and there was little regard for personality alteration in later life and changes in the way life was lived and experienced.

The early developmental phases were tied to biological maturation, with particular emphasis on phase-specific conflict and developmental challenges. The term "adult development" was somewhat ambiguous—not linked to biological maturation and not clearly differentiated from alteration or modification of the personality and its components. Changes in later life were noted but were usually attributed to the regression and revival of antecedent conflicts and phases of development.

This chapter considers the continuity of the personality and of unconscious conflict throughout the life cycle. However, it also considers the adult modifications of the personality during the ageing process, and that continuity and change coexist often with mutual influence. I consider the older phases of the life cycle, beginning with a review of some of the later facets of the life history and study of the Wolf Man. I then present two clinical vignettes, illustrating both neurotic repetition and personality modification in the transition from late middle age to early old age. It is important to emphasize that there is no standard chronological or psychological definition of the terms "old" or "elderly". These terms have many social, cultural, medical, and economic dimensions, and there are also wide variations in the effects of ageing within the individual and from individual to individual.

The pioneering paper of Abraham (1919) who wrote about successful treatment of patients who were then considered to be in late middle age was followed much later by more contemporary contributions, notably by Pearl King (1980) and others (e.g. Coltart, 1991; Levin & Kahana, 1967; Nemiroff & Colarusso, 1985; A.-M. Sandler, 1984; Settlage, 1996; Valenstein, 2000; Zinberg & Kaufman, 1978).

The only major case where we have a longitudinal study of the person, a psychoanalytic life history, and an autobiographical commentary is Freud's case of the Wolf Man (1918b [1914]), who affords "a unique opportunity to witness a human being's inner and outer life unfold before our eyes from childhood to old age" (A. Freud, 1971, p. xii). The case of the Wolf Man was published in 1918, although it was written shortly after the termination of the treatment in the winter of 1914–15. The recollections and reconstructions of the Wolf Man's childhood in Freud's longest, elaborate case history are supplemented by the Wolf Man's own recollections of his own childhood and later life, as well as his recollections of Freud. Freud remained productive and creative throughout his life, and it is regrettable that although there are scattered references to the Wolf Man in many of Freud's later writings, he did not choose to review the case or his other classic case histories in the light of later psychoanalytic experience and knowledge. The Wolf Man had further analytic treatment with Ruth Mack-Brunswick and periodic contacts with psychoanalysts, including Muriel Gardiner, Kurt Eissler, and others; he was the only one of Freud's patients willing and able to cooperate in published follow-up studies and in the process to contribute new material.

The Wolf Man began treatment in January 1910, terminating in June 1914; he was then treated again by Freud from November 1919 to February 1920. The Wolf Man had good reason to believe that he was a favourite patient and remained of interest, not only to his analyst, but to succeeding generations of psychoanalysts. In many respects, he represents a borderline adult and narcissistic personality with a preceding borderline childhood and adolescence (Blum, 1974). Many important features have been reviewed (Mahony, 1984), and analysts of every school have commented, criticized, and contributed to the understanding of the case over the years. With the help of analysis and psychoanalytic psychotherapy, the Wolf Man was able to survive severe stress and traumata. However, he continued also to demonstrate personality fragility and regressive vulnerability, as well as personality modifications over his life. Muriel Gardiner (1971) gave him personal assistance, encouragement, and emotional support. She published her observations with those of the Wolf Man, depicting him in later life.

The Wolf Man was born on Christmas Eve in 1886 and died on 1 May 1979. Preoccupied with the problem of ageing, he had been forced to retire in 1950 at 63 years of age. In 1953 his mother died at the age of 89. Dependent and needy, he had grown closer to his mother and his housekeeper, who was also quite elderly, since his wife's suicide in 1938. He would thank Drs Gardiner and Eissler for their helpfulness, only to disparage them to others deceptively. Despite his ambivalence and ego passivity, much of the memoirs have a ring of authenticity and contain poignant observations relevant to this study. Compared to the initial obliging apathy that Freud (1918b [1914]) described, the Wolf Man's powers of observation, discrimination, introspection, and inference indicate areas of favourable personality change. In other respects his life had been rather joyless and depressed, and he complained about many health problems. He also lamented about not being able or even motivated to paint, losing a significant sublimation. On 18 August 1948 he wrote:

> and I, too, am always growing older, although I must sadly confess, not wiser. For many years I've thought that I would through the many hard blows of fate which I suffered, would at least in age become somewhat more mellow and would acquire some sort of philosophic outlook upon life. I thought that at old age I could at least spend my last years at a distance from the emotional struggles of which I've had so many in my life. But it seems that these are illusions also. [in Gardiner, 1971, p. 337]

Retirement had a deleterious effect, and the Wolf Man wondered whether this was the melancholy of old age. He had no sense of accomplishment and complained about his misfortunes and being condemned to live for many years alone without purpose. He later reported to Dr Gardiner between her visits to Vienna during the 1960s that writing—and, we may infer, appreciation of his memoirs by psychoanalysts—gave purpose to his life. A more positive interest and pleasure in life may have begun after his first publication in a psychoanalytic journal in 1957, although he had also been occasionally meeting with a local psychoanalyst.

Gardiner wrote to the Wolf Man in 1963 with questions about his growing older. He noted that his conflicts were the same but had acquired a more chronic character. His sexual drive had lost intensity, but his aggressive drives, in contrast, had become stronger. Asked about being more or less narcissistic, the Wolf Man replied, "In a positive sense, less narcissistic, because one is no longer so vain in old age as in youth but in a negative sense, one's narcissism has increased, as one has become more sensitive to any criticism of one's person, suspecting that it contains references to the signs and shortcomings of age, of which one does not wish to be reminded." Asked whether his life was more or less harmonious, he replied, "definitely less harmonious. With increasing age, interest in life grows less and, therefore, interest in the world around one and its manifestations lessens also. All our goals are subject to the limitations of time, and the time which remains to one or which one can hope for becomes ever smaller and shorter" (in Gardiner, 1971, p. 348). Reflecting that with advanced age, life lost much of its charm and value, the Wolf Man at the same time observed that

> the problem of ageing depends very much on the individual. My mother, for instance, told me that she was happier in her old age than in her youth, although she had lost her entire fortune and lived as an older woman in poor surroundings and among strangers. Her relatives, to whom she was deeply attached, either remained in Russia or had died ... in age she could live a quiet and contemplative life to which she had always been inclined ... after all, in youth one asks more of life than in old age, and must therefore experience many disappointments. It is not uninteresting that earlier my mother suffered markedly from a severe hypochondria, which however, disappeared completely after her sixtieth year. [p. 350]

The changes described by the Wolf Man for both himself and his mother are not atypical. These changes are not radical alterations of the personality and represent modifications, albeit sometimes in new directions. The period under discussion was during the Wolf Man's sixties rather than his late eighties or nineties, when there was far more severe geriatric alteration of the personality.

Advanced old age is too often synonymous with chronic illness, often associated with progressive loss of physical and ego function. In addition, there are often losses of loved ones and friends, so that at advanced age, physical dysfunction, object loss, severe narcissistic injuries, and regression severely impact on the personality. During the early older period under discussion, there was a diminution of the sexual drive and an increase of aggression, but also the loss of dignity, status, income, and work. Work had represented investment in object relations and reality adaptation. Retirement for him was associated with feeling superfluous and cast aside. Separation reactions and depression are not uncommon, and the Wolf Man reacted with reactivated and intensified depression. At the same time, as noted in the case of his mother, there are usually lessened expectations of the older person. Harsh internal demands to live up to personal ideals and values may be lessened with age. In addition, cultural pressures for achievement may be removed, so that demands for social and intellectual achievement and sexual performance are less pressing. The mellowing seen in some individuals with the onset of ageing may be associated with more benign personal and cultural tolerant attitudes towards standards and values. Changes in the self-representation are found with changes in the ideal self and ego ideal during the lifecycle and the ageing process.

The masochistic depressive dispositions of the Wolf Man persisted with continuing extreme ambivalence. His wandering into the Russian Zone in 1951 on the anniversary of his sister's death risked dire consequences. Even before the subsequent death of his mother and housekeeper, he was involved in a sado-masochistic relationship with an avaricious borderline woman. This self-punitive, tormenting, punitive relationship endured for more than a quarter of a century. His interview at an advanced age (Obholzer, 1980) cannot be regarded as very reliable because of his geriatric condition.

In some cultures, older persons are highly respected; in others older persons are considered to be infirm, lacking in vitality, a potential burden for themselves and their families. Actually, a great deal depends upon the continuity of intact personality resources and, particularly, ego strengths to deal with the inevitable biological, psychological, and social changes. The capacity for accepting change, mastering change, and flexibly adapting is crucial to ageing gracefully or fitfully. In former years the literature emphasized drive alterations rather than structural and dynamic modifications in the total personality. I shall particularly emphasize the importance of adult traumatic experience. The severely traumatized person is never the same (Blum, 1994). Trauma not only leaves a relatively permanent influence, but alterations in the personality occur. There is a vulnerability to reactivation of the specific traumatic experience and a vulnerability to retraumatization and regression. The psychic influence of trauma and psychic damage persists long after physical injuries have healed. There are identifications with victim and aggressor and in the process of recovery with rescuer, protector, and comforter. Trauma also leaves residues in the form of a proclivity to repetition and acting-out of the trauma, rigid defences against re-experiencing the trauma, and a predisposition to anxiety, "daymares" and nightmares, sleep disturbance, and somatization. Disturbances of memory, affect regulation, and alterations of consciousness may persist and coalesce with psychological and neurobiological changes due to the ageing process.

The first clinical vignette concerns a patient with severe traumatic experience of young adult life reactivating and amalgamating with childhood and adolescent traumatization. The patient could be described as a survivor of Nazi persecution.

The patient was about 60 when he started his analytic treatment with me, having had psychoanalyses with different analysts, which, in turn, had followed an initial period of wild analysis. He gained a great deal from his previous analytic work with three "renowned analysts", all of whom helped him with his severe obsessional disturbance and preceding preoccupation with cleanliness versus contamination. The focus of the previous analyses has been on his childhood, his unresolved oedipal conflicts, and self-punitive, self-denigrating tendencies. What had become clear in re-analysis was that he tended to accept insults, was overly compliant, did not protest or pursue disagreements, and tended to accept analytic interpretations without exercising his own critical judgement (Blum, 1985).

In certain respects, the years of analytic treatment, beginning with a wild analyst, had dealt far more with his characterological rigidity than with his passivity, compliance, and fear of aggression. None of the analysts had regarded his adolescent experience in an anti-Semitic European community during the rise of Nazism as important. When denial and isolation of his adolescence and young adult life had been interpreted, he was stunned by the interest of the analyst, the flood of memories, and the avoidance of this whole period during his prior analyses. Furthermore, one of his former analysts had also been a refugee from Nazism. Each spoke to the other in a similar accent without ever mentioning the accent, nor any reference to the Nazi or refugee experience or the Holocaust. There was a silent collusion with an analyst of similar background not to refer to Nazism, anti-Semitism, or Jewish issues. The prior analysis of his adult neurosis and its translation into infantile neurotic forerunners had largely excluded his adolescence and early adult life. His adolescence was a psychosocial crisis, and the patient and his close-knit family suffered in silence in a state of siege. At first there was parental denial of the forewarnings of the reign of terror ahead. By the time the patient reached puberty, there was daily abuse. Jews were treated as if they were enemy aliens. There were repeated experiences of shock trauma, with ongoing strain and fear of family imprisonment. He was savagely humiliated and was terrified when a group of fellow students mocked his exposed circumcised penis and conveyed castration threats with jeers and gestures. The patient later recognized the blocking of any affective re-experience of this whole terrible period of his life. The traumata and developmental strain had many pathogenic consequences, reinforcing his passivity, compliance, and sadomasochistic identifications. His Jewish identity and self-representation had been deformed by the enemy, who was now within. He was guilty over his devaluation of his family, friends, and relatives, some of whom perished in the Holocaust. Jewish religious observance had purportedly contributed to his obsessional neurosis. But there had been no attention to prejudice and persecution having contributed to his fears of being unclean, contaminated, dirty, and undeserving. Parental inability to protect or protest had been associated with a conspiracy of silence in the family, the community, the media, and so on.

The process of ageing in this patient represented a giving-up of certain adult prerogatives and, in the context of the analysis, revived certain features of adolescence and retreat from adulthood. There was narcissistic regression and a revival of conflicts associated with unconscious rage and hostility. As in adolescence, sadomasochistic sexual fantasy was revived, although with diminution and pressure of his sexual arousal and interest. A prostate condition activated castration fears. He no longer had quite the same energy as before and was concerned about diminution of his visual and auditory acuity. The spectre of gradual retirement was reminiscent of his young adult dislocation and of the need to redefine his identity, relationships, and life goals.

Two major problems connected with ageing also appeared. His younger wife reacted with an exacerbation of anger, dissatisfaction, and depression. Implied threats of divorce reactivated the patient's adolescent experience of separation, dislocation, and humiliation. He could be considered unwanted, undesirable, to be despised and excluded rather than loved and included. He could fantasize his wife as a closet Nazi, a domineering, phallic woman. He rationalized his own masochistic need for a powerful parent who could alternately protect or punish him.

The threat of divorce evoked feelings of separation and loss, persecution and depression. The patient imagined that he would not be attractive or desirable to younger women and he would again lose social status. He had not had a mid-life crisis but a crisis in the transition from middle to older age, with revived panic, depression, and self-denigration. As in the past, he again demanded more of himself—grand achievements to compensate for earlier losses, disappointments, and humiliations. His new inability to remember names and his diminished powers of concentration were associated with an "ageing brain". This catalysed perfectionistic demands in other spheres. He thought of a "brain drain" and of inevitable neurobiological decline. His adolescent and young adult expectations had been thwarted. He was now concerned that he would not really be able to maintain a sense of acuity and stability concerning his life. He anticipated older age feeling displaced, declining, and apprehensive.

In this setting, the analyst's perspectives about ageing and awareness of his own personal and cultural values were very important. Countertransference collusion may appear in either denial or reassurance concerning age and its conflicts. His elderly analyst died during his analysis. Both analyst and patient had denied and avoided any question about the analyst's age—a repeated pact of silence. The patient's traumatization continuing into adulthood reinforced his fear of hostile aggression towards a fragile, elderly analyst, and his passive compliance. It may be too easy to compete with previous analysts and to foster passive compliance with the present analyst.

Did the analysis provide new opportunities for missed adolescent experience such as protest and rebellion? Was the analyst a protective new object who enabled the patient to re-experience adolescence and adulthood in a way that had been impossible during the patient's actual development? Did the analyst replace the patient's parents as the powerful protective parent who could help him to confront and master persecutory anxiety and repeated traumatization? In adolescent analysis, the analyst is a new object as well as a transference object. In this particular "younger" older age group as compared with advanced old age, and in this particular case, I infer that transference analysis, genetic interpretation, reconstruction, and reintegration were far more important than the experience of the analyst as a new parental object.

In reviewing his adolescent and young adult life from the vantage point of his sixties, his reminiscence was now bittersweet. He was consciously bitter about the adolescent persecution he suffered. He was pleased about his active escape and more tolerant of his refugee regression and passive timidity after emigration. The shaping influence of the ageing process on the way the present and past are experienced is a relatively contemporary emphasis. It is complementary to the traditional emphasis upon the persisting influence of past, unconscious conflicts and trauma upon the present and the future. Conversely, present meanings may be retrospectively transferred to the past, as well as to the neurotic behaviour of later life.

* * *

A woman, who had been analysed as a young mother many years before returned for further analytic treatment because of intense personal distress, depression, and marital discord. As a young woman she had been very eager to please and appeared over-controlled in speech, manner, and etiquette. A lifelong constipation was related to fear of loss of control and object loss. She was afraid of losing love, self-esteem, power, security, and securities. Her bowel control and retention kept all feelings of resentment and anger inside, and loss of faeces also meant various forms of castration and deprivation. Intensely ambivalent, she was afraid of retaliatory aggression. As analysis progressed, she was able to challenge and disagree, to hurl insults and invectives, to joke, and to feel safely sarcastic and critical. No longer constipated and inhibited, the tendency to be self-critical and critical created difficulties in her marriage and friendships. She could be loving and giving, but also withholding, demanding, and disdainful.

Many of the gains of her first analytic experience endured. She was never again subject to chronic constipation, and she retained the improved spontaneity and vivacity, which were characterological by-products of her analysis. However, with the onset of ageing and transition into older years, there was a regressive revival of old symptoms, as well as marked tendencies towards depression. She re-entered analysis and then psychotherapy in her sixties, superficially struggling with the issue of "generativity versus stagnation" (Erikson, 1959).

Since generativity is concerned with the care of offspring in future generations, it may be extended to grandparenthood as well as parenthood. Erikson (1959) also indicated that preparation for ageing begins with the child's representations of himself and others at later ages and stages of life, and stated, "A child in the multiplicity of successive and tentative identifications thus begins early to build up expectations of what it would be like to be older and what it would feel like to have been younger" (p. 114). To this may be added how it feels to be the older parent, the grandparent, and to be married to an older spouse who has also changed in the course of life.

Symbolized by her prior chronic constipation, this patient had always engaged in "holding on" and had difficulty in letting go. Separations were always conflictual, and the later analysis now involved separations and individuation as an older person. While she could be described as illustrating the conflict of identity versus despair and disgust—Erikson's (1959) designation of the typical challenge of mature older age—this patient seemed more concerned with problems of loss: of her sense of importance, purpose, respect, and feeling loved and appreciated. She did not represent or regard herself as those of the older generation who are highly regarded for their maturity, wisdom, and judgement. Rather, she felt superfluous, a "fifth wheel", and separated from her loved ones, beginning with the marriage of her child. The "empty nest syndrome" was one facet of a larger problem of loss. Analytic work revealed that prior to the departure of her child, the deaths of her parents had actually left her feeling depressed and frightened—a vulnerable, unprotected orphan. Her experience of loss, validating her fantasies of destruction and retaliation for hostile death wishes, and the constipation of youth were associated with the fantasy of loss. The depression of ageing evolved when the loss fantasies were anchored in reality; loss was complicated by cosmetic and bodily change and health impairments. She could do everything she had done before, but with greater effort, more fatigue, and less satisfaction. She both feared and wished for dependency more intensely.

One major effect of the new situation was the intense appearance of regressive longing for a nurturing, comforting, feeding mother. At times she presented in the transference like a whining cry-baby. She was eager to have the exclusive possession and affection of her mother in the transference. The idealized oedipal father of the transference in the previous analysis had now given way to a transference split between her comforting, consoling mother and the disappointing, rejecting, envious mother-figure. The patient tried to hold onto sessions and was intensely resentful at the end of sessions or at the weekend separations. She was ever more dependent upon her husband and jealous of any attention given to her husband and child. Grandparenting, too, had both its gains and its losses. She could experience the continuity of family and a sense of restitution and immortality, while at the same time feeling that her child was ever more involved in her own new family.

The appearance and experience of these reactions was far more intense than in her earlier life. She had then been more optimistic, more ready to take on the tasks of the moment. Her conflicts had elements of the anal regression of the older woman who becomes "quarrelsome, vexatious and overbearing, petty and stingy ... traits which they did not possess earlier during their period of womanliness" (Freud, 1913i, p. 323). Freud noted the radical alteration of the personality of the formerly charming girl, loving wife, and tender mother. I do not think that such transformations are limited to one developmental phase or that they particularly characterize women, at least in contemporary society. The role of women in other eras was often severely restricted and devalued. Until relatively recently, most women did not live long enough to experience the menopause, and many women were depleted and traumatized by their own chronic illness and the mortality of their children within large families.

My patient viewed her losses and disappointments through the crucible of ageing. New conflicts and personality problems stood out in relief, and old problems were re-experienced in terms of her being an older woman who had lost loved ones, her youthful attractiveness, and her earlier determination, vigour, and vitality. Her reluctance to terminate was less a fantasy of stopping the clock and not further ageing and more of a problem of separation and further loss of object and love. Unlike the more geriatric and advanced-aged patient concerned with death and immortality, termination would be a real object loss, though not actual death (King, 1980). She was much more concerned with having and holding her love objects and overcoming loss. The unconscious is indeed timeless, and it was important for her to understand the recapitulation of unconscious conflict and trauma. But it was also important for her to recognize the meaning of her conflicts in terms of her current life and her reactions to changes ensuing with the ageing process. The analyst's own countertransference to his/ her own ageing, and to his/her own ageing love objects may all be helpful in understanding the patient.

Unlike the senescent patient or the dying patient whose time is very short, the recently older patient is concerned with the length and quality of longevity. These patients may be helped with analytic work to have a more meaningful, productive, and gratifying life. The patient is also a changed person—not simply his or her former self psychologically and physically. Some analysis may better prepare them for the inevitable changes that follow. It may be noted that Freud's creative contributions were produced in his middle and later years. The patients who have been previously analysed may be especially accessible to the resumption of analysis.

Other older patients, sometimes including those who were refractory to therapy at earlier phases of life, may be ready for introspection and dispassionate reflection and may beneficially utilize psychoanalytic psychotherapy.

CHAPTER NINE

Some reflections on D. W. Winnicott's ideas

Carlos A. Crisanto (Lima)

L et us begin by remembering the essential elements in the Winnicottian way of approaching a clinical problem. These elements are:

- preoccupation with the understanding and management of the regressive states, explicit and concealed;

- interest in the authenticity or otherwise of what the patient produces in the analytical situation;

- the importance of holding and mutuality between analyst and patient;

- consideration of the factor of need, apart from wishes and fantasies (Khan, 1986).

According to the above, psychoanalysis consists of the establishment of an understanding and trusting human relationship that leads to the earliest stages of emotional development of the individual, where a traumatic "heritage" exists that will have to be resolved. In other words, it is a process of interaction between two individuals who work together in order to achieve a spontaneous and free emotional growth (Guntrip, 1975).

Winnicott says that when a retreat of the patient is produced, the important thing is to transform it into regression to dependence (on the analyst, that is) in such a way as to obtain an opportunity to correct the patient's inadequate adaptation to need that occurred in his earliest years of life. Winnicott remarks that the important thing— once the need is recognized—is not so much the concrete provision of its gratification as to let the patient know that we have understood what his need is. This is done through the interpretation—says Winnicott—but I would add that this transmission of experience can be accomplished without the use of words (Winnicott, 1954b).

For the regression to occur, the presence is necessary of an organization that is constituted by:

- a failure in the environment's adaptation that will determine the development of a false self;
- a belief in the possibility of the correction of the original failure;
- a provision of a specialized environment (the setting and the analyst); and
- a new emotional development.

To all the above, Winnicott adds the threat of chaos. He also mentions the expectation that new and more favourable conditions, this time, will allow a normal development.

We should not consider regression as something negative or pathological but as something healthy that could happen in normal people. Here Winnicott refers to an unconscious assumption (which reminds one of Bion's basic assumptions in the function of groups) that the "frozen" original failure could be "unfrozen" by a more propitious emotional environment. He considers regression as a process of normal healing. When anyone faces difficult problems, he may regress to previous healthy stages of development, so he can restart from there. Thus, there are two classes of development: one healthy and the other to developmental stages of the ego. How do we face the needs of our patients? This is a fundamental question because the success or the failure of the therapy will depend on it. The therapist's capacity or skill in adjusting to his patient's needs is an art. Nevertheless, Winnicott advises us to try to understand its mechanism, no matter how difficult the task may prove to be (Winnicott, 1954a).

Winnicott emphasizes the distinction he makes between the patients he considers to be "complete" human beings and those who are not—in other words, between neurotics and psychotics. Among the latter, he takes account of those whose defences are in a chaotic state and those in whom the defences have been organized into an illness. Another Winnicottian conception of psychosis tells us that it is a defensive organization structured to protect the true self. In psychotics need predominates over wishes. Also, in their case interpretation is not the most important instrument in the cure. The analyst, besides, must be tolerant with the acting out (Winnicott, 1954a).

The false self is part of the true felf, and it must surrender itself to the analyst during the analysis. The behaviour of the analyst is fundamental because the provision of a good-enough environment will change the groundwork from the false self to the true self. Only then will the patient learn from the errors of the analyst, becoming capable of grasping reality and thus being able to achieve the benefits denied to him during his infancy (Winnicott, 1955).

The existence of the true and false selves could be conceived as a consequence of dissociation. The patient could play the role of the true self as if it had had a real existence. It is supposed that the true self is hidden so as not to be annihilated by exploitation. Unthinkable anxiety could occur if the latter were to happen. The false self could renege on its "duty" to protect the true self. The function of the first is to find the best conditions for the latter to manifest itself. When this is achieved in the analytic setting, the false self hands over the true self to the care of the analyst. As from that moment, the analyst takes charge not only of the care but also of the handling of the true self. The analyst makes contact with the latter only at the moment of extreme dependency. The real and fundamental work of the analysis is made with the true self, otherwise the creative originality of the individual would be missing (Winnicott, 1960).

The person of the analyst—who he is—his countertransference, the psychotic transference, and the treatment process are fundamental elements to be taken into consideration—above all, the non-verbal elements that are taken for granted in the treatment of neurotics, that go beyond the interpretations as conceived in classical analysis. Psychoanalysis provides a degree of integration, of socialization and self-discovery that would not be possible to obtain without it. Self-discovery is more bound to a process of unveiling that produces astonishment than to intellectual factors (Rubinstein, 1993).

According to Marion Milner—whose ideas are very much related to Winnicott's—the psychoanalytic process is the expression of the patient's capacity to accept the symbolic playing of representative figures of the external and internal realities, as well as the capacity to move freely within their limits. This author conceptualizes this experience, by itself, as curative—apart from the interpretations (among which she tries to include all the above—she confesses that she does not always succeed).

This makes one think of the importance of the non-verbal aspects of analysis. Very basic experiences from the pre-verbal stage of emotional development occur concomitantly with the rest of very well known factors that influence any analysis. Many times—if not always—they are taken for granted; at other times they become evident to the needs of the case. The point is that they play a fundamental role in the development and end result of an analysis.

As Marion Milner very rightly says, these are factors that are very difficult—if not impossible—to explain in words. It is a matter of sensibility, so much so that interpretations are often unnecessary. Everything is implicit, and the least said, soonest mended. It is a question of becoming aware of the playing of the variables of reality/unreality (fantasy). "Playing" and "movement" are fundamental elements to take into consideration. Other elements this author ushers into this topic that help us to understand these very severely emotionally damaged cases, are "concentration"/"focusing" (self-absorption) and the capacity to create illusions about our own experiences. Personally, I think that just like children in the course of their play and artists at work, patients in analysis must fully surrender to the experience (Milner, 1952).

According to Winnicott, the analysis of psychosis must provide an active adjustment to the needs of the patient and also a great respect for the process. This is crucial because it entails respect for the person, the Self of the patient. If we want to help him, we must respect his own timing in his evolution of the analytical process. We must show great patience and understanding. We must help him to unfold his ability to use illusion, which means to stimulate his creative potential, his readiness for a hallucination (Winnicott, 1952, p. 223).

In the stage of utter dependency—according to Winnicott—verbal interpretations are insufficient. Sometimes one can do without them. In cases of profound regression, we play the role of the good-enough mother, so that in our analytic work we are always evaluating and re-evaluating the ego strength of the patient (Winnicott, 1960, p. 249).

Failure in the basic provision of care and affection results in the annihilation of the individual. This difficulty can be observed in most—if not all—of the mothers of psychotic patients. Countertransference is important not only because of its symbolic meaning but also for its value as a "link of lost experience". The essence of Winnicott's communicative dexterity was to consider his own thoughts as subjective-objects to be placed between himself and the patient and not only as instruments for decoding his unconscious world (1963, p. 252). The facilitation of emotional growth is based not only in the sense of security provided by the interpretations, but also on the quality of the experience of mutuality. The "playful revelation" is much more curative that the "intelligent" interpretations provided by the analyst—according to Winnicott. The analyst must be capable of tolerating the "amorphous quietude" of the setting before embarking on the "anxious searching for the form" (Goldman, 1993).

Here I must repeat what I have said on other occasions about the sense that the analysis shares the characteristics of what is considered a normal and usual relationship and dialogue; the only difference is that it occurs at a different psychic level, where phenomena such as transference and countertransference meet. The countertransference/total response of the analyst occurs, according to Winnicott, through the body-ego/light and conscious effort, submitting ideas and feelings to a rigorous scrutiny and selection before proceeding to the interpretation. It is important to be aware that a transference with psychotic overtones is going to be produced in the case of borderline, schizoid, and narcissistic patients, a sort of subjective-object relationship where words are not the most important things but a silent, direct communication—primary identification—is (Painceira, 1993).

The silence of the analyst is very valuable for these very disturbed patients. They feel comforted, reassured, and held by it. Of course, the quality of the silence is decisive (Giovacchini, 1969).

The interpretations must be the patient's creation—according to Winnicott—formulated with the backing of the presence and support of the analyst (Segal, 1993).

Not only the content of the interpretations is important, but their symbolic value also. Winnicott spoke of "linking interpretations" and their structuralizing effect—all of which is subsumed under the "operational composition of the interpretations" (Giovacchini, 1969).

"Be careful not to be intrusive with the patient", Winnicott used to say. The therapeutic encounter, for him, consisted in being more the midwife of the development of natural processes. More than to provide health, Winnicott was interested in helping his patients to restore their capacity to be themselves, to feel free, real, and complete as human beings (Goldman, 1993).

CHAPTER TEN

Technical problems in the analysis of a young adult

Rose Edgcumbe (London)

T his opportunity to contribute to a *Festschrift* for Pearl King is very welcome as it provides the impetus to reconsider some areas of her work that have been of special interest to me.

In her 1973 paper on the therapist–patient relationship, Pearl King stressed the importance for psychoanalysts of research, both by analysts and by developmental psychologists, into childhood development, especially the role of the child's relationships in nurturing and facilitating healthy development (p. 6). She placed herself among the many analysts now influenced by this understanding in their technique and theory: "the analyst–patient relationship . . . is beginning to be seen as a setting within which psychological growth, self-discovery and learning can take place" (p. 7). As a child analyst much influenced by Anna Freud (e.g. 1965) I have always found myself in sympathy with this point of view.

In a subsequent paper, King developed her interest in the lifecycle as it is manifested in the transference (1980). She pointed out that the way an individual has dealt with the challenges and anxieties of each developmental phase will influence his or her capacity to cope with later ones (p. 153). I particularly want to pursue one point King made:

> the developmental phases that most often need to be worked
> through in the transference of middle-aged patients are those of
> puberty and adolescence, the analyst being experienced, (what-
> ever his actual age) as significant adults from those phases of the
> patient's life cycle. [King, 1980, p. 155]

She gave examples of patients who, whatever infantile material had
to be dealt with, also needed to re-experience and work through
various adolescent difficulties before they could move on to resolve
the issues of middle or old age. She suggested:

> One reason for this may be that the middle-aged individual is
> having to face many of the same problems as he did in his ado-
> lescence, but this time in reverse, for it is a period of involution.
> At both phases of the life cycle he has to adjust to sexual and
> biological changes in himself; awareness of these changes can
> arouse anxiety as basic sources of security are threatened. These
> are exacerbated by role changes and their socio-economic conse-
> quences . . . leading to conflicts about dependency and independ-
> ence . . . old defences may break down as socio-biological and
> psychological pressures shift, often precipitating an identity crisis
> . . . and necessitating changes in his self-image, accompanied by
> possible narcissistic trauma and wounds to self-esteem.
>   I think that it is the existence of these parallels that often ex-
> acerbates the conflicts between parents and their adolescent chil-
> dren, and leads to their mutual scapegoating. [pp. 156–157]

Analysts who are aware of the importance of distinguishing conflicts
from different levels of development all recognize the issues Pearl
King has enumerated.

From her work with older patients, Pearl King has been able to
demonstrate the possibilities of helping people to achieve ego growth
and creativity even quite late in life. But in so doing, she has also
underscored the devastating effects that failure to resolve adolescent
conflicts can have on adult life, so that many middle-aged and elderly
patients are faced with the task of mourning lost opportunities and
unfulfilled life wishes before they can achieve the belated ego growth
and creativity of which King (1980) writes. Her work thus links up
with that of analysts who approach the problem from the point of
view of working with patients during the phases of adolescence.
Their work also stresses the issues specific to this period of life: the
internal re-organizations that permit the incorporation of a mature

sexual body into the self-representation, the "second individuation" or separation from infantile objects that leads to independent functioning, the structural re-organizations that allow modifications of ego and superego identifications, and so on (e.g. Blos, 1962, 1967; A. Freud, 1958; Laufer & Laufer, 1984). If these steps are not successfully negotiated the adolescent cannot move on into full adult functioning. Many years of work with adolescents at both the Anna Freud Centre and the Brent Consultation Centre have convinced me of the importance of intervening to prevent deadlock in development from blocking the adolescent's move into adulthood. More recently, a research group at the Anna Freud Centre has studied the developmental problems of a group of young adults.

I would like to describe some technical problems in handling the transference and countertransference with one of the patients in this group. Here Pearl King's work is again relevant, especially her paper on the analyst's affective response to the patient's communication (1978), in which she discusses how disturbed mothering may damage an infant's sense of self- and viable ego-boundaries. She stresses the importance of knowing not only what aspect of the object is being transferred onto the analyst, but also what affects the object was experienced as having felt towards the patient. To understand this requires careful monitoring of the transference and countertransference (pp. 330–331) and disentangling the patient's psychopathology from that of his parents (p. 332).

"Louise" was 22 when she came for analysis, which lasted for four years. She was one of the least disturbed of the patients in the young adult research group. To outward appearances she had managed the major developmental tasks of adolescence: she had left home, was living in a stable relationship with a man, and was working for a degree. Her overt symptomatology was limited to difficulties in getting on with her work, some readiness to feel criticized, and difficulties in her relationships with women. These difficulties were soon apparent in the transference and countertransference, both of which seemed somehow thin and tenuous. This was in spite of the fact that her material was often interesting, and sometimes she could work well, developing themes, identifying conflicts and finding ways of solving them, and appearing to enjoy our joint enterprise. But at other times she would get stuck, becoming boringly repetitive. She always seemed to keep a distance from me, often missing sessions, never putting analysis before her work and study commitments; yet at times she was dependent and clingy, evoking a degree of protective concern in me which she could not use.

Her paradoxical behaviour was especially striking when she rearranged her work timetable without consulting me during a break four months into treatment. Four of her five times needed to be rescheduled, and she lost one session altogether as we could not find an alternative time. She accepted this as inevitable. Nine months later she asked for the session back at a time when she felt a special need for my help with difficult decisions about work. I was now able to offer her a suitable time, but not the original one. She seemed shocked, unable to believe that I had not kept the original time for her. I was surprised, having no sense that the lost session was so important for her or that her transference included an image of me preserving the space for her. We reinstated the fifth session, but she rarely managed to come for all five.

What Louise knew of her history included some potentially distressing and disruptive events, of which she initially spoke with indignation, but no strong feelings of any other kind. She had been cared for by various minders for her first two or three years, seeing little of her foreign parents who studied and worked long hours to better themselves. At one point they lived in accommodation where children were not allowed, so when the rent collector called, Louise and all her possessions had to be hidden and she had to be silent.

She had memories of her mother's inept handling, for example not stopping to let Louise go to the toilet on the way home from school, so that she wet herself on the bus. Or giving her scratchy crisps as a "treat" when she had a sore mouth after dental treatment. Or refusing to hold her hand when going through immigration, so that she would cry and the family could jump the queue.

Regarding education as important, her parents urged her to study hard and provided extra coaching to improve her chances, which she understood as implying that she was not doing well enough. They warned her that she had to work twice as hard as white children to get anywhere. As a schoolchild she spent long hours during holidays alone at home, supposedly doing homework set by her parents or practising the piano. But she would do "naughty" things like letting the dog loose. She felt guilty about such things, being strongly imbued with the belief that she should be "good" and hard-working.

When she was studying for O-levels her parents returned to their home country and could not understand that for their child, born and raised in England, it was not home. Louise could not settle and insisted on returning to England for her A-levels. In analysis it became clear that she did not really feel that she had left home— rather, that her home had left her. She lived with family friends but did not get on with them and moved into student accommodation as soon as she began her degree studies. She rapidly became involved with one of her tutors and moved in with him in her second year.

It quickly became clear in the analysis that Louise's work difficulties were part of a widespread difficulty in thinking and verbalizing. She would "get stuck", panic, and feel stupid. Although capable of being clear and articulate, at these moments she would stammer out repetitive and meaningless phrases. At the worst times her grammar would disintegrate altogether so that she could only string together disconnected words and phrases, inadequately trying to describe an event that had upset her but unable to elaborate on causation, meaning, or context unless I asked specific questions to help her sort out the sequence of external and internal events. She had a vocabulary for feelings but seemed to lose it at such times, as if unable to name or differentiate affects. I thus found myself labelling feelings or suggesting possible alternatives in what she might be feeling. At first I thought of such interventions simply as clarifications or verbalizations to help a patient with obvious developmental deficits in addition to the neurotic conflicts from which her anxious upsets stemmed (Edgcumbe, 1993, 1995; Fonagy et al., 1993; Hurry, 1998). From this point of view, my role could be conceptualized as that of a "new object", or a "developmental object", trying to help her to link experiences with feelings and thoughts, so as to contain them within herself instead of being shattered by them. I wondered whether the words she did use for feelings had any real meaning for her, since she could only use them in an intellectual way at times when she seemed to feel little or nothing.

But I was also struck by the transference–countertransference element at times when she seemed to be describing herself as if from the outside rather than the inside and quite eagerly using me to find the inside feelings. For example, trying to describe a feeling, she stammered: "I felt . . . I was . . . I had lines on my forehead." I suggested: "You were angry?" "No." "Puzzled?" "Yes. That's it." There were many moments like this when she seemed to be describing herself from an outside point of view, perhaps comparing herself to an outside object such as a frowning mother, but not sufficiently identified with such an object to be able to interpret her own behaviour. Or perhaps she was seeking help from a mother she did not expect to be in tune with her; and I often found myself struggling to get in tune.

From the very beginning of treatment there was plentiful evidence of her expectation that I would be a critical and demanding mother. There was also much material about her expectation of being left abandoned and unhelped by her angry or rejecting object. For example, one Monday early in the analysis, she was anxious about a practical test the following day, and I felt I had not been able to understand or help much by the end of the session. The next day she arrived extremely upset and tried to describe what at first seemed an inexplicable incident. Her boyfriend had accompanied her to her test, to help her carry all her equipment. She realized she had left something behind. Suddenly he jumped out of the train and left her alone. From her tone and manner I could sense her distress, and I assumed that she felt bewildered, angry, and helpless about being left to manage alone. Simple links with my own absence at the weekend or failure to help her yesterday did not seem relevant or helpful. She was quite unable to explain how she felt, how she coped with the situation, or how she understood what her boyfriend was doing. She simply repeated over and over in a shocked voice that he had jumped out of the train and left her alone. I therefore asked specific questions about what she had left behind, was it important, might he have gone to get it for her, and so on. In this way we established that he had, indeed, returned home for the missing item, in order to bring it to her at her college. But this outcome had in no way diminished her sense of shock, incomprehension, and outrage.

I said that perhaps she often experienced as being abandoned something that might have been intended as helpful. She then recalled how her mother used to sit with her while she practised the piano. Her mother had nagged her to keep playing but could not read music and therefore could not correct Louise's mistakes. It was different with her father, who could have helped her with her maths but did not. He went off and left her to do it alone. I wondered if she feared I would be either like a mother who could not understand enough to correct her mistakes, or like a father who did understand but refused to help. She agreed that she often doubted whether I could or would help; and a subsequent theme in the material elaborated her fear that I would have my own agenda for her analysis, like her parents pushing her to study but not attending to her needs and wishes in the matter. This theme was to become more and more important as she recognized how hard it was for her to know what she did want for herself. She was much better at responding to the cues given by others about their expectations of her than at examining her own feelings and wishes. She expected punitive anger if she did not comply with the object's wishes—a theme that ran through all her relationships.

She continued to make good use of me to help her identify feelings and wishes. Sometimes, especially in the early stages of the analysis, I felt we were doing this on a very infantile and primitive level. For example, following a missed session, she was struggling to describe various difficulties, made worse by not seeing me. She said: "And I felt . . . I didn't come." I asked what sort of feeling that was, and she replied: "Bad." I was powerfully reminded of a young child who cannot verbalize feeling lonely, frightened, or abandoned but can only say: "I want my Mummy." Such feelings are so inseparably bound up with the object that they can only be experienced as, for example, the "I-want-my-Mummy feeling" (Hodges & Edgcumbe, 1990).

At other times we were dealing with far more mature and complex issues, which nevertheless reduced her to the same incoherent state. For example, much later in treatment she was trying to describe her reaction to receiving many birthday presents from friends. But she could only stammer: "I was . . . like . . . oh really?" We were able on this occasion to explore many fears, for example that no one would come to her party, they would all pair off and leave her alone, she might be attracted to someone other than her boyfriend, and so on. She was then able to reformulate her reaction: "I was excited and surprised that so many people wanted to give me presents."

It was clearly an important question for the analysis to what extent she had failed to develop differentiated and identifiable affects and defensively abandoned her capacity to understand her own experiences. There was certainly material at an oedipal level indicative of conflicts over jealousy and competitiveness with rivals. But her paralysis of thinking also seemed to stem from an inability to resolve what she experienced as endless contradictions in the demands of her internal objects. For example: "You must work twice as hard as white people in order to do well" versus: "Success ought to come naturally and easily, so if it doesn't there is something wrong with you." Or: "You must be independent and manage alone" versus: "You must do the tasks mother sets you." Or: "You must sing/play/perform excellently" versus: "You must be silent and invisible." Unable to reconcile these conflicting demands, she was often in a state of puzzled anxiety and seemed to experience much of her life as a series of disjointed and inexplicable happenings.

Early in the analysis I began to think that there might be a confluence of her developmental need to continue to use objects as sources of structure and motivation and a defence against an internalized sado-masochistic, destructive relationship with mother. She often presented herself as the helpless victim, but it also became clear that Louise feared becoming effective or influencing other people because she perceived that as involving aggression. She found it particularly difficult to deal with demanding or assertive women, be they friends, teachers, or parent figures. It was a long time before she could recognize envy of their assertiveness. What she was more readily aware of at first was her fear of something destructive and evil that might emerge in herself. Many of her dreams portrayed this fear, together with her mistrust of me, who might bring to life something bad in her since I said I wanted to help her discover her own wishes and feelings. She both hoped and feared that I could help free her from the superego demands she found confusing and limiting.

It became an important question in the analysis to what extent she did what she "ought" because she feared her "wants" were sadistic and destructive or because she feared a punitively sadistic, revengeful internal object, or because she had not developed a sense of a self as having intentions. I began to wonder whether it was loss of the object she feared most or loss of self, and to what extent her view of me/mother as not supporting her self-development, but as requiring her to pursue my/mother's aims, could be understood as her awareness of a false self distortion (Winnicott, 1960) or of the object's refusal to let her separate/individuate (Mahler, Pine, & Bergman, 1975), and to what extent it derived from a later, defensive need to deny responsibility for her own hostility, sadism, and destructiveness.

She could gradually verbalize that when not given support and help, she assumed that what she wanted to do was "wrong". She often referred to herself in childhood as "naughty". But she gradually became able also to say that she felt her naughtiness was important to preserve, being as near as she could get to self-assertion. She wanted to become happy and self-confident but feared that she might become "bland". This was the sort of thing that made her afraid of my "agenda" for the analysis and put her in a dilemma about trusting me to help her. She likened it to making a pact with the devil in which you get more than you bargained for—specifically: "You find out things about yourself you'd rather not know. What do we do about them?"

"What do we do about it?" became a frequent question. The classic analytic approach—helping her to see a conflict or understand the elements of some dilemma she was in—was not enough to allow her to find a solution for herself; and I began to realize that her question was not simply a resistance, but a real request for help, perhaps a sort of testing out. She needed to know whether I was a mother who really wanted her to know her own mind and who would help her find a way of acting on what she found, or one who was implicitly forbidding her to think and act for herself, or one who did not understand what she was asking. I was struck by a paradigmatic incident she described from her childhood. Louise had been playing in the house of a friend who wanted to light matches, and this child's mother showed her how to do it safely by lighting them in the sink. Louise reported this incident to her own mother, who told her she could light matches, too, but did not offer to show her how to do it safely. This left her feeling it was dangerous, and she ought not to do it.

Her view of change as an aggressive act was exemplified in a dream at the beginning of the second year of analysis. At the time she was in an adolescent-like rebellion against working hard, which she labelled: "rejection of the work ethic". In the dream, *with sadistic pleasure, she told a work-mate; "I've killed Alice"*. Associations led to her anger about having been forced into emulating the successful middle-class white child epitomized in *Alice in Wonderland* and her envy of such children.

There followed a phase in which the transference focused on her wish to be loved "however bad I am". By this time it had become apparent that her boyfriend was mainly a mother substitute, not a heterosexual object on a mature genital level. She tried to pluck up courage to leave him and had a dream in which she was struggling to get off his lap. This reminded her of her mother saying: "You can go out to play, but the door may be shut when you get back." Further associations led to her fear of being "found out" by mother discovering Louise's secret fantasies of stringing up and torturing mother. At the same time she was angry with her boyfriend for what she experienced as his hiding her in a dark corner when she attended a film lecture he gave. During this and other similar accounts a new variant of her stammer occurred, in which she mumbled so indistinctly that I could not tell whether she was saying: "I was angry" or "He was angry"—as if she needed to conceal the ownership of feelings.

Such material allowed me to link her fear of being criticized or rejected for her wish for independence to her fear of being found responsible for bad wishes and her shame about the bad things in herself that had to be kept hidden or blamed on someone else.

Over the next year or so there was a good deal of acting out as well as in the transference, much of which posed for me the dilemma one has when analysing an adolescent: how to encourage the moves to independence without letting the patient run away from resolving essential issues. Much of her acting out served to work through conflicts, especially those around being hidden. In the sexual sphere she indulged in some exhibitionistic and scopophilic relationships before finally leaving her boyfriend and experimenting with more ordinary relationships. In her work she gradually lost her enthusiasm for video and film work and began a shift to dance. She became aware that she was shifting from being the observer to being the performer. Dancing often allowed her to express feelings better than she could verbalize them.

For some time she seemed to need to keep me as a benevolent external superego, approving of the changes she was making. I was unsure whether this was the only way she could moderate her internal superego objects or whether it represented a refinding of a lost internal representation of a containing and more kindly mother. That it was, at least in part, the latter seemed indicated when she eventually began to find it easier to talk to her real mother and to sort out her mother's anxieties about work and money from her own. She also began to recognize her mother's good intentions in her childhood and even to recall nice things her mother did, like providing her not only with homework to do when alone but also with interesting toys and games.

Louise was still prone to retreat to a distance from me when conflicts in the transference grew too threatening, but gradually she became able at least to return from her detachment to complain that I left "blanks in the conversation" by remaining silent instead of giving her a verbal thrashing for her disobedience. So she ended up thrashing herself. She commented: "I was well trained for that by my mother."

Leaving her boyfriend and going to live on her own intensified her fears of involvement with me, leading to increased detachment, including missing many sessions and an intensification of the thinness of the transference and countertransference. This was in spite of the fact that she was now often using me very well, when she did come for sessions, to help her explore her own discoveries about her inner world and her new-found pleasure in her own body and its functioning. There were often, however, sessions in which she chattered on, adolescent-style, about her doings in a rather superficial way. I found this rather irritating in a by now 25-year-old woman and was at first inclined to think of these as resistant sessions. But I gradually realized that they still represented her need to have me approve of her doings, even when they were not directed to serious matters like working hard. It seemed to me that her readiness to feel criticized was part of an internal scenario in which she tried but failed to please coercive objects, not only because of her own contradictory wishes, but also because she found the demands of her objects confusing and contradictory and was unable to make sense of them.

As she became able to talk to her mother more directly and to differentiate her mother's anxieties from her own, it became clear that in Louise's childhood her mother had probably been too anxious about the difficulties she and her husband were experiencing to focus much on Louise's developmental needs. But she had also been absent a great deal, leaving Louise either alone to bring herself up as best she could or in the care of changing and possibly insufficiently involved child-minders. Louise had developed an apparent self-sufficiency that in adolescence allowed her to leave her parents, but only for parent-substitutes. Her apparent self-motivation for study and work proved fragile, still based on a wish to please the infantile object.

From the early days of the analysis it had seemed to me that Louise must have an unconscious doubt as to whether she was even meant to exist. But her descriptions of having to be hidden and keep quiet were detached, without real feeling. Her real anger, and wish to be seen and heard, only began to emerge in the acting out that began in the second year of analysis, after I had, as it were, given her permission to find out what she wanted. This "permission" remained conflictual for her and was, I think, responsible for the continuing sense of distance between us. The thin transference and countertransference may be seen as reflecting several layers of self–object interaction. The helpless self expects no appropriate response from the coercive, critical object and attempts pseudo-independence; the hidden self feels forbidden to be seen, to perform, and to interact with others but also feels safer

when wicked and sinful aspects are hidden; the angry, disap-
pointed self fears her murderous rage to the object. Louise was,
perhaps, caught in an insoluble internal situation: she needed me
in her internal world as a supportive, benign, containing object to
help her re-evaluate her past and present experiences and to move
on in her development. But those early experiences had made her
reluctant to let in any object, especially one who told her what she
was thinking and feeling. It was a difficult balancing act for her to
allow me a place in her mind, and equally difficult for me to get
the right balance in my interventions.

What eventually brought about the end of the analysis, in some
respects prematurely, was her enrolment in a full-time dance
course too far away to permit her to get to me—that is, in one way
a repeat of her leaving her parents. But in the internal process of
getting there, she had become very well aware of the roles she put
me into, and that what she really wanted was to keep me in mind
as the one who helps her sort out what is going on and not run
away. She said: "I mould myself around people. I need to prise
them out." But she also said: "I am integrating into myself the help
other people have given me."

I think that my own sense of distance was not only a countertransference actualization of the mother roles I was being put into
(Sandler, 1976). It was also a reflection of my awareness of the
need to hold back: I must not re-enact the mother too anxious
about her child's future to listen to the child's own wishes and
aims for herself; but nor must I re-enact the mother too pre-occu-
pied with her own aims to stop her child doing something harm-
ful to her development.

I recall a piece of advice given to me over twenty years ago by Pearl
King at a time when I was seriously ill. I had to cancel patients at short
notice for an indefinite period. I was especially worried about one
very disturbed patient, uncertain how much to tell her and aware that
my capacity for analytic thought was not at its best. Pearl gave me a
marvellously helpful rule of thumb: "Do whatever does not repeat the
patient's past." I have found this rule useful with other patients since
then. It is, I think, a simple way of summarizing what she elaborates
in her papers. Disturbed mothering may damage an infant's sense of

self- and ego-boundaries. In the transference it is important to understand not only what aspect of the object is being transferred on to the analyst, but also what affects the patient believes this object felt towards her. Not only the transference but also the countertransference requires very careful monitoring in order to avoid repetition of earlier self–object interactions, to disentangle the patient's psychopathology from that of her parents, and to aid the analyst in making the responses that will support the patient in reworking earlier developmental phases so as to move on to resolving later ones.

CHAPTER ELEVEN

Further thoughts on the validation of the clinical process

R. Horacio Etchegoyen (Buenos Aires)

I

Psychoanalysis has recently reached its century of existence, and there is no doubt that it now occupies its own, singular, and certainly definite place within the order of the sciences. It has a manifest influence on our society and on its habits, and it has become a cultural fact that marks all the expressions of our time.

In its beginnings, psychoanalysis (which at that point *was* Freud himself) had to fight against detractors who functioned rather as defenders of—sexual—morality and on that basis refused to assign the category of a science to psychoanalysis. Later on it was questioned and taken as an example of what was *not* science; but in the last few years this debate has been set in a different way, since philosophers of science have finally decided to pay due attention to it. In Latin America, the work of Gregorio Klimovsky is prominent. A man of

A preliminary version of this chapter was read in New York, on 2 March 1993, as the André Ballard Lecturer of the Association for Psychoanalytic Medicine. After my presentation at West Point (Etchegoyen, 1994), some additions were made to the original text, and several points were modified.

wide culture, a graduate mathematician, a professor in logic and philosophy, founder of the Asociación Argentina de Epistemología del Psicoanálisis (ADEP—Argentine Association of Epistemology of Psychoanalysis), he began by teaching epistemology to psychoanalysts in Buenos Aires and ended up learning from them the complexities of a discipline that needs to be studied according to its own standards. In the United States, the contribution of Adolf Grünbaum has been outstanding. He has rigorously investigated the philosophical status of psychoanalysis, concurrently with his studies of the philosophy of time and space and of the cosmological theories. His work is important because it assigns to psychoanalysis the value of a knowledge that deserves to be recognized and it also allows us, as psychoanalysts, to listen and respond to his critiques. I believe that Professor Grünbaum, of whose talent and enthusiasm I have had repeated evidence, will gradually come to realize that it is necessary to become acquainted with our *modus operandi* in order to be able to understand us, and only then criticize us.

In Europe, there is no doubt that, influenced by Jaspers' monumental *Allgemeine Psychopatologie* [*General Psychopathology*] (1913), psychoanalysis has been regarded as a hermeneutics—that is, as a science of meaning—following Dilthey's perennial classification into natural sciences [*Naturwissenschaften*] and human sciences [*Geisteswissenschaften*]. The work of Jürgen Habermas and of Paul Ricoeur has been noteworthy in this direction. In Germany, Alfred Lorenzer is prominent in this field. Very close to the Habermas of *Erkenntnis und Interesse* [*Knowledge and Human Interest*] (1968), Lorenzer has developed an important body of work that is firmly rooted in clinical psychoanalysis and has become known in Latin America through his disciple, Hilke Engelbrecht, who currently lives in Peru. Hermeneutics has also influenced the thinking of George S. Klein, Merton M. Gill, and Roy Schafer in the United States, where Donald P. Spence is also worth mentioning. Osvaldo Guariglia, an in-depth connoisseur of critical philosophy, also situates psychoanalysis unhesitatingly in the field of hermeneutics.

In any case, we have reached an interesting point—a convergence that promises to be fruitful, since philosophers of science now recognize that they must study us, and we, psychoanalysts, have relinquished the comfortable refuge of considering that "our science" is beyond the scientific method, a point of view that is, however, supported by eminent colleagues. It is sufficient, for instance, to read *L'Inconscient et la Science* (see Dorey et al., 1991), to remark that many French psychoanalysts maintain that psychoanalysis bears no relation to science. In the introduction for the book, Roger Dorey (1991) considers it vain to wonder whether psychoanalysis is or is not a science, since the question is insoluble, and he marvels at the vigorous revival of the debate today, for psychoanalysis does not comply with the customary requisites of the scientific method. In this sense, Dorey agrees with Popper and other philosophers in their criticism of psychoanalysis, and he states that the misunderstanding was first introduced by Freud himself. After giving the reasons that, in his opinion, led Freud to maintain the affinity of psychoanalysis with the natural sciences—which he critically qualifies as scientificity—he asserts that Lacan, Bion, and, of course, the ego psychologists fall into the same error. The use psychoanalysis makes of the scientific models, Dorey adds (Dorey et al., 1991), is purely metaphorical, and detrimental to its own integrity (p. 12): "The realm of psychoanalysis is, indeed, that of meaning, which is proper to the unconscious inasmuch as radically *an other*; it is in *another scene* that the game is played, in another field that is different from the one in which scientific research is carried out" (p. 13).

Dorey ends his brief and sharp essay stating not only that the two terms (the unconscious and science) are radically separated, but also that the unconscious hates science, in the same way as the primitive ego hates the object, as Freud expressed in his 1915 metapsychological writings. This anthropomorphic metaphor, however, completely ignores the two principles of the functioning of the mind (Freud, 1911b) and Ferenczi's (1913) profound reflections when he goes over the different stages in the development of the sense of reality and beautifully marks the culmination and the decline of omnipotence, since, in his own words: "the sense of reality attains its zenith in science, while the illusion of omnipotence here experiences its greatest humiliation . . ." (Ferenczi, 1913, p. 232).

Equally strong are André Green's (1991) theses in his witty paper for Dorey et al.'s book. Unlike Dorey, Green is not amazed at the debate between the unconscious and science, which is not the result of chance or of a vogue but, rather, the orientation that science followed after the Second World War, further to the discovery of the genetic code, the development of molecular biology, and the advancements attained in the field of brain physiology. In this way, "the theory of knowledge might finally be applied to that which made knowledge possible, i.e.—according to scientists—the brain" (Green, 1991, p. 168). Thus came to an end—Green continues—the peaceful coexistence of science and the other branches of knowledge. Green claims for psychoanalysis the status of a knowledge that is not subject to the scientific method, and he reminds us that there are other forms of knowledge besides the scientific one, as the majority of philosophers assert. The strongest point in Green's argument is that only psychoanalysis can validly address the study of the subject that, by definition, is outside the field of science.

In Green's view, there is an insurmountable abyss between science and the subject: the fundamental problem is how to situate the subject of science in a global conception of the subject of the psyche (1991, p. 175), for "science stops at the threshold of psychic functioning" (p. 177). In fact, the discussion between scientists and psychoanalysts originates in a radical misunderstanding inasmuch as scientists regard the world as an object of knowledge and disregard the cognizant subject, whereas psychoanalysts turn to the psyche as the object of knowledge and disregard everything except the knowledge of psychic reality in an effort to "obtain an *objective* knowledge of *subjectivity*" (p. 180, emphasis in original). Green categorically separates this diverging orientation of science and psychoanalysis towards the external or the internal world; but, in my judgement, he forgets that the psychic reality that psychoanalysis studies is also part of the world, however much it may diverge from it formally.

To my mind, the insurmountable abyss is to be found not between science and psychoanalysis, but between psychoanalysis and traditional philosophy, which attempted to study the mind—then a synonym of conscience—starting from introspection. As Green rightly points out, Freud discovered a new field—the *unconscious*—and when he perceived that his approach met with *resistance*—that is, with a wish not to know—he proposed a radically different method in which "all observation" became fundamental.

Thus the psychoanalyst appears as the observer who, with the help of the analysand, may reach—in the field where transference and countertransference operate—the facts of the psychic reality he intends to study. Green regards this field as irreducible to that of science; but I affirm, like other colleagues do, that the research method applied by the clinical psychoanalyst is entirely scientific, irrespective of the fact that difficulties may be greater when observing psychic reality than when doing so with Mendel's sweet peas.

Green considers that the refutability (falsifiability) of a hypothesis (related to psychic reality—allow me to emphasize) demanded by Popper (1953, 1962) cannot be applied to psychoanalysis, since the analysand and the analyst are not actually on the same level of rationality. This assertion, however, oversimplifies the matter. It is true that the analysand initially operates with the tools of the primary process, and it is also true that the interpretation is formulated in terms of the logic of the secondary process. If these conditions were to remain fixed, the psychoanalytic dialogue would be tantamount to a conversation between deaf people. The actual fact is that it changes continually; it has an amazing fluidity, as her genius allowed Melanie Klein to note in *The Psycho-Analysis of Children* (1932), and in other works of that time. As Lagache (1964) stated in the course of the "Symposium on Fantasy" at the Twenty-Third IPAC, Stockholm, in 1963, the fundamental rule invites the analysand to abandon him/herself to the primary process, giving free rein to his or her fantasy; yet interpretation is a logical operation. While the fundamental rule tells the patient to "talk nonsense", what interpretation proposes is "now let us talk sense" (Lagache, 1964, p. 186). Do not all of us indeed think that the psychoanalytic procedure consists in making the unconscious conscious or, as the structural theory puts it, "where id was, there shall ego be"?

In short, I believe that interpretation may be tested if we proceed accordingly—which is not always easy—and that interpretation is a hypothesis that operates *per via di levare* and not *di porre* [by way of discovery, not of invention]. In his recent work, "Counterinduction in Psychoanalytic Practice", Jorge L. Ahumada (1997) develops this subject in depth and clearly demonstrates that the ostensive insight is inherent in Strachey's (1934) mutative interpretation, which always operates *per via di levare* [by way of discovery].

The subject of interpretation has a prominent place in contemporary philosophy. Gadamer's contributions are well known. Not so well known, but perhaps much more pertinent to our subject, are the reflections of North American philosopher Donald Davidson on what he terms "radical interpretation", the principles it assumes, and the theoretical marks it sets to work (Davidson, 1984, especially chaps. 9,

13, 17, 18). I cannot dwell upon this point, but I believe it is very interesting, and I intend to enquire into it further.

After this digression on a collection of stimulating works, I return now to the central theme of this chapter.

II

In order to approach psychoanalysis as a body of knowledge intended to be recognized as a science—a claim that is present throughout Freud's work—it is essential to accept the premise that we must study the psychoanalytic process and the psychoanalytic situation separately. The *process* is diachronic, it is inscribed in time and presents different difficulties for an epistemological approach, especially if results are to be measured. The *situation*—that is, the session, synchronic and precise—is, to my judgement, more adjusted to the requirements of the scientific method.

I establish a difference between the situation and the process because all analysts accept this difference either implicitly or explicitly from the clinical point of view, although they tend to forget it when they expose their theories and attempt to sustain their validity; but I do not do this out of a belief in the existence of an impassable breach between them: the situation— the analytic session—has, in fact, a duration (which has been set at around 45 to 50 minutes all over the world), and the process is no more than an orderly succession of well-defined events. Yet, the fact that it is not possible to draw a clear division between one and the other does not entitle us to confuse them; on the contrary, it allows us to reach a final synthesis that notoriously reinforces the epistemic justification of psychoanalysis. I shall come back to this later.

Thus, the validation of the clinical process, as the title of this chapter proposes, should be understood as the study of the process in a strict sense on the one hand, and of the session on the other, and simultaneously as a strategic attempt at bringing them both together in a reinforcing integration.

All analysts think that the psychoanalytic process leads to slow but stable changes; and almost all of us consider that these changes (which we sometimes term "structural") have a quality that makes them different from those achieved through other psychotherapeutic methods. Nevertheless, it has not been possible to confirm this statement, which reaches us through Freud himself (1905a, 1916–1917, 1937c), either by the follow-up methods (Wallerstein, 1986) or through so-called empirical research. As Thomä and Kächele (1985) say: ". . . complex (and thus parameter-rich) theories, such as psycho-analytic theory, are difficult to test empirically. . ." (p. 364). Despite its great advancements and its undeniable value, empirical research—considered in its narrow sense—into the psychoanalytic process has not yet succeeded in answering these questions. (The expression "em-pirical research" is a synecdoche adopted through its use among psychoanalysts, since clinical research is also empirical.)

Two examples from my own practice demonstrate how difficult it is for empirical methods to evaluate the results of psychoanalysis and psychotherapy.

A long time ago, during my first years of practice in the city of La Plata, a friend of mine sent me his newly pregnant wife so that I would treat her. She had already had two spontaneous abortions to which emotional factors were determining factors, according to the obstetrician's judgement. I will not go into detail as to why I decided to assume the treatment of this friend, but the fact is that I saw her three times a week, face to face. As she spoke to me very sincerely about her desire to carry on with her pregnancy and exposed her conflicts with her husband and her mother, I interpreted her fears of repeating some of her mother's behaviour as well as her rivalry with her husband. The pregnancy and the psychotherapy were completed, with the couple's genuine gratitude. A beautiful girl was born, but, two years later, my ex-patient came to tell me that she treated her daughter with inex-plicable cruelty. Then, I *did* indicate analysis, and certainly not with me.

How can this very successful case of psychotherapy be evaluated through empirical methods? Thanks to the dissociation between a bad husband and an idealized psychotherapist, this woman's strong phallic envy and notorious urethral sadism were controlled for some time, thus allowing her to carry her pregnancy to full term. Once, to my own (and my wife's!) distress, at a party with some friends, she said that her beautiful girl was Horacio's daughter and not X's (her husband's). She was able to accept her pregnancy as long as it came from the idealized penis of her doctor. Once the therapy was over, her conflicts were directed at the girl (baby = faeces = penis) with such an intensity that, when she came to see me again, she even said that it would have been better to have had another abortion rather than the child.

A middle-aged woman who was in analysis with me for many years on a basis of five sessions per week, also had great phallic envy and strong urethral sadism. She once told me, at the beginning of her analysis, that she had had a fight with her husband and her daughters during the weekend. While they were placidly waiting for lunch-time in the rural house where they spent their weekends, it occurred to her to water the garden. She brandished the hose and sprayed everybody. When they reproached her for it, she felt very offended and insulted her family, now doing with her mouth what she had previously done with the hose. She also sprinkled me as she was narrating this during the session, and the only thing I could do at that moment was to listen to her in silence, without finding a suitable interpretation. Yet, I was able to predict—accurately, as time proved—that this patient would present great problems with the analytic setting, and there would be difficulties in analysing her conflicts with her sphincter control in the transference.

The analysis of her phallic envy and her urethral sadism, intertwined with the problems of her sphincter training, took several years. That episode with the hose was never analysed again; but, according to Hartmann's (1951) "principle of multiple appeal", the weekends in the countryside became much more pleasant and peaceful. For this lady's relatives, it was much easier to accept that her temper had changed than to attribute any effect to the treatment. (Her husband always believed that psychoanalysis was an entertainment for her, which he could pay for without it being an economic burden.) I mention the relatives' opinion because it follows the same reasoning as that of an empirical researcher: who can be sure that the changes in this good lady were a result of the psychoanalytic treatment and *not* merely of the time gone by, of the circumstances of life or simply of her (good) relationship with the analyst? After all, what was this patient cured of? Of the symptom of spattering her relatives with a hose!

These are two extreme examples of everyday practice in which urethral sadism and phallic envy appear. In the former case, the symptom ceased, but its causes did not; in the latter, there were not even any symptoms, but something was "cured". It is evidently difficult to detect these changes with empirical methods, though no analyst will doubt the firmness of my reasoning and no epistemologist will take them—in principle—as valid.[1]

In short, I totally agree with what Merton M. Gill said in a talk entitled "Current Trends in Psychoanalysis", on receiving the Heinz Hartmann Award in 1992: "It will be a long time before the efficacy of analysis and its value as contrasted to other methods of treatment will be demonstrable."

Empirical research could be led, I think, through less hackneyed paths. As I have just said, it is very difficult to prove that the changes produced in the lady mentioned above were due to the psychoanalytic treatment; but an experiment could be designed to test whether my prediction of the appearance of (anal and urethral) problems with the analytic setting was fulfilled and whether the transference of her sphincter conflicts could really come to occupy a unique position in her analysis.

In this same way, more specific research methods could be designed in order to test diverse psychoanalytic theories. During my long professional career I was consulted many times by analysts who had taken relatives and close friends of a patient into analysis for treatment. I do not know of a single case in which this circumstance did not precipitate a violent crisis of fraternal jealousy in the transference, which in most cases was actually impossible to analyse.

I remember a schizophrenic patient whom I treated while he was hospitalized in the Clínica Charcot of La Plata. After a year of treatment he reached an apparently steady remission. Then he asked me to analyse his wife as well. His petition was so insistent and sensible (and I was so inexperienced) that I agreed to interview her. A few days later, the patient suffered a new breakdown, this time an irreversible one. I remember that he felt he was being

---

[1] My good friend Merton, however, wrote to me in 1993, saying he could not disagree more with me.

persecuted by the ants in the Clinic's garden. I then remembered—too late—Abraham's (1924) essay, in which a hospitalized lady with a bout of melancholy (during which she was completely identified with her prolific mother) accused herself of having filled the Clinic with lice, which symbolized her siblings.

In other words, a sort of epidemiological study could be carried out to check whether it is true that, when an analyst takes someone who is very close to one of his or her patients into treatment, a strong jealous reaction breaks out within the transference. If this were so, then several psychoanalytical theories would be well supported.

It is also legitimate to point out that the so-called structural change is very difficult to define and even more complex to evaluate clinically. That is why a discerning and critical observer such as Weinshel (1988) prefers to speak of "psychoanalytic change" and not of structural change, in an attempt to be more moderate and realistic. It is not so easy, however, to determine precisely what we are to call psychoanalytic change.

In a recent article, "A New Intellectual Framework for Psychiatry", Eric R. Kandel (1998), makes a serious attempt to establish a connection between neuroscience and psychoanalysis and attributes a literal meaning to structural change: the changes produced by psychoanalysis and other forms of psychotherapy are inscribed in the brain "by producing changes in gene expression that alter the strength of synaptic connections, and structural changes that alter the anatomical pattern of interconnections between nerve cells of the brain" (p. 460). This certainly deserves to be given some thought, considering that Kandel justifies, from another field, the importance of a prolonged and intense treatment such as psychoanalysis.

III

To my mind, the possibility of contrasting the facts is higher, or at least more immediate, in the psychoanalytic session; this singular dialogue where the analysand offers material from his free associations to the analyst, who receives them with his evenly suspended attention so as to arrange them into a proposition aimed at accounting for what is happening in the unconscious.

Of course, I am speaking of an ideal situation, because the analysand does not always associate freely, nor does the analyst listen with evenly suspended attention all the time: sometimes the analysand cannot make himself understood and the analyst is subject to error; but these difficulties are not insurmountable.

The human deficiencies of analyst and analysand are not the only factors that complicate the psychoanalytic dialogue; there are also the conflicts inherent in every relationship, always crossed by misunderstandings and ambiguity (Money-Kyrle, 1968, 1971). In this sense, psychoanalytic dialogue is just like any other, but there is something that distinguishes it substantially: that it is, by definition, specifically directed at solving those difficulties, those conflicts. These arise, as we all know, from transference and countertransference; and it is the analysis of the always complex transference relationship that gives psychoanalysis not only a unique character among all other psychotherapeutic procedures, but also its most solid credential as a scientific discipline and method: transferential repetition offers the analyst the possibility of testing his/her hypotheses over and over again. Sometimes the transference repeats a determined pattern or conflict so thoroughly that it takes the shape of a true experimental design.

> I remember an intelligent young woman whom I analysed many years ago. She showed neurotic symptoms and was also afflicted by ulcerative colitis, flaring up regularly each time I proposed to increase the fee to keep up with inflation. Since I was not experienced enough then, it took me some time to put together the relationship (money = faeces) hidden behind her symptoms, of which she was obviously unaware. A more experienced analyst would surely have anticipated what was going on much earlier; but then, the experimental design, of which I was a naive witness, would not have taken place.

The psychoanalytic setting is designed for the analysand to display his conflicts in the most ample and natural way and for the analyst to offer in an interpretation the information that is supposedly missing. There are many of us who think, like Zac (1971), that the contrivance established by Freud for psychoanalytic treatment is one of the highest accomplishments of his genius (though he did not always abide by it in his practice!). The analysand repeats his/her usual conflicts with the analyst, but, thanks to the setting, he/she can recognize them as his/her own. In different circumstances, the participation of others makes them unrecognizable. The analytic asepsis that, as that of the surgeon, keeps the field of work free from contamination, consists in this.

From his earliest papers to his recent book, Bernardo Álvarez Lince (1996) has always maintained that interpretation is a scientific proposition. Psychoanalytic interpretation raises the knowledge of the existing psychic reality to the level of consciousness; and, therefore, "the practice of psychoanalysis depends on the peculiarities of the logic of knowledge" (p. 14). In other words, to interpret is to formulate a hypothesis within the framework of a scientific theory. For interpretation to be a real hypothesis, it must be constructed and formulated in a precise and rigorous way. We are now reaching a key point in this chapter.

In full agreement with Álvarez and with Edelson (1984), I maintain that what is being tested in the session is the unconscious content in the mind of the analysand at that moment, Liberman's casuistic or protocolar statements (1970–72), the dyad-specific truth of Thomä and Kächele (1985, chap. 10), and not the great theories of psychoanalysis; but I also believe that there is no impassable breach between them. If psychoanalytic technique is consistently and rigorously applied, we will suddenly witness the appearance the high-level theories, in the form of specific dyadic knowledge, protocolar or casuistic, in the analysand's mind. This I was able to illustrate—convincingly, I believe—in *Psyche* (Etchegoyen, 1993).

IV

To my mind, there exists a definite gap between interpreting and voicing an opinion. "Opinion" is obviously a more encompassing word; but actually, interpretation differs completely from any other opinion. As far as what the analysand thinks and feels is concerned, interpretation never alludes to events, as opinions do. In the same way in which a judge only expresses his opinion through his verdict—otherwise he would be at fault (if not indulging in acting out)—so the analyst's unique valid opinion is his interpretation of the material. An opinion is a judgement one expresses for the other to share or to question; an interpretation, on the other hand, only awaits a decision about its truth or falsehood. As Bion (1977) once said, "a psychoanalytic interpretation does not speak of facts but of what the analysand thinks about them. An opinion is a statement about things; an interpretation is a statement about what someone thinks about things" (Etchegoyen, 1989, p. 380). Liberman used to say: "*I* (the analyst) *think that you* (the analysand) *think that* . . .".

If we were to abide by Austin's (1962) and John Searle's (1969) ordinary-language philosophy, we might say that the psychoanalytic dialogue implies a communicative interaction in which illocutionary acts—that is, the actions that we perform when we say something—take place; but I would dare to propose that interpretation is in itself a singular illocutionary act that consists in proposing to the analysand a hypothesis of what the analyst believes is active in the analysand's unconscious—not to warn, or comment, or command, or approve, or apologize, . . . (Searle, 1969, chap. 2).

The difference between giving an opinion and interpreting often goes unnoticed, and yet it is an implicit requisite of the setting, since the analyst is only called to give testimonies and not opinions.

Like those of any other person, the analyst's opinions express that which he/she thinks, not what the analysand thinks; and in this sense, in giving an opinion, he/she is growing distant from his/her technique (because he/she violates neutrality and the analytic reserve) and also from the ethics of his/her profession, as he/she is expressing his/her values, thus influencing the patients. Analysands often seek our opinions or our advice, thinking that we are better prepared than anyone else to provide such counsel; but, indeed, they are mistaken, and any analyst who thinks this is true will also incur in the same fallacy. Our opinion is not better than that of others; on the other hand, our interpretation can bring the light that others are not able to give. From this it follows that the analyst is actually a mirror whose role is only to reflect what is projected onto him or her: "The doctor should be opaque to his patients and, like a mirror, should show them nothing but what is shown to him" (Freud, 1912e, p. 118). I quote these well-known words by Freud because, in spite of the negative criticism they have received from a lot of psychoanalysts, they are, to my mind, the axis of psychoanalytic technique.

I know quite well that the distinction I am proposing here is not shared by many first-rate analysts. To give an example, in the first chapter of their valuable book, *Psychoanalytic Practice*, Thomä and Kächele do not doubt for a moment that interpretation is the analyst's opinion, and thereby they conclude that it unavoidably influences the analytic process: "The information gathered by means of the psycho-analytic method is influenced to a high degree by the ideas which the analyst conveys" (1985, p. 23).

Previously, I stated that the analyst does not speak about events but about what the analysand believes these events to be. Our endeavour is not to suggest or indoctrinate our patient, not even to help him/her to think, but to see why he/she thinks this or that way. In this sense, psychoanalytic technique—as far as I understand it—is completely the opposite of what Grünbaum (1984) thinks when saying, in *The Foundations of Psychoanalysis*, that "the epistemic decontamination of the bulk of the patient's productions on the couch from the suggestive effects of the analyst's communications appears to be quite utopian" (p. 128).

From this point of view, as I said in my contribution to Leo Rangell's *Festschrift*, our technique is directed "toward discovering the misunderstandings that can lead the analysand to feel we are influencing him" (Etchegoyen, 1989, p. 378). The rigorous application of these technical rules has led me to discover, with surprise, how unshakeable some of the analysand's ideas and, more generally, those of normal people are, and how far they belong into an overvalued or even to a delusional category (p. 378). I do now believe that the mind of the normal person often harbours in cryptic ways a genuine transitive delusion with all the attributes of the influencing machine described in 1919 by Victor Tausk's masterly pen. Often, I have also been witness to the fact that analysts with little experience impede these developments through erroneous interpretations, supportive measures or confrontations with reality. These statements of mine only prove once again the presence of psychotic anxieties in normal person (e.g. Klein, 1932) or, to be more specific, the presence of a psychotic part in the structure of personality (Bion, 1957; Bleger, 1967); but it is relevant in relation to epistemic studies, as it forces us to see the "bête noire" of suggestion from a different point of view, if not from an opposite one, in relation to that wielded by numerous epistemologists: the suggestive influence of the analyst over the analysand must not be understood simply as something that comes from the analyst but as the product of an extremely regressive conflict in which the desire of influencing and of being influenced act jointly in both participants of the dyad in the dialectic of projective identification (e.g. Grinberg, 1956; Klein, 1946). Needless to say, this perspective also applies to political, scientific, and even philosophical discussions.

V

Since the analysand's material is always vast and protean, it faces us with the difficult task of choosing what we are to interpret. Given the multiplicity of choices open to us, if we allowed ourselves to be guided simply by our momentary preferences, the analytic task would be exposed to arbitrariness, to the whimsicality of our theories, and even to our conflicts. This risk can be furthered if we employ a technique I have been using for many years, which consists in reducing the field of variables in order that interpretation may be tested further.

As the analysand's ways of communication are multiple and some of them quite spontaneous, there fortunately exist means to avoid these risks. Associations can be verbal, paraverbal (i.e. phonic), and non-verbal (gestures, mimicry), in terms of Liberman's (1962) classification, and we also have countertransference information which, as was avowed by Racker (1960, *passim*), is to be considered part and parcel of the material. To this must also be added the *insistence* of certain linguistic signifiers (Lacan, 1957, 1966, *passim*).

Under these circumstances, the context of discovery of the interpretation will be found where these elements converge, and then its choice pertains to rational factors and not to arbitrary decisions, which are unavoidably open to subjective and personal influences. It is true that the clinical material open to us is always vast and inexhaustible, and that each time we choose an interpretation, we leave others aside; but if our choice is a rational one, as I have just tried to convey, then we can rest assured that transference repetition will relentlessly bring up anew what was previously left aside.

Contrarily, many analysts think that in selecting our material we do impose a peculiar bent to the analysis; but I think they are wrong and that they fail to distinguish the session from the process: our options on interpreting will influence the session, but what was not included in our interpretation now will come up by itself in the course of the treatment. On the other hand—and this is an obvious fact—*every* interpretation implies selecting the material.

For an interpretation to be testable, it is necessary that it be clear and precise and without ambiguity and that, if possible, it should contain only one hypothesis. Over the years, I have become an enemy of long and complex interpretations, as well as of brilliant ones. The former offer the analysand more than he or she can think of, and sometimes they are contradictory in themselves; the latter call for admiration and envy rather than for reflection. If the psychoanalyst has a long and complex interpretation in mind, it is better for him/her to offer it section by section, waiting for the analysand's response at each step. If the first segment of the interpretation is rejected for good or for bad, what is the sense of going on with the following ones?

VI

If interpretation could (and it should) be defined as a *hypothesis*, then it is logical to think that the analysand will evaluate it and that his/her new associations will transmit, not only their answer to what has been said, but also their opinion on its content of truth. It is hardly worth clarifying that I am not referring to the conventional answer, but to the one that comes from the unconscious and emerges through free association, as Freud says in "Constructions in Analysis" (1937d).

All analysts concur that the analysand's response to interpretation has a great informative and heuristic value. On the other hand, only a few believe that the analysand evaluates what has been said, and even fewer analysts think, as I do, that this is correctly done most of the time. I shall stop at this point because, if this were so, the (*unconscious*—I repeat) judgements of the analysand would acquire a great epistemic value. I categorically maintain that the analysand's response to our interpretation often contains the objective data that we need in order to decide upon its validity. In his well-thought-out paper "Psychoanalysis and the Uses of Philosophy", Hanly (1997) takes my idea on the testing of interpretation as an example of critical realism in psychoanalytic clinical work. He states most clearly: "The critical elements of this idea is the psychoanalytic acknowledgement by Etchegoyen of the complexity and hazards of the analysand's evaluative activity, complicated and not infrequently compromised as it is by the derivatives of the very conflicts within the analysand that the analysis is seeking to resolve" (p. 281).

As a consequence of the above, validation of the psychoanalytic process may be attained *during* the session, as maintained by Wisdom in his fundamental papers (1956, 1967). I personally think that interpretation may not only be tested in the session, but also that the session is the privileged occasion for doing so. Most analysts (Bianchedi, 1990; Bion, 1963; Liberman, 1970/72; Thomä and Kächele, 1985) do not share my position, since they believe that testing during the session disturbs the evenly suspended attention. On the contrary, I consider that evenly suspended attention is precisely what makes us able to apprehend the deep message of the analysand's unconscious on the truth or falsehood of what we have interpreted. To be open to what the analysand says or transmits about our interpretation is very different from expecting a confirmation or a refutation. In the first case, evenly suspended attention is at work guarding or correcting our bearings; in the latter, there is a countertransferential conflict, where interpretation becomes a valued (or idealized) product of our mind, loaded with narcissistic libido and alienating us from our analysand and our task. Feed-back is negative in the former and positive in the latter.

To show how rigorously the analysand evaluates us, I want to start with an example of my recent practice, though it makes me feel a little bit embarrassed.

In a Monday session a female patient expressed jealousy of the person whom she sometimes sees coming out of my consulting-room. She assumed that the latter was an analyst, and, once again, she thought that I treated this supposed colleague with interest, while I only treated her dutifully. This was followed by a long part of the session in which I interpreted that her search for affection derived from the feeling that she was not loved: if she thought that I was analysing her out of obligation, it was because she could not trust other people's love, etc. She accepted these interpretations but then stated that relationships with patients were not the same as with common human beings.

A [*Ironically*]: Well, we have finally reached an irreproachable conclusion. Analysands are not human beings. That is just right! [*Seriously*] There is a huge contradiction in what you are saying, though, since you are so intelligent, you are trying to make it seem logical and normal.

P: The analytic relationship is a relation between two people, but it is not exactly the same as the other ones. That is clear.

When the session was over, I felt very uneasy. I thought that I had let myself be taken to a ground that was scarcely analytic, where seduction and rivalry were mixed in the interpretations: I gave opinions, I contradicted the patient, I praised her.

On the following day the analysand arrived late and said:

P: If we continue with yesterday's subject. . . . The only thing I remember is that I dreamed that *I came to the session . . . I don't know how it was. You were setting the table to have some tea. There were cookies and orange marmalade. My daughter appeared in the dream too, and she asked: "How come? Do the two of you have tea together?" I said: "It seems so."*

The manifest content of this dream speaks for itself. "Ladies' tea" is what we call an insubstantial meeting in my country. Despite this evidence and her first and spontaneous association, "If we continue with yesterday's subject", the analysand never suspected that her dream evaluated—in such a negative way as, in fact, I myself did—the previous session. At first she thought it was a nice dream, though she admitted that her daughter had a strongly critical attitude towards what I was doing. Only near the end of the session did she admit that Carmen, her daughter, stood for a part of herself that criticized the previous session. Then she was able to remove the repression from something that she had thought of repeatedly when leaving the previous day: it called her attention to the fact that I had qualified her as intelligent; she thought that it was praise or even a compliment. On this point, her unconscious evaluation coincided with mine, when I thought that I had flattered her instead of interpreting.

When such a coincidence occurs spontaneously (what I thought after the session and what she herself thought and dreamed), we have a very strong element to validate our work. Only that, in order to do so, both analyst and analysand must bear mental pain, which is sometimes very strong; in the same way that at first the patient did not even suspect that she was criticizing me, I must confess that, despite the great value of this example, I almost avoided including here.

I do not want to be too hard on myself, but I associate myself with that candidate from Max Gitelson's paper in the 1952 *International Journal of Psycho-Analysis*, who interviewed a woman who complained about not being attractive. The candidate immediately told her that he did have a good impression of her, and that night she dreamed of him exhibiting himself with a flaccid penis (p. 5). Incidentally, neither the great analyst that Max used to be nor anybody else would have thought that this girl was assessing the candidate's technical error in her dream, that he had shown his analytic impotence; and yet, how could she have dreamed this had she not noticed that the candidate's words were a grievous mistake? If the candidate would have interpreted the dream accordingly, it would have been possible to re-establish the analytic situation (or, to be more precise, to establish it) without having to go through a change of analyst, as Gitelson indicated,

In the 1927 *International Journal*, Ferenczi published a review of a recently published book by Otto Rank, *Technik der Psychoanalyse* (1926). Ferenczi quotes a fragment of a dream:

> "I was being analysed and was lying on the sofa. The analyst was very familiar to me, but I cannot say who he was. I had to tell him a dream of a journey that I was to undertake to visit some common friends. When I had begun, I was interrupted by an old woman who was sitting on a stool and wanted to interpret the dream in a popular manner (in an old wives' way). I told the analyst that I could tell the dream better if she did not interrupt me. Then he told her to be silent, got up, took hold of the hammock, in which I now seemed to be lying, with both his hands, and shook me hard. Then he said: "When you were born, you were quite red (in the face). Then you were laid on a sofa, and your father sat down beside you'. I was surprised in the dream at this explanation, and thought: 'This is very far-fetched. . .', etc."

Rank brought this dream to prove his theory that the analytical experience is isomorphic with birth, but Ferenczi rightly thought that the dream showed the patient's ridicule and scorn against the analyst's theories and interpretations. May I add that in this scorn, the analysand is also expressing a strong and negative evaluation of Rank's work?

In several passages of "Notes upon a Case of Obsessional Neurosis" (Freud, 1909d), we can also see not only Freud's mistakes but also the masked critiques that the Rat Man made on more than one occasion, as can also be noted in David Rosenfeld's excellent paper (1980) and in *Freud and the Rat Man* (Mahony, 1986).

The examples could be many, but I am interested in pointing out that if it is true that the analysand evaluates us and gets this right most of the time, keeping in mind that he or she can do it with a bad intention—then we can count on much help for contrasting our theories.

The decisive part of the analyst's work is the moment when he or she must evaluate the evaluation of the analysand. In this assessment he or she will certainly find the deep, unconscious response to his/her interpretation, which rarely coincides with what is said consciously and must always be sorted out from innumerable misunderstandings that turn our interpretation into a self-predictive hypothesis (complacency, seduction, positive transference) or into a suicidal hypothesis (aggression, envy, negative transference) (Etchegoyen, 1989, p. 394; Hanly, 1992, 1997; Klimovsky, 1986, fifth paragraph).

VII

The validity of the clinical process is best reached at the point of convergence where the findings of the session are extended into the slow but persistent changes that appear in the process. These changes sometimes occur half-way through (or at the end of) repetitive episodes, where the strength of the transferential phenomenon imposes itself powerfully to our reflection.

At a certain point of her analysis, the lady of the hose, whom I mentioned earlier, was worried about her old mother's loss of sphincter control, annoyed because her refrigerator leaked, wetting the floor, and angry at me because I interpreted her lack of emotional control. There was a moment when the tension of my countertransference was so high that I found myself obliging her to accept my interpretations like a mother who imposes cleaning habits on her child against his or her will. To this was added cystitis accompanied by intense frequency, a swollen wrist that provoked a severe hypochondriacal anxiety in her ("where does this fluid come from?"), and, at last, the remembrance of the fact that when her little sister was born (she was under 3 years old at the time), her mother had soiled her panties. This screen memory (Freud, 1899a) had appeared many times in her analysis, always expressing her denial of her jealousy for the new-born baby and envy for the creative capacity of her denigrated mother. This time she was able to regain those painful infantile feelings and to view her mother and her new baby from another perspective, while she oscillated between admiring and envying my analytic work (which at times also seemed creative to her).

I thank Grünbaum for the precision of his paper, "'Meaning' Connections and Causal Connections in the Human Sciences: The Poverty of Hermeneutic Philosophy" (1990). I concur with him in that psychoanalysis searches for causal connections and not *only* for new meanings, and I understand his criticism of the constructions that Freud (1909d) offered the Rat Man. I do not know whether the example I have just brought is more satisfactory; but no analyst can deny that my labour with this patient would have been impossible if "Notes upon a Case of Obsessional Neurosis" had not been written. Freud's understanding of that man, which surprised all the "Freudian Doctors" who listened to him in Salzburg in 1908, brought about an explanation of obsessional neurosis that no one else had been able to think of up to then, even though his countertransference with Dr Ernst Lanzer could be criticized if viewed in the light of today's knowledge.

On the other hand, on reading or criticizing this great clinical document, one must not leave aside the fact that it shows Freud's creativity at a unique moment, which surely deserves the gratitude of his readers. The way in which he puts together the past and the future of Dr Lanzer's life is not beyond the epistemologist's criticism and is, no doubt, technically faulty at times; nevertheless, it shows the mark of a genius.

Clark Glymour (1974, 1980) has also taken the clinical record of the Rat Man to see up to what point Freud's theories could be tested during the session using his "pincers strategy" method, which can also be applied to Newton's or Kepler's laws. In an addendum to his work of 1974, Glymour (1982) states that some of Freud's hypotheses can be tested, while others are only "rhetorical devices masquerading as arguments" (p. 31). He concludes that his paper is an attempt to separate the two things. I agree with these viewpoints and believe that my technique is aimed precisely at detaching the psychoanalytic interpretation from the analyst's assertions, which, no matter how inspired and creative they may be—and beyond their heuristic value—are no more than his/her subjective and personal opinions. I find it very satisfactory when I hear Glymour say that ". . . the theory Johannes Kepler proposed long ago was strong enough to be tested in the observatory, and the theory Sigmund Freud developed at the turn of this century was strong enough to be tested on the couch" (p. 29). On the other hand, can a science really be a science if all its hypotheses must be tested in a field that is not its own? Klimovsky's thinking moves in the same direction as Glymour's, not only in his paper on the epistemology of the psychoanalytic interpretation (Klimovsky, 1986), but also in his extraordinary book of 1994, when he states that "although in a more intricate way, the deductive hypothetical method also seems to account for the validation of interpretation, something that had, somehow, already been pointed out by John O. Wisdom and other epistemologists" (p. 316, translated for this edition).

I also wish to point out that I appreciate Grünbaum's critiques of psychoanalysis because I find that they are a new and more precise version of Nagel's, Popper's, and Bunge's. Yet I think it is necessary to keep them apart from his polemic with hermeneuticians, in which psychoanalysis loses its autonomy and becomes the battlefield of two major philosophical currents of our time. The facts with which psychoanalysis deals are in part factual and in part semiotic (Klimovsky, 1980, p. 37), they have meaning and thus depend on the personal codes applied by analysand and analyst; but beyond these codes, we have the facts of psychic reality posited by psychoanalytic theory, which, however difficult to attain, are not beyond the reach of our technique. If I personally tend to consider psychoanalysis as a natural science, as Klimovsky (1989) does, it is because I believe—and in this I completely agree with Charles Brenner—that although psychoanalysis works with elements that have meaning (words, wishes, symbols), it does not deal with them exclusively as mere meanings or words within a hermeneutic circle. "The method of observation and the data of psychoanalysis have very much to do with language and meaning, but it is a mistake to conclude from this that psychoanalysis is *sui generis* as a science" (Brenner, 1980, p. 205).

I wish to conclude my exposition by remarking on the enormous explanatory value that the theory of transference has for me, in so far as we consider it, as did Freud (1905e [1901], 1914g, 1950 [1895]), an intermission of the past into the present, a repetition that is neither simplistic nor isomorphic and that allows us to compare what is happening now with what happened long ago and far away—as William Henry Hudson would say.

CHAPTER TWELVE

What do our terms mean?

Anne Hayman (London)

For more than fifty years, Pearl King has played an increasingly vital part in the world of psychoanalysis, working her way from student to President of the British Psychoanalytical Society, contributing vastly to work in the IPA and to every existent aspect of organization and functioning of the British Society; and outstandingly, in creating new projects, of which the British Society Archives are perhaps only the most important and significant among many contributions. Given the extent and range of her creative activity, she may perhaps differ from many outstanding psychoanalysts in being more renowned for things she has done than for things she has written, with perhaps the one exception of the volume mentioned below. But the distinctive originality that made her think of doing things no one else had thought of doing has also made her think and say and write down things that no one else has managed to say and write. I shall report at a little length on something she wrote of this nature—not to discuss it, but to give an indication of her capacity to notice and then bring theory to bear on a difficult and potentially contentious clinical issue.

In 1992, the topic of the English-Speaking Conference held in London by the British Society was "The British Controversial Discussions: The Issues of Unconscious Phantasy and Conflict 50 Years Later". It followed the publication the previous year of the now famous massive volume *The Freud–Klein Controversies, 1941–1945*, edited by Pearl King and Riccardo Steiner. Pearl King opened the conference with a challenge. She noted that in 1942, prior to the Controversial Discussions, Marjorie Brierley wrote that "one way of stating the problem before us [of the then current theoretical disagreements and disharmony] is to ask the question: 'is a theory of mental development in terms of infantile object relationships compatible . . . with a theory in terms of instinct vicissitudes?'", and that Brierley felt that the answer was in the affirmative, quoting Freud's most recent definition of instinct in support of her opinion: "an instinct may be described as having a source, an object and an aim" [Freud, 1933a, p. 125]. But, King continued,

> when I listen to some members of the British Society now [fifty years later], I wonder if she was right, as they tend to work in terms of the analysis of the vicissitudes of the current object relationships of the patient and the analyst, and there is little reference to the vicissitudes of instincts, indicating that perhaps the two theories have not proved compatible, but that one theory has replaced the other.

In 1996 King elaborated on this issue in a paper (as yet unpublished) entitled "What Has Happened to Psychoanalysis in the British Society?" She explained in detail why she believed that analysts too frequently focus on the immediate assumed unconscious relationship between analysand and analyst, and that this so-called "here-and-now transference" gives far too little attention—often none—to each individual moment of the past. Instead of wondering "with whom the analyst is at any one moment unconsciously identified by the analysand", for many analysts the central or only question is: "What is the analysand unconsciously doing to the analyst?" The concept of transference, whereby affects, memories, experience from the past still exist in the mind of the patient and are what is transferred—this is ignored and replaced by equating the transference with the (immediate) relationship. King believes that a whole range of concepts, ideas, discoveries of Freud and also of Melanie Klein, that only make sense if taken together with an appreciation of the patient's past history, include free association by the analysand and free-floating attention on the part of the analyst (both interfered with if the past is firmly ignored in favour of the present); repetition compulsion and regression (both inherently connecting the transference with the past); and likewise the developmental approach, infantile sexuality leading to adult sexuality, and the superego. (Regarding the concept "here-and-now", she thinks the term was first used by John Rickman, for whom the patient's timeless unconscious past was very much present in the here-and-now, and part of the analyst's task was "to discover the age or developmental stage the patient was experiencing at any one moment".)

King's central criticism is of the way the concept of "transference" is frequently understood now, in contrast to the way she understands it and the way(s) she understands Freud and Klein to have understood it. She describes rather appealingly how she searched through Klein's writings, looking for a quote that she could use to blame Klein for the (present) state of affairs (and) to her "chagrin" realized that Klein described transference in the same way King herself thought and thinks about it; and King gives a long Klein quotation from 1943 illustrating this. The clinical practices King describes critically probably stem from the gradual acceptance of Heimann's (1950) theory of "countertransference" and especially its being adapted to the Klein canon (Klein initially rejected Heimann's idea) through Klein's concept of "projective identification", subsequently expanded by many others, including Joseph (1989). King felt she had touched only on the fringe of the problem, and welcomed further suggestions. If what follows is not exactly a response to this invitation, it was stimulated by the example of King's courageous originality.

The issue of Pearl King's concern (the common use or overuse of the "here-and-now" transference" as currently often conceived) can be seen from at least two directions. Her focus is on how a new and essentially more limited concept apparently replaces the original, much richer and more consequential meaning. A second way of looking at it is that a new meaning has been silently accepted for a long-established technical term. If seen from this second viewpoint, then what King criticizes in some practitioners apparently involves their unacknowledgely *changing the meaning of an item of psychoanalytical terminology*. This is the theme that I follow, to note and illustrate a few types of change in psychoanalytic terminology, with some emphasis on their value or the opposite. This is anything but an exhaustive enquiry, as it deals merely with a few random examples that have come the way of the author. But it is felt that they can exemplify a wide problem that requires recognition.

There are a number of ways in which changes in psychoanalytical language occur. The first group of ones that are entirely acceptable are those for which new terms are added to the existing vocabulary because they are necessary for naming genuinely new ideas. There are a number of obvious local examples, such as those within the Kleinian corpus, the ideas of Fairbairn, Winnicott, Bion, as well as those further afield, including, for example, Kohut. Whether or not the new ideas are accepted, the need for special terms for them is not an issue. At the very least they make clear that the new idea *is* new, so that when understanding or agreement is not achieved, there is at least clear certainty on that point. New ideas are, of course, very important—the life-blood of any discipline. Like any growing body of knowledge and ideas, psychoanalysis has its own concepts expressed in its own terminology, and there can be absolutely no argument against these inevitably expanding to accommodate new knowledge and new ideas. The more enthusiastically new ideas are embraced, the more will the new concepts and terminology be used.

The first examples of changes in psychoanalytic vocabulary naturally came with Freud, who, as his creative ideas developed and evolved, used some terms in new ways so that their meanings stretched. Consequently, their meanings were not always consistent, and one term could ultimately have in effect more than one meaning. This has long been recognized as a problem, which means that the subject of this chapter has respectable antecedents. "Ego" is the best-known example; and the topic of the evolution and expansion of the uses by Freud (as well as later writers) of the term has engaged a number of thinkers over the years. It has been accepted as if defined, *inter alia*, as personality, as person, as central agency, as psychic agency, as subject, as substructure of the personality defined by its functions, as self, and so on. There are various approaches to the consequent multiplicity of meanings and inevitable confusion and even contradictory nature of some descriptions. They include exploring the multiplicity as a historical fact; accepting or even validating multiplicity as perhaps reflecting a parallel existing psychic multiplicity; presenting one or another new model offering new meanings to terms, sometimes to solve contradictions, sometimes to offer new ideas (an example is mentioned below); and at least recognizing and describing the existence of uncertainty of definition as a continuing evolving problem. This last approach resembles that of the present investigation.

There are certain difficulties or paradoxes in this pursuit. Not everyone is bothered by differences in definition or meaning of current terms, many people either ignoring or not noticing any difficulty by simply adhering to a chosen model. But in one way this "solution" probably applies to everyone, because, however they arrive at it, all practitioners will surely have a chosen model or models on which they rely clinically (even if it might change at times for some). This means that whatever the theoretical recognition of different meanings of terms and concepts, some reliance on a certain validity of the meanings is more or less automatically taken for granted. Unless this were the case, it would simply not be possible to do any work at all. So paradox exists, in this way. Secondly, analysts are well accustomed to the utter necessity of working clinically with a great deal of uncertainty and ignorance about immediate processes within the analysand, to an extent within the analyst, and between the two of them—but at the same time, in order to make the best analytic use they can of whatever they perceive as happening, they will inevitably rely on some hoped-for safety or security—even near-certainty—of experience and knowledge; if not of those ongoing processes *per se*, then at least of the usefulness of the analyst's very ways of trying to understand. So there may be two different challenges to any analyst's feeling at home or at ease with what he or she is doing. Remarkably, this might not interfere with the analyst's capacity to work without too much anxiety or rigidity or whatever. (Problems about this last paradox, which might be lauded as non-rigid fluidity of mind, described as defensive unconscious splitting, or lamented as stupidity or woolliness or dishonesty of thought, will be left for a later investigation.)

To return to terminology: it is far from unknown for thinkers other than Freud to change terminology by using established psychoanalytical conceptual or clinical terms for new and different meanings. A well-known historical example is the then new meaning accorded the term "phantasy" by Klein, as well explained by Susan Isaacs (1943). Briefly, Freud's main probable meaning of the term "phantasy" (conscious *or* unconscious) was the construction of an imagined situation of gratification to defend against the pains of frustration. Klein expanded this meaning enormously, to denote phantasies as "mainly unconscious, the primary content of unconscious mental activity; phantasy as psychic reality, the mental representative and corollary of instinctual urges which cannot operate in the mind without phantasy." They say that Freud's postulated "hallucinatory wish-fulfilment" and his "primary projection" are the basis of phantasy life; phantasies are the subjective interpretation of experience, early becoming elaborated into defences as well as wish-fulfilments, expressing the specific content and showing the specific purpose of an urge or feeling or a defence. Phantasies exert an uninterrupted and omnipresent influence throughout life, with individual and age difference lying in the mode of elaboration and expression. In terms of this definition, "phantasy" ultimately comes to mean well-nigh every single aspect of unconscious mental activity. This vastly differs from the earlier much more focused meaning of one specific mode of defence against pain; but, somehow, within the British Society this difference is hardly noticed. The term "phantasy" is quite widely used in the expanded (Kleinian) meaning as well as in the more focused limited meaning. This involves an oddity that is ignored; that is, of including under one name, in one category, the functions of imaginary gratification, of perceiving and realistically interpreting experience, of hallucinatory wish-fulfilment and primary projection, of thinking and judgement, and the primary content of unconscious mental processes. This problematic point is mentioned again below.

Another example of established terms being used with new meanings (which includes a new meaning for the term "ego") is found when Winnicott explained his view on the relation between "ego and id". Freud used the terms to denote items in his 1923 model of the mind (1923b). *Inter alia*, he described the individual as "a psychical id . . . on whose surface rests the ego . . ." adding, "the ego is that part of the id which has been modified by the direct influence of the external world. . . ." It is clear from these descriptions (as it was from his 1915e description of System Unconscious, *inter alia*, as earlier than the higher organized system later called "ego"), that for Freud "id" unquestionably preceded "ego", even if only briefly. Winnicott would appear not to contradict this when he wrote that ". . . id functioning is collected together. . . and becomes ego experience". But he went on to state that ". . . there thus is no sense in making use of the word 'id' for phenomena that are not covered . . . and experienced . . . and eventually interpreted by ego-functioning. What instinctual life there may be apart from ego-functioning can be ignored, because the infant is not yet an entity having experiences. There is no id before ego." What

Freud named "das Es" [the id] he saw as preceding what he named "das Ich" [the ego]; what Winnicott named "ego" he saw as preceding what he named "id". This contradiction, too, is further mentioned below.

A third way in which psychoanalytic terminology can change comprises those situations where new terminology disguises the loss or the unacknowledged part-duplication, with or without contradiction, of ideas long established in earlier terminology. What follows are some examples of an idea described in new language that has been offered as new but turns out to be, or to include, ideas long familiar (or that should be long familiar) when couched in older terminology—that is, the use of new words for old ideas.

1. In his 1912 "Recommendations for Physicians on the Psycho-Analytic Method of Treatment" (1912e), Freud recommends "evenly suspended attention". In summary, he explains that in this way a strain that could not be kept up for several hours daily and a danger inseparable from deliberate attentiveness are avoided. For as soon as attention is deliberately concentrated in a certain degree, one begins to select from the material before one; one point will be fixed in the mind with particular clearness and some other consequently disregarded, and in this selection one's expectations or one's inclinations will be followed. This is just what must not be done, however; if one's expectations are followed in this selection there is the danger of never finding anything but what is already known, and if one follows one's inclinations anything that is to be perceived will most certainly be falsified.

This should be compared with Bion's 1970 statement in *Attention and Interpretation*:

> The memories and desires to which I wish to draw attention have the following elements in common: they are already formulated and therefore require no formulation: they derive from experience gained through the senses: they are evocations of feelings of pleasure or pain; they are formulations "containing" pleasure or pain. Insofar as they are Column 2 statements their function is to prevent transformation of the K→O order. . . . The first point is for the analyst to impose on himself a positive discipline of eschewing memory and desire . . . what is required is a positive act of refraining from memory and desire.

These two statements are identical in their advice to analysts, and well-nigh identical in the meaning of their reasons for giving this advice. To some extent the same would apply to yet another new formulation.

2.   In Britton and Steiner's 1994 paper, "Interpretation: Selected Fact or Overvalued Idea", which relies heavily on Bion's thinking, the view is given that the new model the paper promotes has the effect, *inter alia*, that it "protects the analyst from overactive participation".

Essentially, the difference between these three aids to practice lies in the different background theories producing different ways of giving what is virtually or even absolutely the same advice. This sameness might have the advantage of confirmation—a confluence is arrived at from different theoretical sources and therefore in different languages. (Although it should be remembered that without conscious intent, "original" thinking does sometimes plagiarize. It is far from unusual to discover a "forgotten" source for something that had been cherished as an original idea; and it seems fair to assume that all analysts have read Freud at some time in the past!)

There are, of course, reasons for the new formulations. Bion's is in the context of his model of the Grid and so forth, explaining an important idea of his own. However, there is no reason to think that the particular piece of advice to analysts stands or falls by the acceptability of those theories or that particular idea. Often enough the idea of operating "without memory or desire" is spoken of as if it is accepted as an idea in its own right. Freud's words of advice could be preferable, not just because they "are Freud's", but because Bion's could be taken as suggesting that the analyst actively eschew all memory of previous sessions, which effort would certainly be counterproductive clinically, as actively choosing not to think of anything is as much a contrivance as actively choosing points of personal interest. In fact, it seems quite possible that Bion did not mean this but meant exactly what Freud meant.

3. Another example comes with Bion's 1967 statement in *Second Thoughts*. He writes that there is in the analyst's thinking

> an *evolution*, the coming together, by a suddenly precipitating intuition, of a mass of apparently unrelated phenomena, which are thereby given coherence and meaning not previously possessed. . . . From the material the patient produces there emerges, like the pattern from a kaleidoscope, a configuration which seems to belong not only to the situation unfolding, but to a number of others not previously seen to be connected and which it has not been designed to connect.

Bion is explaining how his attention could be arrested by what he calls the "selected fact", which could emerge as the centre of a hypothesis in which different elements in the patient come to be integrated in the mind of the analyst . . . which could then be formed into an interpretation.

This can be compared with words written more than a decade earlier. In 1951, writing "On Counter-Transference", Annie Reich describes ". . . confusing incomprehensible disconnected presentations [which] suddenly make sense and become a *Gestalt*". Bion seems to have arrived at his "selected fact " in exactly the same way as Annie Reich arrived at her *"Gestalt"*, and aside from the descriptive detail, it is difficult to see any difference between her *"Gestalt"* and his "selected fact".

As mentioned, the above examples were given to illustrate the theme of "old ideas presented as if new, in new terminology". Important corollaries to this are the possibilities of new terminology disguising contradictions of ideas and theoretical losses of long-valued insights. Regrettably, although there is something approaching conviction that significant examples of these are available, in the rush to get this chapter written there was not enough time to get full details of them; and this is a task for the future.

To consider what has so far been stated: there are differences in the ways different workers understand the concept "transference". One way of formulating the "difference" is to note that it involves a change in the meaning of the term, in such a way that long-valued insights accruing to the older meaning may have been lost. This leads to noticing changes in some other items of psychoanalytic language, achieved either by the creation of new terms or by established terms being treated as having different or additional meanings. New terminology is unarguably acceptable when new terms are created to name a new idea—as, for example, with a Kleinian term like "depressive position". There is, however, room for argument when new meanings are added to an established term, as with the Isaacs/Klein definition of "phantasy", the question here being whether the older and the newer meanings are really sufficiently within the same category as to be meaningfully definable by the one term (i.e. imaginary gratification as the specific defence against pain of frustration, *and* well-nigh every single aspect of unconscious mental activity). Obviously, the new meanings require to be stated, but whether it helps clarity to lump them together with the meaning of the old term rather than giving them a new term altogether, is another matter. (During the Controversial Discussions, Brierley suggested that Isaacs should use the word "meaning" for what she was newly defining as "phantasy".) It was claimed that the new additions enriched the older concept of "phantasy". Alternatively, it could be felt that there is a loss, because a term denoting just about "everything" ultimately means just about nothing, whereas phantasy meaning "imaginary gratification" is far more specific and thus useful as a term.

When Winnicott said "there is no id before ego", in one sense he, like Klein and Isaacs, was adding to the established meanings of the terms, because he still went along with major aspects of what Freud meant by the concepts, in seeing id as the source of instinctual drive and ego as the seat of mature functions like memory, thinking, organized action, and so on. But in another sense (again like Klein and Isaacs), he was using the terms for a new meaning. He wanted to say something new, about how he conceived of early development, arising from his experience in analysing a few borderline or psychotic patients, and in observing hundreds of infants with their mothers. All these were clinical observations, of the same conceptual order as the clinical observations Freud made on his patients and on himself. But the topics of observation were not "ego" or "id"—they were people who were talking, struggling with feeling wretched or guilty or loving or furious, remembering and forgetting, fighting or complying, and so on. The psychoanalytic "Ich" and "Es" (or "superego" or "depressive position" or "projective identification" ... etc.) are not matters of observation to be described. They are concepts to explain what is being and has been observed and described. They cannot be treated as pieces of natural science to be noted and categorized. If this distinction is kept in mind, it might help to resolve the apparent contradiction of Freud's and Winnicott's "ego and id". Clearly, Winnicott wanted to change something of Freud's concept because he felt it did not adequately explain what he felt he had observed; but his generalization using the terms was at a different level from Freud's. For Freud, "Ich" and "Es" were abstract metapsychological concepts. Winnicott said (personal communication) that he couldn't use metapsychology and he was using the (metapsychological) terms to describe the infant's *experience*. So, rather than modifying Freud's concept the better to explain new findings, it might rather be said that Winnicott was actually using the terms to describe something significantly different. They were the wrong words, in contrast to the meaningful and resonating and useful words with which he repeatedly described the infant's experience.

The distinction between observation, as in natural science, and abstract theorizing about what is observed parallels a distinction made over half a century ago by Marjorie Brierley (1939) when she distinguished between two independent aspects of psychoanalytic theory that she related to two different modes of thinking in psychoanalysis. One was "used in the consulting-room [where] we understand the individual personal subjective experience of our analysands by thinking and feeling *with* them by identification". The other came into play "when we theorize, thinking metapsychologically, and feeling objectively *about* the patient". Descriptions of the sequence of the patient's actual experience, was "something *different in kind* from theoretical generalizations about experience", and Brierley was of the opinion that to avoid ambiguity or even mistakes, the two should be described in different terms. For one example she quotes Strachey describing a patient who may say that "his self is falling to pieces"; but this *subjective* experience might or might not reflect what could be described *objectively* as the "stability of his ego". If the patient is schizophrenic, ego stability might be threatened, if he is hysteric, it might not be, "despite his feelings". To describe the patient using only that patient's subjective description "is not a merely linguistic mistake but may result in capital confusions or errors in our views of the real events". It is a sad reality that little regard has been paid to Brierley's clarifying distinction, with the result that confusions between what she called "perceptual" and "conceptual" language abound in our literature; of which Winnicott's misleading use of the *metapsychological* terms ego and id, to describe what he believed was the *experience* of the infant, is a telling example. So while he had much to *add* to psychoanalytic terminology in describing his new ideas (e.g. "transitional states and objects", "true and false self") his "new" use of the terms "ego" and "id" arises, in this view, from a misconception.

It is a different matter with the rather startling resemblances in small details of differently conceived theories that have been illustrated with examples of Freud, Bion, Britton, Steiner, and Reich arriving at what seems the same idea in different ways and along different routes and using different terms. It makes a difference as to when each arrived there in relation to when the other did. It is certainly not unknown for different researchers in any discipline to get to more or less the same idea at about the same time, the resounding example being Darwin and Wallace; and it would appear that when relevant thoughts and ideas are being exchanged and known about in the scientific community, it is quite possible for them to stimulate similar responses in more than one perspicuous worker. Winnicott and Bion, working at the same time in London, produced ideas about earliest development that were somewhat different in their languages and concepts, but by no means always so different in meaning. To take one example, papers first including Winnicott's "unthinkable anxiety" and Bion's "nameless dread"—obviously referring to just about the same thing—were published within the same year (although I have a recollection, for which I cannot find the reference, of Winnicott grumbling that his was first and not acknowledged!). In Annie Reich's aforementioned paper, published in the same year as Heimann's renowned "Countertransference" paper, which Reich was therefore unlikely to have read before she wrote hers, there are clear references to something of the very same idea about countertransference that Heimann was presenting.

It is less easy to guess about the source of similarities in two publications when there is a decade or more between their appearance. On the other hand, if such an identity of ideas does not irritate too much ("that was said ten or twenty years ago by X—why isn't it quoted?") it can be seen as a rewarding or even reassuring confluence. Psychoanalysis has far too little in the way of testability or refutability of theory not to feel that identical conclusions by different workers, working separately, constitute at least some substitute for statistical confirmation.

Finally, while there are obviously occasions when a change in meaning of a psychoanalytic term is justified because new knowledge of the relevant topic shows the need for change in the concept, there are others when this is not the case. The first problem is to recognize when this is so and then to try to understand why it has happened—that is, why an unnecessary, confusing contradiction or duplication or other muddle of terminology is accepted. How can it be that terms *can* be used with so niggardly a regard for the function of terms, which is to communicate, clearly and unequivocally, which function includes the clear and unequivocal communication (rather than the dramatic enactment) of muddle, unclarity, and equivocation, if that is the subject of what needs to be communicated.

There may be a number of contributing factors. One is the situation when the change is part of an exciting new idea that may engage so much interest that earlier ideas are left behind and forgotten, which can be a serious loss. This might sometimes have been the case with the concept of "transference", as King illustrates; and another example might be of how the concept of "repression" is sometimes lost when relevant clinical findings are subsumed under the heading of "splitting", thereby losing the distinction of ego intactness, if repression is *by* ego and splitting is *of* ego. One factor might be a problem inherent to our study. There is no way at all of testing our theoretical concepts *per se*, and their usefulness or otherwise depends entirely on whichever set of words resonate with any one psychoanalytic community at any one moment, which is shown by the fact that they differ in different countries and in different groupings and at different times. Furthermore, there are differences between those using abstract metapsychological formulations as well as clinical experiential ones and those preferring to theorize only in clinical experiential terms, with the added difficulty that the difference is not always noticed. An overall disadvantage of most workers relying on their chosen, immediate modes of communication and theorizing is the lamentable paucity of serious attempts to contrast different ideas, to compare and contrast and measure their comparable usefulness, which goes together with the great difficulties that many experience in seriously considering criticism of their own ideas, as if considering alternatives is a disloyalty, rather than a welcoming of new ideas.

* * *

To summarize: there are a number of ways in which psychoanalytic language changes. While some are certainly acceptable, the emphasis has been on some that are regrettable, because of duplications and contradictions and consequent confusions that ensue. Valuable ideas may be blurred or totally lost; or great difficulties can accrue in that vital "scientific" need, the communication and especially the comparison and evaluation of theoretical ideas. A few examples are given to illustrate these various problems. No grand solutions are offered. All that has been attempted is an indication of the nature of a serious problem, in the hope of this being a step towards some further understanding. It is offered in tribute to Pearl King, not because it reflects her ideas, but because her admirable capacity to present ideas that she might not think popular has encouraged me to do likewise.

CHAPTER THIRTEEN

Love relations in later years

Otto F. Kernberg (New York)

Falling in love is the first stage of the development of a love relation. In the psychoanalytic literature as well as in general psychological literature and in poetry and the arts, it is typically represented by the love relations of adolescents. Romeo and Juliet constitute the paradigm for falling in love, for the mutual idealization of the lovers, establishing, as Alberoni (1987) has suggested, a "revolution or two". Yet, clinical experience and, indeed, life experience reveal that the process and experience of falling in love and establishing a passionate love relation is not restricted to adolescents or young adults but may occur at any point throughout the entire life span. Passionate love relations may develop in old age, with all the characteristics of love relations in adolescence—the mutual idealization of the couple and their sexual intimacy, their implicit rebellion against the daily life of the group that surrounds them, against the social network that pursues ordinary work activities while the couple in love creates a secret, transcendent world for themselves (Kernberg,

Presented at the San Diego Psychoanalytic Society and Institute, San Diego, California, 31 January 1998.

1995). These features can be observed in couples in their sixties and seventies, and probably even beyond. The question that concerns me is whether such love relationships in later years have particular characteristics that differentiate them from earlier ones and whether these characteristics may illuminate aspects of love relations not sufficiently recognized in our observations of love relations in adolescence and early adulthood.

The first observations that strike one in exploring this issue are a peculiar resistance to exploring it, a sense of embarrassment, as Martin Bergmann (personal communication) has pointed out, along with awareness of the shadow of the limited time span of life ahead for the couple—with illness, incapacity, and death as a realistic dimension quite different from the theme of love and death in adolescence that is reflected in the literature on romantic love. Having had the opportunity to study the love relations of elderly patients as well as those of healthy couples in their sixties and seventies and the privilege of observing such developments within the social network of a generation of older adults, I have been struck by several regularities of the love relations in this age group.

To begin, the intensity of the erotic experience of falling in love in the second half of life is remarkable, the frequent statements of adults in their fifties, sixties, and seventies implying that the sexual experiences in their newly found love relation were unmatched by previous, even satisfactory involvements. The early encounters of the new couple are often marked by timidity and insecurity, by women's typical fears of not being attractive enough, of showing the marks of the years in their bodily changes, their fears of disappointing a new lover with their body, as well as with whatever sexual inhibitions they still experience or are afraid of re-experiencing. Men experience similar worries—fear over their potency, over disillusioning a woman who may have had many other gratifying sexual experiences, and concern about the changes in bodily appearance that reflect their age.

But at this point there is a sharp divergence between healthy couples and those with pathological defences against the narcissistic lesion implied in real or fantasized sexual inadequacy, or with severe masochistic tendencies, who, not surprisingly, defensively withdraw when their security is challenged, narcissistically devalue the partner, experience a new commitment as an invasion and a loss of autonomy, or become resentful of their involvement in the complex life patterns and relationships of another person with a full and different life experience. Severely masochistic patients tend to repeat their unconscious impulses to ruin the new relationship by their inordinate demands or hypersensitivity to any disappointment, their infantile clinging or the perpetuation of their sexual repression rationalized in terms of conventional rejection of the erotic in old age.

Healthy couples, by contrast, may have an unexpected new experience of mutual openness and a tolerance of their own initial insecurity, and they may develop the capacity to share their feelings of insecurity with their loved partner. This reflects a new openness towards oneself, as well as a growing capacity for a trusting relationship with a loved partner. At a deeper level, a growing idealization of the body of the other develops, as the appreciation of his/her personality translates into the combination of erotic desire and tenderness. Their initial insecurity and timidity tend to resolve rapidly through their mutual empathy and understanding and to shift into an intense and remarkably liberated sexual experience that tolerates the integration of polymorphous perverse infantile sexuality into their sexual play, fantasy, and activity.

These couples in the later stages of life typically evince a decrease of the inhibitions derived from unconscious prohibitions against sexual activities, with enjoyment, for example, of oral and anal sexual play and activity that may not have been possible for them in earlier relationships. There is a decrease of internal superego pressures as well as of the tendency mutually to project superego prohibitions, fostered by the intimacy of their communication about past fears and old restrictions. As they contemplate their future, they experience acutely the passage of time, the limited duration of life, and the conscious or unconscious awareness—in Jacob Arlow's (personal communication) words—that time itself is the eventual oedipal victor. In protest, they enact a shared rebellion against this ultimate oedipal enemy. In concrete terms, they see their remaining time as being too short to be spent in nourishing inhibitions or postponing new experiences, and they may share a maturing sense of the irrationality of the infantile prohibitions against sexuality that have ruled them to one extent or another in the past. In short, these couples may experience an expansion of the realm of the self in the context of their exciting sense of rebellion against the conventional attitudes towards sexuality in old age.

In fact, conventional morality directs sexual prohibitions both against infantile sexuality in the assumption of the "innocence" of childhood and against the sexual life of the old, whose eroticism is often depicted as shameful, decadent, or ridiculous. The cultural association of sexual intimacy with the perfect bodies of adolescents reflects the projection of the oedipal prohibitions experienced by children, who assume that their own parents don't enjoy sexual intercourse, and by young adults who harbour the same assumption about their ageing parents. Conventional morality, reflecting the culturally shared oedipal prohibition and guilt, thus denies fully fledged sexual enjoyment outside the narrow age band of the pre-parental gender images of childhood and early adolescence.

The implicit rebellion against the conventional assumption of controlled, measured, decorous, and passionless behaviour of the older generation is expressed in the older couple's erotic play and their excitement in the face of the sexual freedom of the partner, an excitement heightened by the contrast of that freedom with the partner's conventional social behaviour. It may well be that the contrast between the stripped-down version of sexual intimacy tolerated by conventional clichés and the reality of the secret relation of the sexual couple reaches its height in the love relations of later years. The erotic collusion of the older couple is a replay of the forms that oedipal rebellion takes in adolescence, now suffused, however, with a sophisticated knowledge of the discrepancy between conventional adult behaviour and a private world of ecstasy and playfulness. This oedipal rebellion now may sweep away the remnants of sexual prohibitions and promote the search for extremes of previously unexplored pleasure, in defiance of the limited nature of time.

The idealization of the body of the beloved other now may include aspects of ageing linked to the images of the oedipal figures, in a shift that, by incorporating a life history into the aesthetic appreciation of the body, runs counter to the conventional standards of beauty. One patient, during his adolescence, had admired the wife of an idealized former teacher. He had developed a social relationship with that much older couple and had always been afraid of the sharp criticisms of his professor's wife, whom he remembered with a particular expression of her eyes surrounded by wrinkles. About forty years later he met a woman whose sharp intelligence and gracefulness had first attracted him, and with whom he then fell in love. Separated from her for extended periods because of her professional commitments in other parts of the country, he spent much time looking at her photographs in his studio. He particularly loved the expression on her face, the wrinkles around her eyes, which at some point she had complained about, concerned about her ageing. He had assured her that her eyes were one of her most endearing features. He only became aware weeks later, in the course of a session, that the loved features of her eyes resonated with the image of his professor's wife, thus linking his beloved to his adolescence and to the revival of his oedipal romance.

Donald Meltzer (Meltzer & Williams, 1988) had suggested that the infant's libidinally invested idealization of the surface of mother's body is the origin of the capacity for the sense of aesthetics, and that the counterpart of this idealization is the projection of aggressive wishes and fears into the interior of mother's body, leading to a broad spectrum of potential hypochondriacal fears as well as the most primitive manifestations of castration anxiety in patients with severe, aggressively infiltrated psychopathology. I have suggested in earlier work (Kernberg, 1995) that this dynamic constellation explains the greater fear that men have of women's ageing bodies than women have of men's ageing bodies that—on the contrary—may more directly evoke the erotic components of women's oedipal strivings. In both participants of the love relationships in later years, we may find that idealization of the other now includes aspects of the manifestations of the ageing process *per se*, possibly as sublimatory idealization of the previously feared manifestations of time as symbolically representing the effects of aggression. One might speculate that the acceptance of the inevitability of old age and death, now incorporated into the mutual erotic idealization of the body, expresses the affirmation of oedipal triumph and of the gratitude for life in the context of an awareness of its limitations.

A curious development occurs in later years in the relationship between erotic desire and passionate love. I have proposed in earlier work (Kernberg, 1995) that male and female development of the integration of sexual excitement and tenderness differs. The little boy usually experiences an uninterrupted awareness of genital excitement from infancy throughout the masturbation of early childhood, eventually continuing in men's relative freedom for sexual intercourse and orgasm. At the same time, the oedipal prohibitions and ambivalent relationship of the little boy to the mother are transferred establishment of an object relation in depth that would integrate the erotic and idealized, the libidinal and aggressive aspects of the internalized relations with the maternal object—a difficulty typically expressed in the Madonna/prostitute dichotomy of adolescence and its pathological fixation in the adulthood of men. For men, therefore, sexual freedom predates the capacity for the establishment of an object relationship in depth with a woman and for integrating sexual freedom within such a love relationship.

In the case of women, on the contrary, the unconscious, typical lack of maternal stimulation of the female infant's genital leads to early inhibitions of vaginal sexuality, as described by Braunschweig and Fain (1971), with inhibition of the little girl's erotic relationship with mother. This contributes to the transfer of her erotic longings to the father—that is, the establishment of the capacity of a relationship in depth with a distant object. This "courageous" step facilitates the capacity for a loving object relation in depth in the case of women, and the later achievement of the rediscovery of her full vaginal sexuality in the context of an adult love relationship. The most frequent pathology of women, in this regard, is some degree of sexual inhibition in the context of the establishment of a satisfactory love relationship. I concluded, in earlier work (Kernberg, 1995), that eventually, coming together from contrasting pathways of development, men and women achieve the same capacity for a synthesis between sexual liberation and an object relation in depth, and that, in fact, passionate love is precisely the hallmark of that synthesis between erotic desire and tender love.

Now, in the light of the observation of love relations of older couples, I suggest that this development continues into old age, with a surprising role reversal. Men falling in love and establishing a passionate love relationship at late stages of their lives frequently have the exhilarating experience that their intense love for a woman transcends in new ways their erotic desire, so that love becomes the bridge to sexual intimacy. In their fusion in love with the woman they desire, they experience a sense of total security and certainty about their love and an overwhelming gratification at having found the love object of their lives. Love, it would seem, becomes a means for the achievement of erotic desire, replicating, we might say, the early maturational characteristics of younger women. Women who fall in love in later stages of their lives may, on the contrary, experience a freedom of sexual desire that becomes the bridge to love for the man they have now found. One male patient in his sixties said jokingly to his new girlfriend: "I fear, at times, that you are only treating me as a sexual object and that my feelings and personality are of no relevance to you."

A man's idealization of the body of the beloved woman may acquire such a focused, exclusive linkage of erotic desire to this specific love object that a sublimatory transformation affects the sexual arousal that, earlier in life, would have been evoked in him by the observation of other women's bodies in art and nature, leading to a new sense of total gratification and completion of life's desire in the sexual intimacy with his lover. In women, a new "reconciliation", one might say, between clitoral and vaginal sensuality may be observed. Whereas throughout a significant segment of adulthood they had experienced a subtle incompatibility between clitoral stimulation as self-gratification and vaginal excitement as passionately giving themselves to a man, they now achieve the capacity to integrate intercourse and self-stimulation, clitoral, vaginal, and anal eroticism.

From the viewpoint of the permanency of the structuring of the love life by the oedipal constellation, it is significant that many love relations in later years are a re-encounter with a love object from much earlier in the individual's life. Such cases include rediscovering a childhood or adolescent friend or sweetheart after the death of a spouse or a divorce, sometimes by chance but often by actively searching for encounters with a significant other after decades of completely separate and unrelated lives. This selection of a love object represents in part an effort to resolve still active aspects of oedipal longings or prohibitions when that particular object had seemed forbidden or unavailable in the past. It now may represent the sublimatory resolution of an incestuous object choice. Martin Bergmann (1987) has suggested that all new love relations are steps towards the resolution of aspects of an incestuous relationship, and he proposes that, if there is no more incestuous desire available as a motivation for the id, there no longer exists the capacity for developing a new love relationship (personal communication). Implicit in everything said so far is my view, derived from a perspective contributed by French psychoanalytic approaches, that the oedipal constellation is not only a phase of psychosexual development and the dominant unconscious infantile conflict, but a permanent structure that organizes unconscious dynamics throughout the entire life span (Mijolla & Mijolla, 1996).

> One female patient in her late sixties fell profoundly in love with a man who had been a father figure of her deceased husband, and she developed a fully satisfactory love relationship with this significantly older man for the rest of her life.

> Another woman in her middle sixties, met by chance, after many years of unsatisfactory relationships with various men, a boyfriend from her early adolescence and developed a relationship that evolved into what she experienced as the great love of her life.

> One male patient in his early seventies found a deeply gratifying relationship with a woman from the country where he had spent the formative years of his adolescence.

Two elements—the re-encounter of a lost love object, and a new encounter that contrasts with the traumatic frustrations of a past relationship—are ubiquitous in love relations late in life. In the context of the new love relationship, aspects of past oedipal frustrations and longings may be relived and overcome in sometimes dramatic ways.

> A patient who established a new love relation in his late sixties with a woman from a foreign country speaking the language of his childhood, found himself softly humming childhood melodies as he was happily resting in her arms in the middle of the night.

> A female patient found herself crying in the arms of her new lover, remembering the death of her father, and rather intimate erotic fantasies about him that she had struggled with during the last weeks of his illness—a painful memory that had remained practically unavailable to her over many years and from which, by now sharing it, she could free herself at last.

A major finding that emerges throughout everything said so far about late-life love relations is their liberating effect upon superego restrictions of erotic desire and intimacy. This shift in equilibrium between ego and superego probably reflects the confluence of a lifelong, ongoing psychological maturation, the conscious and unconscious awareness of the passage of time, the wisdom derived from life

experience, the gradual freeing from submission to conventional ideology that I have referred to in earlier work in analysing the relationship between the couple and the group (Kernberg, 1995).

Undoubtedly, there are many cases where such a development
does not occur, where the ageing process and old age only seem to
accentuate and worsen character traits derived from the immature,
rigid, and punitive superego. These elderly people express a rigidly
defended submission to conventionality and a cynical and bitter devaluation of the possibility of a happy love relationship that reflects
the combination of unconscious envy of happy couples and implicit
recognition of their own life-long failure to love and be loved.

When contrasting pathology with normality at the beginning of
this chapter, I was really stressing my interest in the implications of
maturity in the realm of sexuality and love. Maturity in the sexual
realm is a reflection of learning from the experience of love relations
in the past, coming to terms with one's own personality as it may
have evolved in the context of a long-lasting love relationship such as
marriage over many decades, the capacity to learn both about one's
own behaviour and that of one's partner.

As an expression of emotional maturity, falling in love at later
stages of life includes a romantic idealization of the person one loves,
the expression of a profound intuition regarding what is still missing
in one's own life and requires completion, and the assessment of the
other person in depth as a complement to the knowledge of how one
can envision developing further within such a new relationship.
There is, of course, always an element of the unknown in all new love
relations, but there is also a growing intuition of what a life lived
together may promise, and the excitement of that promise dispels the
shadow of frustrated expectations in the past. Further, love relations
in the context of emotional maturity include a deep interest in the life
experience, the personality, the approach to people and politics, to
nature and art, to leisure and work of the person one loves, and the
profound gratification of sharing an internal world with a partner
who thus may bring it to new life and help to preserve a personal past
from extinction. To reconstitute for oneself and for the couple the
entire life experience of the loved partner may provide an extraordinary expansion of an individual's life experience. Also, the awareness
of the limited time ahead, the threat of illness, crippling dependency,
and death as an unavoidable perspective for the future of the elderly
couple enriches the appreciation of daily life lived together, helps to

brush aside the small conflicts of everyday experience, and consolidates a joint defiance regarding time and the future.

Love relations in later stages of the life span also test the extent to which pre-oedipal issues, conflicts around dependency on a maternal object, and the identification with a giving mother have been satisfactorily resolved. The possibility of loss of autonomy through illness, with prolonged dependency on the other, is a realistic possibility, and the couple's capacity and willingness to face this threat becomes an additional implicit aspect of their relationship. An early stroke, crippling arthritis, heart disease, or cancer may radically affect the equilibrium of the couple and put the maturity of its members, their capacity to depend and to assure dependency to the other, to a major test. Obviously, social and financial security, the maintenance or re-establishment of a significant social network that can support the couple and protect the one who has to take care of the other from exhaustion are key elements in any couple's survival in old age.

The capacity to depend on the loved other and to let oneself be taken care of may be severely hampered by unresolved early oral frustrations and aggression and the resulting defences against dependent longings and relationships. For women, under optimal circumstances, having to be taken care of by the man they love and taking care of an ailing partner both fit into traditional cultural patterns; but they also require maturity in order not to be seduced into an equally conventional pattern of masochistic sacrifice to impossible conditions.

For men, to have to renounce autonomous functions and, particularly, being taken care of by the woman they love is a direct reproduction of the early infant/mother relationship. Furthermore, such a dependency runs counter to the conventional ideology of the patriarchal society that forces men into a "fatherly", dominant role that protects them against deeper oedipal and pre-oedipal anxieties. The need to be taken care of tests the man's tolerance of dependency as opposed to a narcissistic sense of humiliation, a paranoid fear of being hated or resented because of this dependency, or feeling devalued because of the loss of oedipal attractiveness. These are major challenges to the love relationship in advancing age. The mutual awareness of these threatening possibilities and the tranquil certainty of one's disposition and passionate commitment to take care of the other, based upon a solid knowledge of oneself as well as of the loved one, constitute significant dimensions of a growing intimacy that enriches the couple's sexual freedom: one's weaknesses, fears, and inhibitions are a part of what, courageously, one has to accept in oneself and, with love, accept in the other.

The growth of ego identity throughout the entire life-span is reflected, as I have proposed in earlier work (Kernberg, 1995), in the capacity to identify with a broadening spectrum of generations and a broadening incorporation of both one's extended past and a projected future for one's life. This sense of where one belongs and of the aspirations for a life lived together helps to consolidate the mature couple and flexibly to combine their different cultural, political, and social backgrounds and commitments. The coincidence and complementarity of their viewpoints form a harmonious constellation, and the curiosity and wishes to learn from the other are matched with the wish to integrate the other into one's own commitments. I have mentioned that the possibility of learning about another life in depth, to acquire a deep knowledge of the entire life-span of another loved human being, is an exciting development for the new couple. Yet learning about each other includes the challenge of overcoming oedipal rivalry and jealousy sufficiently to tolerate the other's enviable past experiences and the idealization of potential rivals that, reaching over from the past, might disturb the future of the couple.

These tasks are more difficult when the oedipal configuration of the new couple is dominant, as when they differ significantly in age. A man's falling in love with a woman twenty to forty years younger than he is nearly always indicates a major unresolved aspect of oedipal conflicts, an effort to resolve in one coup a major aspect of the unconscious oedipal reservoir that, ordinarily, would be drawn upon in much smaller doses. The degree of success or failure of such a relationship obviously depends on the extent to which it is threatened by the unconscious guilt of one or both participants over the breaching of oedipal barriers, or the extent to which the unconscious motivation of the two members of the couple enters into obvious contradictions with the reality of their relationship.

For example, while older men clearly representing a father figure may permit the gratification of the unconscious incestuous wishes of a young woman, severe narcissistic pathology may complicate the situation. A narcissistic woman may be interested in the prominence of the older man, his political, cultural, intellectual, or artistic superiority, his fame or prominence, denying the reality of his personality, insecurities, and human limitations until they overwhelm her in their daily life. She then experiences a growing sense of frustration and resentment when his power and fame can no longer compensate for her frustrated dependency expectations in the relationship. If, in addition, such an older man in turn presents significant narcissistic pathology and severe restrictions in his capacity to depend on the woman who selected him, a major tragedy may be forthcoming.

Peter Greenaway's film *The Belly of an Architect* (1987) illustrates this constellation with the suicide of the ailing architect betrayed by his young wife.

A narcissistic older man expecting a young woman to be both an admiring subject and an object selected for public display and admiration may rapidly destroy a relationship with a woman who loves him but whose own social as well as emotional development is crippled by his demands. The relationship between an older man and a young woman, on the other hand, tends to provoke intense social admiration, envy, and resentment, the first two usually experienced by men, the latter by women, who, in addition to thus expressing their own projected oedipal guilt, also react to the implicit provocative display of prevalent cultural power relations—namely, the shared dominance of old men and young women. If such a couple can tolerate their guilt over the unconsciously incestuous implications of their relationship, and are able to enjoy the potentially forbidden rupture of oedipal barriers in their intimacy, standing up against the socially shared ambivalence towards them may heighten the intensity of their sexual liberation.

The relations between older women and younger men, in addition to the corresponding oedipal and incestuous implications, also run counter to the dominant conventional ideology regarding the relations between men and women and may expose, particularly the woman, to men's and women's conventional reluctance to accept the sexual affirmation of a maternal figure. Usually the age difference here is significantly smaller than that between older men and younger women, and I have been able to observe only a few couples with these age-related characteristics. Once again, the significance of narcissistic pathology in one or both members of the couple may be the crucial pathological ingredient tending to destroy it. Older women with unconscious oedipal fixations and resentment against mature paternal men may select effeminate younger men who, in turn, may obtain narcissistic gratification in a dependent relationship that is limited in its mutuality, and potentially threatened by any slackening of the gratification of the man's narcissistic needs. The traumatic effects of the rupture of such a relationship, in which an older woman experiences herself betrayed by a younger man, recreates the oedipal trauma and may be reflected in the woman's experience of a total loss of her value and attractiveness and of the meaning of her life. In all relationships involving large differences in age, unconscious guilt over oedipal and incestuous longings may actualize significant masochistic pathology.

The social reality of major financial and political power invested in older men and the typically greater financial and social insecurity of older women undoubtedly influences their relationships and is an important source of security and insecurity, restrictions and temptations in the love relations of later years. The attitude towards the lovers of their families—their children and grandchildren—may seriously restrict them if the couple have not reached the maturity to free themselves from the excessive dependency on group pressures that dominated them in earlier stages. In fact, if late adolescence is a time that marks the disappearance of adolescent mixed-aged groups and their gradual replacement by a base network of mostly married couples, one might say that late adulthood is characterized by the gradual freeing of the couple from its excessive dependency on such social groups, reinforced by the family ties established with siblings, and children, the spouses and children of siblings and the social networks linked with them.

At a certain point in life the dependency on group structures tends to decrease, and, in fact, a love relation in later years may signal that final autonomy of the couple, symbolized in the couple's enjoyment of solitude and travel and the selection of a small group of friends corresponding to their mutual needs in the context of a significant shift away from the social, political, and family commitments of early adulthood. It is, we might say, a second edition of the adolescent rebellion against the group.

Of course, the couple always need the group for their development and survival. I pointed out in earlier work (Kernberg, 1995) that normally, "unmetabolized" aggression generated in the couple's relationship is dispersed in their interactions with the surrounding group, at the same time as sublimatory aspects of libidinal oedipal urges also are satisfied in these interactions. One interesting aspect of the establishment of a love relation in later years is the excitement, the mixture of envy and gratification by proxy that the new couple evokes in their surrounding social group. This reaction is, of course, amplified when the couple occupies a prominent political, artistic, or social position. It is interesting that often women who had been rather inhibited sexually in the past are now, in the glow of this new love relationship, willing to talk freely of their erotic desire and their sexual gratification and, consciously or unconsciously, enjoy the erotic thrill this evokes in others. A woman who establishes a love relation in later years may create around herself an aura of excitement that increases her attractiveness for men who have known her for years. The men in such a love relationship may, in turn, convey to their surroundings a new sense of security and autonomy, of quiet fulfilment that, in subtle ways, strengthens their authority within their particular social group. Martin Bergmann (1987) illustrates this quality of love in old age with a quote from Bertrand Russell's auto-biography:

> Now, old and near my end,
> I have known you,
> And, knowing you
> I have found both ecstasy and peace
> I know rest
> After so many lonely years,
> I know what life and love may be
> Now, if I sleep
> I shall sleep fulfilled.

Gabriel García Márquez, in *Love in the Age of Cholera* (García, 1985), describes the sense of physical frailty and emotional insecurity in the initiation of a love relation in old age that renews a relationship from early adolescence, in the sudden outbreak of digestive disturbances of the hero at his first new encounter with the woman for whom he has longed throughout most of his life. However, in the culmination of their relationship that follows, they are engaged in an ecstatic voyage in a ship on the river through a land devastated by illness.

The question could be raised, to what extent the ideal state of affairs I have explored here implies a standard of maturity that is unrealistic for a large segment of the population—certainly for many of those with significant character pathology that renders the attain-ment of mature love highly unlikely because of complications and even worsening throughout the years. Furthermore, the efforts of many people without serious character pathology to achieve a satisfactory love relation may be hampered by disappointment and bitterness over life goals that remained blighted, or by frustrations and traumata in the sexual realm. In arguing against that viewpoint, I believe that our observations of optimal developments provide us with a practical view of human potentials that, even if often unfulfilled, constitute a standard against which we can evaluate more precisely the nature of the limitations with which our patients present us when we study their love life. As is true for other areas of human conflict, "normality" really corresponds to an ideal that permits us to focus sharply on the corresponding areas of psychopathology.

This perspective should facilitate abandoning the conventional view of sexual love and passionate attachments as unlikely in healthy old age, while loneliness and disappointments, the giving up of the search for gratifying relationships, are taken as the normal state of affairs. There are undoubtedly many individuals who, through unconscious sabotage of their own interests, narcissistic destruction of their opportunities for love, repetitive setting up of masochistic patterns of love relations that ended up in loneliness and frustration, thus have shut the door to new and different experiences. There are many other men and women who, if we challenge such self-defeating patterns in the light of a theoretical framework of what realistically might be possible in their lives, can be helped to start all over again.

I have been impressed by the effective ways in which creative men and women restructured their lives in their fifties, sixties, and seventies and fought the self-defeating tendencies that are a universal aspect of human psychology. Perhaps an obvious but sometimes neglected aspect of this life task is the extent to which such self-defeating tendencies are expressed not only through destroying the opportunities for gratifying love relations and revengeful patterns of denying the importance of sexuality, but also in unconscious hostility towards their own body, in defiant neglect of physical health and bodily appearance. The normal function of narcissistic concern for one's body is an important aspect of the search for sexual intimacy. Between the extremes of narcissistic enslavement by bodily preoccupations on the one hand and the omnipotent, narcissistic neglect of one's health and appearance on the other is a realistic concern for one's body. The relationship, in clinical practice, between a neglect of physical health and bodily appearance and the neglect of the potential for intimate relations with others is remarkably consistent. The normal narcissistic function of concern for one's health implies identification with a maternal function of concern for the self, taking care of oneself, that also reflects the capacity for concern for another, taking care of another, and tolerating that another take care of oneself. Here oedipally structured sexual intimacy and pre-oedipal intimacy, dependency, caring and erotic desire fuse in a relationship that may represent the key to happiness reflected in Bertrand Russell's poem.

* * *

We started out from a sense of inhibition and embarrassment in exploring the relationship of couples at later stages of their life and have come around to perceive the excitement, the profound gratification of the group in observing a couple that breaks though the conventional view of older couples as passionless and desexualized. The intensity of romantic love persists throughout the life-span as a potential for transforming ordinary daily reality into a private paradise. In the case of individuals whose emotional maturity prepares them for entering into such an experience, romantic love in later years may be as exciting, and possibly sexually freer and more gratifying and emotionally more complex and enriching than in earlier stages of the lovers' life. It complements the life-long unconscious longing for oedipal gratification and breaking through the prohibitions against incestuous temptation and may provide a unique path to the sense that life has been worth living.

CHAPTER FOURTEEN

Unconscious choice and responsibility: an elusive point of psychoanalytic theory

Leo Rangell (Los Angeles)

I am happy to join my colleagues in honouring Pearl King on the occasion of this personal chronological milestone. For my part in this outpouring of good feeling to a friend and respected colleague, to be coupled with some thoughtful reflection on concerns and issues within our psychoanalytic discipline, I go back a few decades to a time when theory was the point of greatest interest, when it was felt and recognized that every application, including therapy, stemmed from understanding. Theoretical issues to ponder and debate occupied centre stage and were more compelling than the pressing problems of economics and turf and the practical fate of psychoanalysis, which command most attention as the field approaches its second centenary and mankind its third millennium.

In the most recent period of psychoanalytic history, group interest, even excitement, has consistently centred around changes in theory by purported new "systems" of thought. Steady accretions to enduring psychoanalytic theory have elicited virtually no significant or sustained notice or adherents. I believe that these trends are not a true or dependable indicator of the progress of psychoanalytic science. The latter runs a course independent of the repetitive rise and decline of mass movements.

This chapter presents a summary of a steady and cohesive theme that has coursed its way through a selected group of papers I have written over the past four decades. What is lost in detail in this summary view may be gained in being able to see the large streams, which have otherwise been rendered obscure or even invisible, by the individual contributions having appeared in separate places over time.

A major theme I wish to highlight—that of the moment of decision and action in unconscious mental life—consists of the exercise of unconscious choice by the ego during what I describe as an ongoing intrapsychic core process of mental functioning. Considered as an advance edge of psychoanalytic thinking, this change—or, to be more accurate, the inclusion of this theoretical emphasis added to those that already exist—has far-reaching consequences for the understanding of human behaviour.

To consider this dimension of unconscious cognitive activity in connection with the main scientific interests of Pearl King, one can readily see its applicability to all three subdivisions of her writings: on psychoanalytic technique, on extending analytic interest to the entire span of life, and on its role in interpersonal relationships, which form the glue of the psychoanalytic movement and its institutional life. Along each of these lines of thought, unconscious processes preparatory to and determining decision and action play a major role.

There are two main thrusts to this contribution, in the configuration of figure to ground, as it were. Each has been an equal focus of theoretical study, an ongoing intrapsychic core process, and psychic derivatives radiating from it. The central armature of this conceptual frame revolves around the postulation of what I (Rangell, 1969a, 1986, 1987) have called "the intrapsychic process"—a sequential series of intrapsychic events operative moment by moment in everyday life. An elaboration of Freud's (1926d [1925]) concept of thought as experimental or trial action, this ubiquitous psychodynamic process consists of some 12–14 steps, which include an initiating stimulus, from within or without, scanning for associated memories and their effects, the receipt by the ego of a signal of anxiety or safety, following which the ego actively executes either a defence, a fantasy or affect, or action or some other form of intended behaviour.

Within this sequential chain of intrapsychic events, anxiety or safety, choice and decision are seen to occur universally in normal operational intrapsychic dynamics. These involve both conflict-free and conflictful situations in normal mentation. Neurotic conflict and pathological solutions enter the picture with the insufficiency of defences and their incipient or threatened breakdown.

Embedded in this unconscious intrapsychic process, which I (Rangell, 1967) have called "the human core", are the postulation of unconscious choice conflict and the contiguous concept of the unconscious decision-making function of the ego (Rangell, 1969b, 1971). This is a view of psychic conflict and its resolutions quite different from the conventional type of oppositional conflict, which leads to a solution by compromise formation. The operation of an active unconscious ego decision, intention, and "will" in the final psychic outcome introduces a significant new dimension into psychoanalytic theory, the psychoanalytic therapeutic procedure, and the elusive questions of responsibility and accountability.

This ongoing intrapsychic testing process is seen to contain and utilize within it all of the metapsychological points of view, the dynamic, genetic, topographic, adaptive, including the economic, the ego having to judge intensities of reaction, and centrally the structural. Far from moving away from metapsychology, the description of this underlying process fortifies it. All the "points of view" are concentrated here. This is, without minimizing meaning and purpose, an argument used by some against the retention of metapsychology but, indeed, enhancing and increasing the depth of these.

Purpose, intention, choice, and decision are by these works included within structural metapsychological psychoanalytic theory. The omission of this stream of motivation from psychoanalysis, which has incorrectly led others to seek new theories to include them, has been obviated by the inclusion of this series of purposeful activities within total psychoanalytic theory. With an extension of ego autonomy into what I (Rangell, 1986) call "the executive functions of the ego", and a place given to ego will comparable to that of the instinctual wish, psychoanalysis joins other psychologies, academic and experimental psychology, learning theory, and other disciplines in including and encompassing purposeful action.

These intrapsychic events constitute a psychoanalytic theory of action that Hartmann (1947) and Rapaport (1951, 1958), after all that both had contributed about ego autonomy, stated did not exist within psychoanalytic theory. With these extended formulations, hermeneutic understanding blends with structural metapsychological explanations. Meanings and mechanisms are fused. The psychic structural systems are the vehicles through which purposive behaviours are expressed and intentions achieved.

Although this unconscious intrapsychic process and its derivatives are a unifying thread underlying human mentation, it does not constitute a new paradigm, as much as these are eagerly awaited to be followed by many. It is also not presented as a new "point of view" of metapsychology. It is, in my opinion, an extension that is added to and comes to reside squarely within the body of existing psychoanalytic theory.

Encompassed within the boundaries of the intrapsychic sequence described, a number of new formulations were arrived at, as well as new emphases not hitherto centred upon. These include:

1. within the subject of unconscious conflict, a new aspect of intrapsychic conflict, choice conflict, the facing of a dilemma, the being "in conflict", in contrast to the conventional oppositional type of conflict between ego and id;

2. within ego functions, related to the above, a new unconscious decision-making function of the ego, not hitherto included within the ensemble of ego functions by Freud (1923b), Anna Freud (1936), Hartmann (1950), or others;

3. among the variety of final psychic outcomes, "the syndrome of the compromise of integrity", on a par with neuroses in human affairs (Rangell, 1974, 1976)—this results from intersystemic ego–superego conflicts and compromises of the superego, comparable to id–ego conflicts from which neurosis and compromises of the id result;

4. within the central activities of the ego, Hartmann's (1939) ego autonomy is extended to the exercising of the will (Rangell, 1986), between decision and action, initiating movement on the path towards external action.

At the centre of this microscopic investigation of the intrapsychic process and series of events, anxiety theory has been advanced and a unitary theory of anxiety (Rangell, 1955, 1968) that fuses Freud's (1900a, 1926d [1925])) two theories of anxiety has been offered. Aspects of both of Freud's theories of anxiety are seen to exist and to be included within separate arcs of the intrapsychic sequence described. The anxiety signal, Freud's second theory, is seen to occur at one stage of the process, and the tension state following unsuccessful defence, which is the phenomenological equivalent of the observations of Freud's that led to his first theory of dammed-up libido, is seen to occur at a later phase of the developing intrapsychic process. Anxiety both precedes repression and follows it, at different stages of the process, accounting for observations made by Freud at different phases of his theory-building. Added to his earlier formulation, defence is now against aggressive instinctual drives as well as libidinal.

Clinical observations and theorizing at this intrapsychic level together point towards an interface with somatic phenomena and mechanisms. The existence within the intrapsychic process of the arc I describe as the tension state links to Freud's first (physiological) theory of anxiety and provides an interface and a merging with somatic phenomena. This can be the dynamic connection linking psyche and soma, possibly via Selye's (1950) stress phenomena and adrenocortical response, up to the kaleidoscopic variety of external psychosomatic outcomes. These include both those that derive from or accompany anxiety and those that eventuate from further development of symptomatology, whether conversion or psychosomatic derivatives in final mind–body outcomes.

Yet, though phenomenologically contiguous and even combined, the two systems remain theoretically separate. Kety (1960) has said that there may one day be a biochemistry of memory but never one of memories. Fisher (1966, 1978) has said the same about sleep and dreams. Sleep and dreaming can be explained, but dreams will always require interpretations. Neurophysiology can explain the one, but the other will always require a hermeneutic approach. Both are necessary, and each plays a part. Psychoanalysis can approach the psychosomatic synapse from its side, but a meeting with those coming from the other direction is necessary to re-study what Freud (1950 [1895]) first approached in his "Project", which he thought to the end of his life would one day come about. Modern neuroscience is accomplishing much in that direction in current scientific life.

Each arc in this intrapsychic sequence fortifies the others, to make for a mutually reciprocal process in all directions. The presence of a choice conflict makes a decision function of the ego necessary. The emphasis of the ego–superego contribution introduces the moral issue and the question of integrity or its absence. This in turn needs to be taken into account within the decision-making process. The introduction of the signal theory of anxiety made a choice conflict inevitable. The recognition of a tension state as one arc of the intra-psychic process made understandable Freud's first theory of anxiety, which resulted from mounting tension.

The intrapsychic sequence comprises an organizing principle of all human behaviour. Anxiety, choice, defence, action occur univer-sally in normal operational intrapsychic dynamics. The same back-ground process exists in common across the nosologic spectrum. What separates one course of conduct and one symptom complex from another are the ingredients that confront the ego and the solu-tions that the latter imposes to effect solutions.

Each segment of the internal sequence has external derivatives, from direct instinctual sequelae, to defence, to free-floating anxiety, to decision or the ego state of indecision, to psychic tension or its somatic derivatives, or external action, or a psychopathological outcome, neurotic, borderline, or a more severely pathological syndrome. Most observable behavioural phenomena, clinically and in life, consist of a combination of fused and interacting elements, either compromises or various aggregates of contiguous or sequential intrapsychic inputs.

An important new concept for psychoanalytic discourse is that of human "will". "Will" has, until now, been ensnared in the automatic phrase "free will", from which I (Rangell, 1986) state it needs to be extracted; as I (Rangell, 1959) have previously separated "conver-sion" from "hysteria", so "free" needs to be separated from "will" and each considered on its own. Ego will is no more nor less free than ego autonomy, both of which are relative. Yet both of these, and psychic determinism, are all present and to be accounted for. Within the demands of the id, the restrictions of the superego, and the limita-tions of reality impinging from three sides, the ego chooses the direc-tions of behaviour. Determinism and reality constrain and limit it, in the strength and characteristics of the ego itself and the deterministic history it has undergone, but with what remains—human will does survive and emerge—the ego chooses, directs, and acts. In fact, it must choose. If it elects not to, that is also a choice.

Who, or what, does, thinks, feels or acts? That is the nub of the question, which intersects psychology, psychiatry, neurology, phil-osophy, and psychoanalysis. It is the perplexity and ambivalence or indecision about this dilemma that has kept this subject from being met head-on in psychoanalytic theoretical discourse. To this question, psychoanalysis has a specific contribution to offer.

The ego is the agent, Freud's (1923b) rider on the horse—not the drives, or the superego, or the external world, or the self, but the ego. Active unconscious ego choices determine the selection of defences and the nature of external behaviour, whether the choice of one element among several, such as specific instinctual wishes, or of the particular compromise formations, either into the interior of the organism, as affects, fantasies, or psychosomatic symptoms, or into outer actions, normal or abnormal, and the types of each.

While it perplexes or even offends some that the ego can "do", to me this is the acme and fruition of the structural point of view. In an introduction to the posthumous publication of a seminal paper by Rapaport (1953b) on activity and passivity, Gill (1967) notes the surprising fact that Rapaport had never published this paper, although it had been in careful, finished form since 1953. This was attributed by Gill to "the extraordinary scope of the concept of activity and passivity in Rapaport's mind, [which] he regarded . . . as at the very heart of an adequate conceptualization of the human psyche" (p. 531). This "heart" of human behaviour, with major consequences for the direction and outcome of life, has in my opinion never been properly pursued or advanced at the core of psychoanalytic theory.

The implications of these new, or at least for psychoanalysis unfamiliar theoretical foci of choice, decision, and will need to be integrated, with intellectual conviction and clarity, with the basic psychoanalytic tenet of psychic determinism. The execution of will and of directing activity on the part of the ego does not speak against causation and exists side by side with psychic determinism, both of which are soft and relative. Man's will, built upon constitutional givens, added to and further developed by acquired life experiences, joins the chain of causation and determinism that exists in nature. Man is subject to causation and determinism, yet can change. Both fit the empirical observations, and both formulations are necessary in theory to encompass the basic tenets upon which psychoanalysis stands, that man can influence and change the deterministic forces that guide him. Speaking of aggression as being part of man's nature, Waelder (1967) has said: "man, though rooted in nature, can transcend it to a large degree. As Denis de Rougemont put it: 'Man's nature is to pass beyond nature'" (p. 47).

By attending to the subject of unconscious ego will, a concept unfamiliar to psychoanalysis, analytic insights deepen the understanding of a human psychic activity that has been stalemated and a subject of endless debate among philosophers and scientists from the beginnings of modern man. The positions I have taken are not incompatible with but extend the views arrived at by Freud. They indeed follow from Freud's (1923b, 1940a [1938]) formulations of the unconscious ego and the operation of secondary process mentation within the unconscious.

The description of this intrapsychic background base of behaviour contains the essences of all other partial and alternative theories, such as of the self, the object, the interpersonal, Kleinian, developmental theory, information processing, systems theories, the findings of direct infant observers, even the concepts of computer analysis or of the brain as the largest and most complex of computers. Information is processed, the object is addressed, the self is preserved, and the earliest and later inputs, pregenital and oedipal, are all given their due place in the automatic scanning that is ongoing within the unconscious intrapsychic process described.

This theoretical addition demonstrates advance by accretion rather than by repetitive new and partial theories—a method I consider to have advantages for a rational development of psychoanalytic knowledge and history. The march of new theories or explanatory systems, which have been alternative rather than additive to existing theory, have typically had a rapid rise, accompanied by excitement and huge followings, followed by a quiet decline and disappearance. During the years of their ascendancy, however, cumulative theory has been excluded or set back, usually for decades at a time. Advances by accretion, such as described here, are typically not furthered by contagious enthusiasm fuelled by group pressures, but are, in fact, more likely to be met by inertia or even resistance. What may be absorbed from the new approaches, which in each case is some partial advance, could have been contributed without an eclipse, stagnation, or even regression of the total accumulated body of theory.

The present additions constitute a major branch, stemming from but not replacing the main trunk. Some analysts seem indeed to have feared that a deeper acknowledgement and understanding of the activities of the unconscious ego would replace or diminish the roles of other aspects of traditional psychoanalytic theory, such as instinctual drives or psychic determinism, neither of which it does. Instead, more becomes known about the interactions between all psychic elements, and knowledge that accumulates is integrated with the whole.

The need to integrate intention, purpose, and autonomous decision and action into structural metapsychology, in a field of hermeneutic emphasis, became so objectionable to some as to lead to the creation of new psychological theories outside what they felt to be Freud's mechanistic views. Thus, both George Klein's (1973, 1976) clinical theory and Schafer's (1976) action theory described purposeful action as being outside psychic structure and abstract metapsychology, as a function of the self and person rather than the system ego—not unlike Kohut (1971, 1977) years later. In contrast, my own formulations bring both levels of observation and theory together. The fact is that clinical and abstract theories belong together; they are reciprocal and of mutual influence. Hermeneutics and explanations, dynamics and structures, meanings and mechanisms are fused and integrated in total psychoanalytic theory. Neither can be done without in a full psychoanalytic science. I (Rangell, 1997) have written of "total composite psychoanalytic theory" throughout many writings over years. I oppose the terms "classical" or "traditional" as referring ambivalently to feelings of respect, even awe, while at the same time also connoting deteriorating and rigid. The psychology of the self or of object relations is as much a part of total psychoanalytic theory as the theory of drives.

Intellectualization, mechanization, reification have become modern shibboleths. Affective conflict has lead to intellectual blurring. Intellect is confused with intellectualization as a defence. A fear of reification has led to an inhibition to following through to its ultimate explanatory value Freud's immensely useful division of the psychic apparatus into structural systems. Failing to keep in mind their metaphoric nature and their conceptual base as clusters of functions, there is an ensuing confusion over the spurious question of homunculus. The system ego is confused with and fails to be differentiated from a shrunken-down but total "little man". Such a diminutive but reduced clone would still need division into structural systems. The ego, as the agent of action and responsibility, is not a smaller version of the total organism but the psychic executive system acting on the part of the organism as a whole.

In addition to a general reaction away from scientism and intellectuality, a major internal nidus of resistance in this area is against an increase of responsibility. Whereas the earliest psychoanalytic insights wounded man's narcissism in that man was shown to have less control over his actions than he knew, with the present additions the opposite is also the case—that is, that with the introduction of unconscious choice and decision man chooses and acts more than he thinks he did.

Responsibility, rather than being less, may paradoxically become greater than conventionally thought. The developmental block pointed to within as well as outside psychoanalysis is now due to resistance against increased responsibility rather than decreased control. While the two concepts seem to be in contradiction, the two dynamics coexist, as often turns out to be the case with seeming dualities in psychoanalysis. Legal and moral issues that follow become more, not less complex. Of major interest and concern to humankind, this subject requires more definitive study and understanding in psychoanalysis as well. The issues to be further studied and made more clear, in which some of the dilemmas to these questions reside, have to do with the ratio or degree of automaticity versus control, or activity versus passivity in opening up "the sluices to motility and action" (Rapaport, 1953a).

The theoretical exposure and wider acknowledgement of this layer of active unconscious behaviour, which affects issues of responsibility, has applied effects in many directions. One is a natural influence on the therapeutic process. Insight develops in distinguishing properly between what has happened to the patient and what he has contributed, both in a general way, towards his life development, and specifically in the production of his symptoms and pathology. This results, on the one hand, in a lessening of responsibility, with its telltale guilt, and, on the other, in a more mature and realistic acceptance of responsibility. With the latter can come an increased guilt that is appropriate for what one has done to others. Since neuroses, however, produce pain towards the self rather than to others, the recognition of one's own role in bringing this about results in lessened self punishment and a feeling of increased self-worth and integrity.

On a larger social scale, the theoretical change in the direction of unconscious choice and decision brings with it a more complex attitude towards social responsibility for one's actions, which have yet to be understood in their full implications. The fact that there is unconscious motivation does not absolve the individual from social and interpersonal responsibility for his behaviour. While previous insights contributed knowledge of forces that influence man to act outside his control, thereby tending to diminish responsibility, the present addition simultaneously makes a person more—not less—

responsible than he thinks for his choices and actions taken. The two mechanisms are complementary, not contradictory. The possibility is opened for clarification in a field that has been perplexing and inconstant, with expanded psychoanalytic insights pointing the way to new understandings of vexing social and legal problems.

In my structural psychoanalytic point of view, the ego exercise of judgement, discrimination, and thought is carried through in one continuous and consistent series of functions to deciding, choosing, and executing, conveying the results of human mental processes to the effecting motor and other somatic organs. Someone or something has to decide, to put it all together. It is not the arm or the leg or the liver—all parts of the self—nor is it an aggregate of mental and physical structures, giving equal place to the brain and the mind. It is not the brain exclusive of its derivative mind, but the human mind, derived from and supported by the body and brain, that "does" things. Breaking the mind down further into its components, in psychoanalysis this means its topographic and structural divisions, in their relationships to all other mental elements. Within psychic structures, it is the functions of the ego we are pinpointing and enlarging. It is not dehumanizing to recognize and utilize localization of functions. This does not mean that responsibility does not belong to the whole. The ego, the psychic brain, acts as an agent for the self. The entire body— whether a person or a larger organization—is responsible and accountable for what its assigned agent does.

Unconscious responsibility, the concept led into by these considerations, is a term that on its surface seems internally inconsistent and brings its own train of challenges and problems. Whereas at the beginnings of psychoanalysis man resisted insights into the unconscious in order not to feel helpless, even though as a corollary this decreased his responsibility, with the present advances and insights he resists knowing that he acts without knowing that he has acted, threatening to make him more responsible than he knows. Putting these opposites together into a coherent theory, which may then have helpful applications to the social living of man, is no simple or automatic task. But that is what needs to be done. With new insights, a first step is to undo errors of the past and excesses in the opposite direction. In the earlier stages of psychoanalytic knowledge, these were to excuse actions across the board that had unconscious determinants. Perhaps with this accomplished, which was partly necessary, we can begin to achieve a balance towards what psychoanalytic understanding might be able to contribute about unconscious assumptions of too much, but also too little responsibility.

What seems surprising is the block among psychoanalysts themselves to extending knowledge of the workings of the unconscious into the full range of unconscious activity, evaluating, planning, and executing action. The consequences of these insights, which include both the complexities and the benefits, would follow. Psychoanalytic research and discovery did not introduce the unconscious temporarily and partially. Opposition to its findings was never absent and needs the same understanding of the reasons for it now as at the beginning.

Psychoanalysis deals with ambiguities, but hopefully clearly. Fenichel (1941) stated that "the subject-matter not the method of psychoanalysis is irrational" (p. 13). The extraction of theory from clinical findings is far from complete. People decide without knowing why, but people also decide without knowing that they have decided. Each affects responsibility in an opposite direction.

To those concerned about too much secondary process in the unconscious, or an encroachment of the ego over the id, while the goal of psychoanalysis is to apply rationality to the ambiguous, it is also, as Loewald (1978) says, the reverse: to see and permit the life of the irrational in the rational. This leaves room for uncertainty and creativity in the promulgation of human affairs.

CHAPTER FIFTEEN

Developmental and genetic perspectives in psychoanalysis

Anne-Marie Sandler & Joseph Sandler (London)

It is appropriate to start this short presentation by commenting on what we mean by a developmental perspective in psychoanalysis. At the time when Freud's writings were translated from German to English, the term "*genetisch*" was rendered as "genetic", in line with the usage in psychology at the time. Thus what was then called genetic psychology would today be referred to as developmental psychology. Psychoanalysts, following Freud, still speak of the "genetic point of view", and this usage, although in one sense somewhat archaic, is also useful, for we can now distinguish between the genetic and the developmental viewpoints in psychoanalysis; in what follows we should like to spell out what we mean by this distinction.

Freud's specific theory of neurosis was based on the idea that neurosis was the outcome of a regression from a developmentally higher level of instinctual functioning to one in which infantile libidinal wishes and phantasies are revived. These revived strivings were unconscious but created guilt and anxiety in the individual because the adult ego and superego did not accept such infantile impulses. Their pressure towards their gratification was in conflict with the

---

This chapter was written in 1998.

patient's ideals for himself, which had not regressed. This conflict, and the internal defensive struggle that ensued, resulted, as Freud saw it, in compromise formations in the shape of the neurotic's symptoms.

It is Freud's attempt to explain the origin of the regressively revived unconscious sexual wishes and phantasies that he perceived in the analytic material of his neurotic patients that led him to his theory of childhood sexual development. This theory placed emphasis on the division of the child's development into the well-known oral, anal, and phallic–oedipal psychosexual phases, followed by the phases of latency and puberty, all succeeding one another in a very definite sequence. During development what was referred to as libidinal fixation points were regarded as a consequence of over- or under-stimulation, trauma or excessive erotic gratification employed in infancy as means of dealing with anxiety. Thus, for example, an overanxious mother might calm her restless child by constantly placating it by giving it food, and this sort of experience, aimed at reducing unpleasant feelings and enjoyed by the child, could be seen as a potential source of a so-called pre-oedipal or pregenital fixation point.

In Freud's theory the existence of fixation points was not seen as necessarily hampering further development, but represented phase-specific ways of gaining libidinal gratification that could be revived as a consequence of regression. The revived instinctual wishes of childhood would, as Freud saw it, lead to a perversion if allowed to proceed unchecked—that is, if they did not arouse conflict and defence: hence Freud's comment that the neurosis is "the negative of perversion". We want to emphasize the fact that the developmental theory formulated by Freud was based on reconstruction from the material of his adult analytic patients. Thus, in classical Freudian psychoanalysis the terms "genetic" and "developmental" were synonymous, but we will try to show that a conceptual gap has developed between the two and that we can now differentiate between the two perspectives.

First, the *genetic* perspective: very simply, as we have said, this is the view of the specific individual's development as gained from the material of his or her analysis. It is, of necessity, a view of past development as it is relevant to the patient's existing mental structures, unconscious conflictual wishes and phantasies as they exist and affect him or her in the present. Genetic interpretations are an essential part of the analytic work of reconstruction, aimed at providing a temporal dimension to the understanding of the present and to allow the patient to accept aspects of himself or herself that had previously been defended against, which had been a source of conflict. It is as if the psychoanalyst looks at the past through a special optical instrument that focuses on *that which is relevant to the current work of analysis*, with the aim of bringing about structural change in the patient. More properly, we believe, the so-called genetic point of view in psychoanalysis should be called the genetic–reconstructive view.

This focusing is, as far as the reconstruction of subjective experiences and real events in the patient's early years is concerned, very largely theoretical, because it is difficult to recall much with accuracy before about the age of 4 or 5. Such reconstruction allows for a great deal of scope for differences in analysts' conceptions of the significant mental processes and experiences in the child's earliest years.

Now to the *developmental* perspective, so essential for the psychoanalytic theory of child development, as opposed to the genetic–reconstructive perspective, which, because it has been based on the reconstruction of childhood from the analyses of adults, has been too limited: moreover, Freud's schema of *sequential* phases of development has proved increasingly inadequate for a general psychoanalytic developmental theory. Thus, for example, development in the child's object relationships, of aggression, of aspects of the ego and the superego, do not fall into the schema of psychosexual phases, and it is a great mistake to regard the psychoanalytic theory of development as simply being the elaboration of the oral, anal, phallic–oedipal phases. We have witnessed, within psychoanalysis, how such workers as Margaret Mahler, Erik Erikson, René Spitz, Melanie Klein, and Heinz Kohut have all postulated different phases of development, each worker emphasizing those aspects of development which are of particular interest to him or her. Thus Margaret Mahler, who was very concerned with the developmental pathology of psychotic children, was primarily concerned with issues of separation–individuation and elaborated a series of developmental steps linked with the infant's processes of separation–individuation. Erik Erikson was concerned with socio-psychological aspects of development, and as a consequence he considered his theory to be an epigenetic one, linked to certain crises in the individual's life-cycle. Melanie Klein thought that the infant went through subjective phases that paralleled adult psychotic states, and she formulated a developmental theory in terms of the paranoid-schizoid and the depressive positions; and so on.

Clearly, we run into difficulties if we think of fixed, overarching developmental phases. Yet the theory of mental development has an increasingly important role to play in psychoanalytic theory and in the many areas of applied psychoanalysis. It is important to emphasize that the psychoanalytic theory of development is inevitably a multifaceted one, consisting of a number of complementary frames of reference, each to be used as and when appropriate.

The developmental viewpoint has been greatly stimulated by psychoanalytically informed baby and child observation, by observations made during child analysis, and by the work of the so-called "baby-watchers"—psychoanalytically orientated observers and experimenters who have used systematic observation and empirical methods for the study of infant behaviour.

A major step forward in the application of a developmental point of view (as opposed to a genetic–reconstructive one) was taken by Anna Freud in her concept of developmental lines. She saw personality and pathology as being the outcome of interaction between the major mental agencies of id, ego, and superego, in turn in interaction with external reality. This could be seen as leading to progressive structuralization of the personality and in some case to pathological adaptations.

As the interactions between id, ego, superego and the external world cannot be observed directly in the child, they have to be inferred. To facilitate this, Anna Freud devised a model consisting of lines of development in which the developmental landmarks were relatively clearly observable. Thus she spoke of a basic developmental line from *suckling* to *rational eating*, where the steps on the way are: being nursed at the breast or the bottle (apart from the common transient difficulties caused by fluctuations of appetite, intestinal upset, or maternal anxiety); weaning from breast or bottle initiated either by the mother or by the baby; the transition from being fed to self-feeding; a successful move through the phase in which there is a battle over feeding, and so on. Further lines are, for example, from *dependency* to *emotional self-reliance and adult relationships*, the line from *wetting and soiling* to *bladder and bowel control*; from *irresponsibility* to *responsibility in body management*; and from *the body* to *the toy* and from *play to work*. Failure to move successfully through the steps involved in the developmental lines creates a likelihood that developmental pathology could occur.

Special significance with regard to diagnosis can be attached to observed imbalances between the developmental lines; but it is important to emphasize that the lines of development are not in themselves a psychoanalytic theory of development. Rather, they provide pointers to what can be understood about internal developmental processes conceived of within a psychoanalytic theoretical framework.

Work at the Anna Freud Centre based on the assessment of developmental lines and their use in diagnosis has led to the clarification of a conceptual distinction between neurotic (i.e. conflictual) pathology and pathology due to developmental imbalance. In the case of the truly neurotic child, the symptoms are seen as occurring as a result of internal conflict, which brought about regression and consequent further intensification of conflict. Of critical importance in the diagnosis of neurotic disturbance in childhood is the retrogressive pull back along one or more developmental lines as a consequence of regression.

Developmental pathology, on the other hand, is seen as a product of an internal imbalance, a distorted structuralization, inferred from the discrepancies between the different developmental lines. In this the diagnostic emphasis is not placed on individual symptoms but, rather, on the internal developmental factors that bring those symptoms about. Thus the child who manifests separation anxiety with a conflictual—that is, a neurotic—basis may have achieved the capacity to separate from mother but, because of conflict over unconscious hostility to the mother, develops a need to be reassured constantly that she is alive, and because of this needs to keep her in sight. On the other hand, the child who has not developed the capacity to maintain an appropriate internal image of the mother, a so-called supportive internal object, will also show separation anxiety, but the developmental diagnosis will be quite different and the treatment may need to proceed along different lines than for the neurotic child. It would be aimed, in the first instance at least, at fostering the developmental progression of the child or the creation of an appropriate internal compensatory mental structures.

Although we may have made a sharp conceptual distinction between the genetic–reconstructive point of view and the more developmental one, the boundaries are in practice not so clear-cut for the practising analyst. When at times we come to make a genetic reconstruction we are influenced not only by the patient's material and by the transference and countertransference, but also by what we have learned about development from baby and child observation.

Our approach to the analytic process is very much influenced by the view that throughout life we all have to deal with continual conflicts between opposing mental forces, and that an integral part of development is the progressive adaptations we make to these conflicts. However, whereas the so-called normal individual manages to find more-or-less satisfactory intrapsychic adaptations, the patients who come to our consulting-rooms have for the most part fared less well. Their adaptations, their compromise solutions, the best solutions available to them given their inner resources and the state of their psychic reality and of their external reality during development, have left them with neurotic, borderline, character, or psychotic disturbances, which, from one point of view, can be regarded as intrapsychic adaptations of one sort or another, but which cause pain and discomfort. When we speak of the centrality of conflict within neurotic patients, we want to emphasize that we have in mind something far more general than oedipal conflict, or pre-oedipal conflict, or conflict between the different psychic agencies of id, ego, and superego, or even conflict between opposing instinctual urges—sexuality and aggression, love and hate, life and death drives. We have in mind the conflict that shows itself in the patient *in the present* between ways he or she has found in the past to deal with unconscious wishful phantasies and is striving to reproduce these solutions on the one hand, and defensive, self-protective needs, on the other. We will try to make this point clearer, and to put it into a developmental context.

Miss B, a 40-year-old neurotic woman, came to treatment because of an agitated depression and an inability to continue her work as a real estate agent. It became clear very early in her analysis that she was suffering from intense feelings of loneliness and of being, as she put it, "cut off from people". From the start of her analysis Miss B had been very talkative, but gradually her material appeared to have acquired a special quality of urgency and intensity. She poured out her thoughts more or less continuously, speaking over and over again of her various worries about her ageing mother, who was looking after a troubled grandchild but who could never accept the patient's help in this task. It gradually became clear to the analyst that even though the content of her material was revealing and seemed important, the use she made of her analyst in the sessions had to be attended to first. It was evident that by talking endlessly, with a desperate urgency, she cut her analyst off, so that it was difficult to interrupt her with a comment. At the same time by conveying a great deal of preoccupying and conflictual material concerning her mother, she was isolating and protecting herself from the feelings and thoughts connected with any awareness of her dependency on the analysis. This self-protective stance evoked a countertransference feeling in the analyst of being bypassed by the patient, even though she brought a great deal of material to her sessions. As this became clearer, the analyst, who had felt increasingly irritated, recalled that the specific and urgently given material about the patient's mother had appeared particularly intensely shortly before the summer holiday and had invaded the sessions ever since. The analyst then understood that the material this patient was bringing represented a resistance against the awareness of an inner struggle that was not simply between an aggressive or envious urge of some sort directed towards the mother on the one hand, and a defensive manoeuvre that made the patient feel worried and concerned about her mother's welfare and strenuously protective of her on the other. Much as the analyst was tempted to understand her state of resistance as being due to an underlying hostility in the transference, which was replaced by concern, expressed in displaced form, towards the mother, this did not feel right. It became obvious that the conflict was one that existed in the here-and-now of the analysis and was essentially connected with a strong underlying unconscious dependent urge, a strong wish to cling to the analyst, a wish evoked—invited, in a sense— by the very structure of the analytic situation. This wish was felt to be dangerous and was, it became evident, in conflict with the need of the patient to preserve her self-esteem, which she unconsciously felt to be threatened by what she regarded as the childish demandingness inherent in her longing for the analyst between sessions, at weekends, and during other breaks. The solution she found to her conflict took the form of being urgently concerned about her mother, which was, of course, a displacement of the concern she wanted the analyst to have about her. At the same time, by being caring and self-contained, Miss B could be independent and could protect herself from humiliation. This conflict, which emerged as a resistance to the psychoanalytic process, had to be analysed and worked through before we could move to another level of work.

How can we look at this from a developmental perspective? It has been said that analysis is essentially the analysis of resistances to analysis, and we think that there is a great deal of truth in this. However, we would put it a little more precisely and say, rather, that analysis is the *progressive* analysis of resistances and that these resistances emerge in a sequence that is to a large extent developmentally determined. Miss B could be regarded as having been defending in the analysis against transference feelings and fantasies of dependency and attachment, and it would have been a mistake to assume that these were a simple reflection of early object-related oral wishes of one sort or another.

In fact, as the analytic work proceeded, it emerged that when she had started school at about the age of 6 or 7, she had become very clinging and demanding, at which time a close friend of hers had been accidentally killed in a boating accident. For some years she had succeeded in forcing her mother to take her to school every day, even though she could easily have walked there, as many of her classmates did. In adolescence she had turned against her own tendency to cling and her marked dependency, following a love affair that was broken off abruptly by her boyfriend, who had accused her of being too possessive. The circumstances of the break-up were extremely humiliating for her. The anticipation of re-experiencing this in the analysis was a great threat to her, and it was only after bringing this into the open that we could work on the phobic anxieties that had, earlier in her development, motivated her clinging and demanding tendencies. (Here we can see, incidentally, how strongly anxieties and other painful affects can function as motivating forces in development.) The urge to cling had to be made acceptable to Miss B through interpretation, and the conflict over this urge had to be reduced in order to allow further resistances to appear and be analysed—that is, in order to move to a different level of conflict.

What we are trying to show is that an unconscious (and inevitably object-related) wishful impulse, as it emerges in the analysis, is something that has to be viewed from a developmental standpoint, as a tendency that had been, earlier in development, an ego-syntonic solution to conflict—that is, a solution that did not arouse conflict and was acceptable to the patient's consciousness. What was once an effective adaptation to conflict acquired a forceful quality during development, a so-called peremptory quality, in that it was powerfully evoked at the slightest signal that the previous conflict might reappear. In the case of Miss B, the clinging was a way of coping with anxiety, and later in the analysis it was possible to bring to the surface the aggressive and destructive death wishes that lay at the root of the anxiety.

In general terms one could say that the patient is always struggling against an acceptance of some aspect of what has been called "the child within". We aim at freeing what has become *unacceptable* during the course of development in such a way that it is not enacted but is tolerated within the patient's psychic life without having to be defended against—tolerated by virtue of being able to be viewed by the patient from a more mature and tolerant perspective. In this connection it is important that the patient's insight have a temporal dimension, that it be anchored in a developmental perspective. In this context we can differentiate between *reconstruction* (which is the "genetic" approach) and *construction*, which relates to the clarification of the way the patient's mind works in the here-and-now of the analysis, in the transference and outside it. Both approaches are important, although in our view analytic construction should precede reconstruction, unless there are very special reasons for giving priority to reconstruction.

CHAPTER SIXTEEN

Fear of death—
notes on the analysis of an old man

Hanna Segal (London)

> This is an old paper—it belongs to the times in which Pearl King and I were pioneering the psychoanalytic investigation and treatment in old age. I want to dedicate this paper to Pearl in remembrance of those old times we shared and in recognition of her wide-reaching contributions to that field.
>
> Hanna Segal, on being invited to contribute to this Festscrift

This communication is based on the analysis of a man who came to treatment at the age of 73½ and whose analysis was terminated just before his 75th birthday. He had suffered an acute psychotic breakdown when he was nearing the age of 72. Following the usual psychiatric treatments (electric shocks, etc.), he settled down to a chronic psychotic state characterized by depression, hypochondria, paranoid delusions, and attacks of insane rage. Nearly two years after the beginning of his overt illness, when no improvement occurred and when the psychiatrists in Rhodesia, where he lived,

Paper read before the Twentieth Congress of the International Psycho-Analytical Association, Paris, July–August, 1957. First published in the *International Journal of Psycho-Analysis, 39* (1958), pp. 178–181.

gave a hopeless prognosis, his son, who resided in London, brought him for psychoanalytical treatment.

This man's treatment with me lasted for eighteen months. It was not, of course, a completed analysis, but it dealt sufficiently with the patient's outstanding problems to enable him to resume normal life and activity and to achieve for the first time in his life a feeling of stability and maturity. In 1958, the patient had been back in Rhodesia for eighteen months, enjoying good health and having resumed his business.

In his analysis I came to the conclusion that the unconscious fear of death, increasing with old age, had led to his psychotic breakdown. I believe that the same problem underlies many breakdowns in old age.

In a work of this length I cannot give a complete picture of the patient's history or psychopathology, and I shall mention only such points as are relevant to my theme (a fuller case history is now awaiting publication). He came from a little Ukrainian village, from an extremely poor orthodox Jewish family. His childhood was marked by fear of starvation and freezing during the long, cold winters. He had seven siblings, with nearly all of whom he was on bad terms. His mother was, to begin with, portrayed as greatly favouring his older brother, while he himself was a favourite of the father. In contrast to the mother, who was felt as cold and rejecting, the father was idolized but also greatly feared. Following his father's death, the patient, then 17, fled from the Ukraine and, after a long, hard struggle, eventually established himself in Rhodesia as a middleman salesman. He had not tried to keep any contact with his family, which remained in the Ukraine. He also largely broke away from Jewish orthodoxy. He married, and he had two daughters and one son. He idealized his family, but in his business relations he was suspicious and persecuted. For several years he had been addicted to secret drinking.

The circumstances of his breakdown are relevant to my theme. It became apparent early in his analysis that there were three precipitating factors of his illness: the first was his first visit to his son, who was studying medicine in London; the second was meeting (during the same visit) his younger brother, from whom he learned that all the members of his family who had remained in Europe had perished in Hitler's camps during the war; the third and immediately precipitating factor was an incident that happened when he returned to Rhodesia. He had for several years given bribes to a man in order to get business from his firm. During the patient's absence this man had been caught in another dishonest deal. As soon as the patient heard this, he felt terrified that his own bribery would be discovered and within a matter of hours he was in a state of acute psychosis with delusions of reference and persecution, centring, to begin with, on his fear of his deal being discovered, and his being punished and ridiculed. He believed, for instance, that newspapers contained articles about him, that radio broadcasts were being made, people laughed at him in the streets, and so on.

I suggest that my patient was unconsciously terrified of old age and death, which he perceived as a persecution and punishment; that his main defences against this fear were splitting, idealization, and denial. His visit to London had shaken his defences. His idealization of his only son broke down. The news he received about his family had broken down his denial of his family's death and the resulting guilt and fear of retaliation. When he returned to Rhodesia, he was faced with the fear of punishment, which to him at that point represented death.

From the point of view of the patient's anxiety about death, the analysis could be divided into three phases. The first was characterized by complete denial of ageing and fear of death. He described himself as having always been very young for his age, working and looking like a young man and so on, until the beginning of his illness, which, he felt, had robbed him of his youth and health. He unconsciously expected that his treatment would give him back his youthfulness. It soon became apparent that this denial was made possible by the patient's idealization of his son, who represented to him another self, young and ideal, into whom he had projected all his own unfulfilled hopes and ambitions. He used to send him parcels every week, and on these parcels all his interest and love centred. He put himself into these parcels sent to his son, in whom he lived, untouched by age. This relationship to his son was partly a repetition and partly a reversal of his relation to his own father. The father appeared early on in the analysis, particularly as a loving and feeding father. In relation to him, the patient had developed an unconscious, intensely idealized, oral homosexual relationship. He was the father's favourite, and he felt that so long as he had his father's love and could orally incorporate his penis, he would be protected from starvation and cold and ultimately from death. With his son he partly repeated and partly reversed this relationship. He identified himself with his father and projected himself, the favourite son, into his own son, thereby prolonging his own life. This projective identification of his young self into his son kept fears of persecution and death at bay. He also at times projected his ideal father into the son and expected to be fed and kept alive by him for ever.

Accompanying this idealization, there was a great deal of split-off persecution. Parallel to his ideal son there was a son-in-law, like an evil twin, his main persecutor. In the past the father had been perceived mainly as loving, whereas the brothers were remembered for bullying and terrifying him. Any feeling of persecution that appertained to his father was immediately split off and projected onto his older brothers. In the background there was a picture of an unloving and cold mother. The feeling of persecution that he experienced in relation to her has been mainly transferred by him on to the various countries he lived in, which he completely personified and invariably described to me as treating him badly, exploiting him, and refusing to give him a livelihood. None of this split-off persecution could, to begin with, be mobilized in the transference. I represented mainly his ideal father and son, occasionally merging with an ideal feeding mother. He had projected into me all the ideal figures, including his ideal self, in projective identification. His bad feelings and figures he had projected onto remote persecutors. So long as he could maintain this idealization of me, I would protect him from persecutors, and he would be safe.

The second phase of the analysis was ushered in by the first holiday, which the patient acutely resented; when he came back, it was more possible to make him aware of his feelings of deprivation. The splitting lessened; the persecution came nearer to the transference. The bad countries of the past stopped playing such a rôle in his analysis, and the persecution now centred on the very cold English winter that was going to kill him. Death was no longer denied—it seemed to be there, around the corner. The split between his son-in-law and his son also narrowed. To begin with, he could maintain quite simultaneously that his son had brought him to London, where he was going to be made completely well again because he had his wonderful analysis, and, at the same time, that his son-in-law had sent him to London to die of cold. Gradually it was possible to point out to him how much his son-in-law was the other aspect of his son and how much the cold climate and country that was going to kill him was the other aspect of the analytical treatment and of myself. At that point his disappointment in his son during his first visit to London came to the fore. He had admitted that his son had not lived up to his expectations. He kept repeating: "It wasn't the same Harry, it wasn't what I meant for Harry." He admitted that he had felt completely robbed, that he had put his potency, his life, his love into his son and then that in losing the son he was losing his own potency and life and was left to face death alone. Having to face that his son, though devoted to him, in fact led a life of his own was felt by him as losing his greatest hope—namely, that his son would give him a new lease of life.

At this point it became clear to the patient that his ideal and his persecutory object were one and the same person. In the past he had split off his fear of his father onto his brothers. Now he saw clearly that it was his father's retaliation that he was afraid of. He feared that his son would leave him to his persecutors and to death and disown him, as he had left and disowned his family. Earlier on in the treatment he said that before he left the Ukraine, he had to put a stone on his father, and worked very hard to earn the few shillings to purchase this stone for the grave. To begin with it appeared as an act of mourning and piety; now it became clearer that he had to keep under the stone a very frightening and revengeful ghost of his father. In the transference it also became clear how much he had either to placate me or to control me in order to prevent me from becoming a persecutor. The persecution by his mother also came vividly to the fore: it was experienced as cold and starvation and as being abandoned or actively poisoned. He remembered that his younger brother had been fed by a Christian wet nurse. One day this girl had squirted some milk into his face, and he had fled, terrified, feeling soiled and poisoned. Being burnt up or broken inside (a frequent description of his hypochon-driacal symptoms) was also felt by him as somehow connected with his mother. As his experiences of persecution were becoming more explicit and more connected with the real objects—myself in the transference, his son, and finally his experiences with his early family—it was also becoming clearer that these persecutions that he was either expecting or currently experiencing were felt by him as punishments. With his admission of these fears of persecution and punishment, he could overtly admit his fear of death. He felt that his idealization of me was his only protection against death. I was the source of food, love, and warmth, but equally I was the killer, since I could bring him death by withdrawing them. Ideali-zation and placation of me alternated with only thinly veiled persecutory fears.

As this split in his perception of me lessened, so did the projection, and gradually he was able to admit his aggression in relation to me. This ushers in the third phase of his analysis, during which the persecution and idealizations gradually gave place to ambiva-lence, a sense of psychic reality, and depressive anxieties. Slowly he was beginning to realize that if his symptoms now appeared only during breaks and weekends, it was not simply because I, the ideal object, abandoned him to his persecutors; he was beginning to realize that everything I had given him—interpretations repre-senting the good breast and food or the good penis—turned in my absence into bad, burning, poisonous, persecutory substances, be-cause when he was away from me, hatred welled up in him and turned everything bad. He began to admit more freely how greedy he was for the analysis and for my presence, and how impatient and angry he was when away from me. His son and I were becoming more and more the oedipal couple in his eyes, always together when we were not with him, his son representing now the father, now his younger brother—a partner of myself standing for his mother. He recalled vividly the birth of his younger brother and the absolute fury he had experienced not only in relation to the baby and the mother, but also to the father who gave mother this new baby. We reconstructed that he had been weaned at the birth of this brother when he was about two. He remembered soon after that there had been a fire that had destroyed nearly the whole village, after which his family had been practically homeless, living in one room in an inn. It became clear that this fire was felt by him to be a result of his own urinary attacks. These were relived with such intensity that for a few nights he actually became incontinent.

We could now trace the beginning of his secret drinking to the beginning of the war in 1939, that produced in him a severe unconscious depression which he controlled by drinking. The beginning of the war unconsciously meant to him the destruction of his family. He admitted that, had he thought of it, he might have brought his family over to Rhodesia and saved their lives. He felt that he had had all the luck; he took the father's penis, and then he turned against his family in anger, superiority, and contempt, and left them behind to be burnt and destroyed. He unconsciously internalized them and carried inside himself the concentration camp, with its burning and breaking up. But, unable to bear his depression and guilt, he split off and denied it and turned to drink, as in the past he had turned to an ideal homosexual relationship with his father. When in his analysis he began to face what the beginning of the 1939 war meant to him, he experienced a great deal of guilt in relation to his family, particularly his mother. His previous valuation of her had become very altered. He realized what a hard struggle she had had to keep the family alive, and that the bad relations that existed between himself and her were at least partly due to the way in which he treated her, turning from her in anger and contempt to the idealized homosexual relation with his father, thereby robbing her both of himself and the father. He then experienced mourning about his family and particularly about his mother, and with it he relived his early weaning situations with her, his deprivation, jealousy, envy, his urinary attacks on her, which, he felt, had left her empty and bad so that she was unable to feed his younger brother. Together with this changed relation to his mother and family came a very altered relation to the idea of his own death.

The end of the treatment had by then already been fixed and symbolized for him his approaching death, of which he now spoke very freely. It appeared to him as a repetition of weaning, but now not so much as a retaliation and persecution, but as a reason for sorrow and mourning about the loss of something that he deeply appreciated and could now enjoy, which was life. He was mourning his life that he was going to lose, together with his analysis that was ending, and for the first time he was mourning fully the mother and the breast that he had lost in the past. He also felt some longing for death, expressed mostly in his wish to go back to Rhodesia to meet his old friends again, which symbolized his wish to die and to meet his dead parents, of whom he was no longer frightened. But the mourning and sadness were not a clinical depression and seemed not to interfere with his enjoyment of life. In fact, he began to feel that if this life, this life-giving breast, was something that he was going to mourn for so much, then, as he told me, he might as well enjoy it and do his best with it while he could.

In the last weeks, particularly in the last days of his analysis, he repeated some main themes in his associations, but not in symptoms, and I here select a few associations from the last week. On the first day he spoke angrily about somebody who behaves like a cow; he gives one a bucket of milk and then kicks it. I interpreted that I was the cow who gave him the analysis, like the mother who gave him the breast, but by sending him away was kicking it and spoiling it all, and I was myself responsible for kicking the bucket—that is, my own and his death. The following day he came back to this association and said in a dejected way that it was he, in relation to his mother, who often behaved like the cow that kicked the bucket. Later he said that she was the cow, and he kicked the bucket that fed him; and he accepted my interpretation that his anxiety was that when he has to leave me, he will be so angry that he will kick me inside him and spoil and spill out all the good analysis, as he felt he had done with his mother's breast, and that he would be responsible for my death inside him and for his own death. On the third day he spoke about a jug; he said that one must not judge a drink by the jug it is carried in, and he associated that he was the jug—old and unprepossessing, but the stuff that he contained could be good; it could be beer, he said, or milk. In associations it became quite clear that the beer and milk represented the good breast and the good penis, the mother and father, and myself in both rôles, inside him. He felt that he had re-established his good internal objects.

At this point in his analysis he felt hopeful. He felt that his life was worth living and that, however old he was, his internal objects were rejuvenated and worth preserving. It was also clear that his children and grandchildren were no longer felt by him as projections of himself, but as his objects that he loved, and he could enjoy the thought of their living on and growing after his own death.

Conclusions

I suggest that my patient had been unable, in his babyhood, childhood, and later on, to face his ambivalence and the resulting depressive anxiety.

He could not face the death of his object and the prospect of his own death. He protected himself against those anxieties by denial of depression, splitting, and projective identification. Those defence mechanisms, however, intensified his unconscious anxiety, in that all situations of deprivation or loss were unconsciously perceived as persecution. Idealization and denial had therefore to be intensified as a defence against both depression and persecution. When in old age he had to face the prospect of approaching death, the loss of his life appeared to him primarily as a situation of acute persecution and retaliation. He tried to counteract it by intensifying mechanisms of projective identification, denial, and idealization. When his denial and idealization broke down during his visit to London, the persecution became unbearable, and he became insane. The analysis of those anxieties and defence mechanisms in the transference enabled him to experience ambivalence, to mobilize the infantile depressive position and work through it sufficiently to enable him to re-establish good internal objects, and to face old age and death in a more mature way.

CHAPTER SEVENTEEN

Male and female narcissism: a reassessment

Harold Stewart (London)

From his earliest conceptualizing of the topic of narcissism in the paper, "On Narcissism" (1914c), Freud affirmed and re-affirmed that female narcissism is by and large greater than that of the male. A typical example of this comes from the chapter on femininity in the *New Introductory Lectures on Psycho-Analysis* (1933a): "Thus, we attribute a larger amount of narcissism to femininity, which also affects women's choice of object, so that to be loved is a stronger need for them than to love" (p.132). This assessment of narcissism has rarely been questioned, and I wish to argue that a good case can be made for the opposite being true—that men are more narcissistic than women.

This idea first struck me when I was thinking of my own clinical experiences with patients, but this impression might well have arisen from the result of the treatment of a limited number of cases by a single analyst. In view of this, I decided to look elsewhere in an attempt to substantiate this viewpoint and therefore turned to Freud's own writings and examined them more closely in order to see whether he could provide me with any necessary evidence.

I shall start with three quotations from "On Narcissism":

> Here we may even venture to touch on the question of *what makes* it necessary at all for our mental life to pass beyond the limits of narcissism and to attach the libido to objects. The answer which would follow from our line of thought would once more be that this necessity arises when the cathexis of the ego with libido exceeds a certain amount. A strong egoism is a protection against falling ill, but in the last resort we must begin to love in order not to fall ill, and we are bound to fall ill if in consequence of frustration, we are unable to love. [Freud, 1914c, p. 85]

From this quotation, I would like you to notice the phrase "we must begin to love in order not to fall ill"; it is not "we must begin to be loved in order not to fall ill". The second quotation is:

> A different course is followed in the type of female most frequently met with, which is probably the purest and truest one. With the onset of puberty the maturing of the female sex organs, which up till then have been in a condition of latency, seems to bring about an intensification of the original narcissism, and this is unfavourable to the development of a true object-choice with its accompanying sexual overvaluation. [p. 88]

Here I would like you to notice the phrase, "unfavourable to the development of a true object-choice".

The final quotation from this paper is:

> Nor does their need lie in the direction of loving, but of being loved; and the man who fulfils this condition is the one who finds favour with them. [p. 89]

These quotations, from the *New Introductory Lectures* and from "On Narcissism", suggest that the stronger female need is to be loved rather than to love, and that this manifestation of her narcissism renders her less capable than the male of the development towards making a true object-choice, of being able to love. The result of this is to render the female more liable to become ill than the male.

However, against this outcome of falling ill, Freud mentioned in "On Narcissism" that a strong egoism is a protection against falling ill. The relationship of narcissism and egoism is most extensively considered in the chapter on libido theory and narcissism in the *Introductory Lectures on Psycho-Analysis*. I quote:

> First, how do we differentiate between the concepts of narcissism and egoism? Well, narcissism, I believe, is the libidinal comple-

ment to egoism. When we speak of egoism, we have in view only the individual's advantage; when we talk of narcissism we are also taking his libidinal satisfactions in account. As practical motives, the two can be traced separately for quite a distance. It is possible to be absolutely egoistic and yet maintain powerful object-cathexis, insofar as libidinal satisfaction in relation to the object forms part of the ego's needs. In that case, egoism will see to it that striving for the object involves no damage to the ego. It is possible to be egoistic and at the same time to be excessively narcissistic, that is to say, to have very little need for an object, whether, once more, for the purpose of direct sexual satisfaction, or in connection with the higher aspirations derived from sexual need, which we are occasionally in the habit of contrasting with "sensuality" under the name of "love". [1916–1917, p. 417]

Here, Freud is clearly differentiating between egoism and narcissism, and I have discovered no reference in his writings to the effect that females are more, or less, egoistic than the male. In these circumstances, egoism no more protects the female than the male against falling ill, and hence it does not affect our argument in either direction.

The problem of illness is difficult to evaluate since we have to consider not only what is innate and biological in its causation, but also that which arises from the environment. However, I will take a leaf out of Freud's book when he said, in the chapter on femininity:

I have promised to tell you of a few more psychical peculiarities of mature femininity as we come across them in analytic observation. We do not lay claim to more than an average validity for these assertions; nor is it always easy to distinguish what should be ascribed to the influence of the sexual function and what to social breeding. [1933a, p. 132]

I, too, will take the liberty of not easily differentiating the biological from the social, and so if my thesis, too, has average validity, we should expect to find evidence of a higher incidence of illness among females compared with males.

Now, which illnesses should be examined if this difference of incidence is to be ascertained? I would suggest that we look at those used by Freud in "On Narcissism" to illuminate his concept. These are the perversions, particularly homosexuality, schizophrenia, and hypochondria. As my source for the incidence of these illnesses, I have taken the authoritative textbook on psychiatry, *Clinical Psychiatry* by Mayer-Gross, Slater, and Roth (1969), a book that could never be accused of having a bias towards psychoanalysis.

If we examine the perversions, we find that in all those listed—and these include fetishism, trans-sexualism, transvestism, exhibitionism, sado-masochism, bestiality, and homosexuality (if homosexuality is still to be regarded as a perversion or deviation)—the incidence is far higher in the male than in the female. The authors particularly state about homosexuality:

> This preponderance of homosexuality in the male in a wide range of cultures makes it unlikely that the male preponderance in highly-developed societies is wholly the product of social and legal prejudice as some workers have suggested. The differential sex incidence is more likely to have some biological explanation. [Mayer-Gross et al., 1969, p. 171]

The incidence in schizophrenia offers interesting evidence. To quote again:

> There is little difference in the risk of schizophrenia for males and for females except that, in England and Wales at least, the age of onset in women tends to fall rather later than in men. This results in a striking change in the sex ratio of new admissions at various ages, with a marked preponderance of males at earlier ages, especially between 25 and 35, and an increasing preponderance of females at ages after 45. It seems probable that this is a characteristic of the illness which is to be found in Western countries generally; but whether its causes are to be sought for in biological or social factors is an open question. [p. 240]

An important biological factor in women after 45 must be the menopause, which represents a profound loss of part of her feminine biological and psychological make-up, and this must constitute an important etiological agent in this increase of incidence in women. The implication here is that it is precisely her femininity that had protected her to some extent against this severe narcissistic disorder in her younger years.

Hypochondriasis is not really a disease entity but, rather, a symptom. Its onset in the younger person is usually seen in persons with hysterical traits and frequently female, whereas in the older person its onset is usually in persons with anxiety and obsessional traits and frequently male. But although this age of onset and incidence in the sexes is the opposite of that seen in schizophrenia, it does not seem to be the variations in a common narcissistic element that is involved in this instance, and so provides no evidence either for or against my thesis.

Freud mentioned two other groups of people in "On Narcissism" who, although they do not represent illness, do represent narcissism, and these are the great criminals and the humorists. Although I have no authoritative figures to back me up, I have little doubt when thinking of people belonging to these groups that it is largely males who contribute to their numbers.

Lastly, although it is not really evidence, it is surely not merely fortuitous that the concept of narcissism is named after the Greek mythological character, Narcissus, who is himself male. He pined away and died from his frustrated love for himself as his object-choice.

I would, therefore, suggest that the evidence from these various sources provides support for my thesis that the male is more narcissistic than the female and that if this is so, then psychoanalytic theories and psychopathologies based on narcissistic differences between the sexes will be in need of revision. Perhaps, too, the other qualities of feminine character need to be re-examined: that is, feminine passivity, shame, her lesser sense of justice, her weakness in social interests, her lesser capacity for sublimation, and her psychic rigidity.

I would now like to consider possible reasons why the male should be more narcissistic than the female. Freud always considered the absence of the penis and the subsequent penis envy as the main dynamic for his views on female narcissism. Since then the vicissitudes of the boy's earliest relationships with his mother have been charted, and I believe that it is in this area that the narcissistic difference can be traced.

Melanie Klein, in *The Psychoanalysis of Children* (1932), postulated the presence of an early feminine phase in the sexual development of both boys and girls. In both sexes the infant has oral-incorporative desires towards the mother's breast that are inevitably doomed to frustration and disappointment. This leads the infant to turn its desires from the frustrating, disappointing breast to the father's penis as being potentially more satisfying. Thus both the boy and the girl pass through this feminine phase of an oral-sucking fixation on the father's penis, which she considers as the basis of true homosexuality in the male.

It is at this point that this dominant feminine component could be felt by the boy as a potential source of danger to his masculine heterosexual component; to avert this danger, the boy would have to narcissistically cathect his penis and its heterosexual drives, no doubt with the help of a positive identification with the father's penis.

Stoller, in *Sex and Gender* (1968), also advances views on sexual development that differ in some respects from those of Freud. He postulates that the boy's relationship to his mother makes the development of feminine qualities more likely; that the boy, unlike the girl, has to manage to break through the pool of his mother's femininity and femaleness in order to grow beyond the feminine identification that has resulted from his first encounter with his mother's female body and feminine qualities. He considers the prevalence of effeminacy, passivity, and forced hyper-masculinity to be evidence that this task is frequently incomplete.

This view is almost the exact counterpoint, from the vantage point of the external reality of the other, to that of Klein, who considers it from the vantage point of the internal phantasy situation, since both emphasize the initial feminine phase in the boy that represents a source of danger to his masculinity and heterosexuality.

Grunberger (1964) has suggested ideas different from Freud's to explain why females are more narcissistic than males. He postulates (a) that a mother will be more ambivalent towards her daughter than towards her son, a view strongly held by Freud, (b) that unless one postulates a congenital homosexual stage, a true object can only be of the opposite sex, and (c) that awareness of the genital organs, even if unconscious, is present from the beginning of life. These ideas would make the earliest stages of development more frustrating for the girl than for the boy, since the mother would be only a substitute for a true sexual object. The frustration is not sufficiently compensated for by the mother's love and attention towards her daughter owing to the mother's ambivalence, and hence it leads to the girl becoming narcissistic as a self-compensation for the frustrations. Grunberger also remarks that because the mother is of the opposite sex, the son would feel more frustrated than the daughter, but he believes that the mother's greater love and attention to her son—she being less ambivalent towards him than towards a daughter—would compensate for this heightened frustration and assuage his narcissistic hurt.

However, if we regard this in the light of Stoller's views, the mother's greater love and attention towards her son would give rise to the feminine identification that could certainly be intensified by the son's genital frustration with his mother. This could then lead to more, rather than less, narcissism in the boy as compared with the girl, on the lines mentioned above.

To sum up: I would suggest that narcissism may be greater in males than in females precisely because the identification conflicts with the mother occur at an earlier and more primitive stage of development in boys than in girls.

CHAPTER EIGHTEEN

The unconscious:
past, present, and future

Clifford Yorke (London)

Pearl King's clinical and theoretical contributions to psychoanalysis would alone justify this 80th-birthday *Festschrift*. But her work for psychoanalysis goes far beyond her many papers. She has also shown an organizational flair that has enriched the *milieu* in which her chosen subject has developed, and, in particular, she has taken the greatest interest, and played a leading part, in the development of the British Society, of which she is its leading historian. She has been a fine teacher and trained many in the practice of psychoanalysis. In the course of a long professional lifetime she has seen many changes, for some of which she has been responsible and of which she can justifiably feel proud. But there are others—within psychoanalysis itself—for which she neither bears accountability nor gives approval. It will not, I believe, strike a discordant note to draw attention to some of the most important of these, since they are alien to what I take to be her own sustaining psychoanalytic principles.

I cannot presume to speak for her, and in what follows I take full responsibility for what is said. I know, however, that there is much with which she will sympathize, and it is in this belief that I make this contribution to the present work.

I *do* know that she shares with others the belief that, for a great many years, Freud's psychological writings have not been sufficiently or well enough taught in our Society. There is reason to think that this is almost certainly true of other Societies too, but it seems best to speak of the organization one knows best. And it may be as well to say, at the outset, that I am talking about *fundamental* Freudian principles, not about minutiae and obscurities. If, for example, you were to ask students on the verge of qualification—and even members—of this Society to give reasons why Freud thought it necessary to conceptualize his structural model of the mind, many would be unable to do so. This is hardly a state of affairs that makes for a healthy psychoanalytic society. If models of the mind that were developed later are to be accepted or rejected, whether with or without modification, a knowledge of basic Freudian principles has to be taken as a starting point if, that is, the model is to be regarded as a psychoanalytic one. That is a point that Mrs Klein, for example, understood very well. (Klein invariably asserted that her views were a legitimate extension and enlargement of Freudian thinking, rejecting any evidence brought to bear against this conviction.)

The Curriculum Committee are currently working hard to rectify the situation and have made improvements; but there is one significant circumstance against which they may struggle in vain. For Freudian principles are in fact *devalued* in the British Society, as they are in many other parts of the psychoanalytic world. Not many people really *admit* this: instead, they will, for example, dispute the value of metapsychology as an out-of-date nineteenth-century pseudo-scientific and mechanistic theory, which *modern* psychoanalysis has long left behind. But in doing so they will fail to recognize that metapsychology is neither more nor less than the psychoanalytic theory of the mind. Please note that it is not suggested that metapsychology cannot be changed or modified in the light of evidence that calls for such changes, as Freud (1900a) emphasized; but inasmuch as we are dealing with the structure, forces, and relative strengths that operate within and between mental agencies, we are close to irreducible concepts without which psychoanalysis would cease to be psychoanalysis. The way in which these elements are thought to stand in relation to each other, or are built upon, is a different matter. True, there are many who cannot come to grips with these concepts when expressed in *psychological* terms, but they are, as Freud insisted, "no less indeterminate" than the same or comparable terms used in other sciences, such as physics (cf. Freud, 1940a [1938], p. 159).

It is equally fashionable to deplore "drive theory", as if this concept were a legitimate shorthand for Freudian psychoanalysis itself. It is often denied that drives have any motivating force in mental functioning and that affects are the real factors that prompt the human mind to perform its various functions. But the plain fact is that Freudian theory has always acknowledged the motivating power of affects (it is somewhat dispiriting to find that the Sandlers, for example, in the paper discussed below at some length, refer to anxiety as a motivating force, as if the idea had never occurred to Freud), while at the same time insisting on the indispensable and dynamic forces of the drives. Furthermore, the theory has pointed to links between the two as well as important differences, such as the ways they reach consciousness (if at all). These facts are often sidestepped, and sidestepped in the course of honest, but regrettably uninformed, judgements. It is repeatedly asserted, in pursuing some of these criticisms, that "object relations theory" has replaced "drive theory" (a pejorative term nowadays and one that does serious disservice to Freud). This kind of criticism ignores the fact that Freud was the first and by far the most thorough of all object-relation psychologists, and it could not be seriously made if people knew their Freudian theory better. There are many other kinds, and additional expressions, of Freudian criticism common among psychoanalysts today; but few appear to offer any advantage, in terms of basic concepts, over the model of the mind they set out to demolish.

It would be tedious and unnecessary to go through these criticisms at any length. I have tried to deal with some of them elsewhere (e.g. Yorke, 1995, 1996a). But there is one widespread form of attack on psychoanalysis that, for present purposes, I want to emphasize. This is the tendency, in some quarters, to devalue the importance of the personal past and to regard everything that really matters as restricted to what takes place in the so-called here-and-now of the session, strictly within the relationship between analyst and patient. But how a person can be divorced from his past, and still remain a person in the present passes all understanding—or, at any rate, psychoanalytic understanding. Psychoanalysis is, above all, a *developmental* psychology: for that matter, metapsychology is a *developmental* metapsychology. But it has been seriously suggested, and vehemently argued, that since we cannot *know* the true facts of a patient's early life but, at best, *reconstruct* it, we should ignore it altogether. That amounts to saying that when the patient lies on the couch, he leaves his personal history behind and behaves—*and should be understood*—as if his own past were not of the slightest consequence for the comprehension of what he thinks, feels, says, or behaves like *now*. The repetition compulsion can be discarded as a concept of no clinical significance.

Not everyone inclined to such views would go quite as far as this, but, in all the circumstances, it is not surprising that the concept of the "unconscious" itself also comes under attack, at least in the senses that Freud understood it—descriptive, dynamic, systematic, or qualitative. For the Freudian "unconscious" has itself the most sustained and important history in the development of his ideas and one that is worth recapitulating (with due apologies to those who are familiar with it) and perhaps adding a few reminders of the Freudian concepts of the *preconscious* and *consciousness*, as a reminder of what we are in danger of losing, before developing the present critique of contemporary psychoanalysis more fully, restricted though that appraisal will have to be. Freud's first public use of the term "the unconscious" [*das Unbewusste*] is to be found in a footnote to the case history of Frau Emma von N. (Freud, 1895d, p. 76), though it was used by Breuer in his account of Fräulein Emma O. (Freud, 1895d, p. 46) and it had already long been used by other authors. But it is only in *The Interpretation of Dreams* (Freud, 1900a) that Freud gave his impressive account of the "Unconscious" as a *system*. There he set out his detailed description of how the system worked, described the laws by which it operated and how it related to, and differed from, other parts of the mind. But the term was not without ambiguities, of which Freud was clearly aware, and it was in 1912, in his paper for the Society for Psychical Research (1912g), that he distinguished between the *descriptive* unconscious, the *dynamic* unconscious, and the *systematic* unconscious. Whatever mental content is outside awareness at any given moment is *descriptively* unconscious. Whatever cannot be recalled, in spite of every effort, is *dynamically* unconscious, and dynamic because it is not its *weakness* that keeps it unconscious—it is its *activity* and forcefulness, to be kept at bay only by opposing counter-forces. Lastly, whatever is not only inaccessible to awareness (except under special conditions such as sleep, when it appears in distorted form) or to the most intense introspection but is also allocated to a special area of the mind, obeying, and regulated by, its own laws, is *systematically* unconscious: it is depicted in German by *Ubw.* [*Unbewusst*] and in English by the shorthand *Ucs.* It operates with freely displaceable energy and is discharged via the primary process.

Although Freud's *account* of the Unconscious was greatly expanded in 1915 (for which the 1912g account was a preparation), the *definitions* (given in Section II of that major work), designed to reduce the existing ambiguities of the term, are less exact and lack the clarity of the 1912 paper, as Strachey notes in his foreword to the text printed in the *Standard Edition* (pp. 257–259).[1] Furthermore, the meanings of the term "unconscious" are reduced from three to two (descriptive and systematic). The "dynamic" was omitted. The topic was re-addressed in 1923 (1923b), when the structural model was introduced and the three distinctions restored, as they were when Freud returned to the topic in 1933 (1933a).

Freud made a very important statement about the "Unconscious" in his *An Outline of Psychoanalysis*, published posthumously in 1940 (1940a [1938]); but it will be easier to pursue the present argument if we break off this brief outline of the history of the concept before the dramatic changes in the model of the mental apparatus were introduced in 1923 and return to it after a brief look at the development of the concept of the "Preconscious". The connection, as well as the differences, between the two is of vital importance: apart from anything else, *Ucs.* material can only gain access to consciousness if it is first admitted to the preconscious—that is, by negotiating the censorship between these two psychic systems. There is an important exception: an unconscious fantasy can reach consciousness without passing through the *Pcs.*, in which case it is perceived *as coming from the outside, as a hallucination.*

In his first published schematic sketch of the mental apparatus, Freud (1900a) indicated the movement of the excitatory processes through the psychic systems and said that they could "enter consciousness [through the *Pcs.*] without further impediment provided that certain other conditions [were] fulfilled: for instance, that they [reached] a certain degree of intensity, that the function which can

---

[1] Strachey decided to reprint the version of this paper as it appeared in the *Proceedings of the Society for Psychical Research:* it was written by Freud in English and is reproduced without alteration. Strachey rightly considered this paper one of the most important of Freud's metapsychological statements and regretted the absence of any definitive text (cf. Grubrich-Simitis, 1996).

only be described as 'attention' [was] distributed in a particular way, and so on" (1900a, p. 541). Later, Freud added (p. 593) that the "attention" required to bring preconscious material into consciousness was "only available in a specific quantity, and this [might] have been diverted from the train of thought in question on to some other purpose". Here, again, we must regret the absence of a missing metapsychological paper—that on "attention"—though the subject had been prominent in the "Project for a Scientific Psychology" (Freud, 1950 [1895]). Freud, however, in extending the passage just quoted, made it clear that the withdrawal of attention did not mean that the train of thought could not continue unobserved or that, when it again reached a higher degree of intensity, it could not again attract attention in spite of its initial "conscious" rejection. Such thoughts might be completely rational or rejected on rational grounds, though they might, in the process described, come to be re-appraised and accepted.

Perhaps, and for present purposes more importantly, it is essential to note the qualifications of the statement that preconscious material can gain direct access to consciousness—that is, that "certain conditions" have to be met in order for this to happen. In this connection, Freud made an important point a little later: that the excitations of the *Pcs.* can reach consciousness "after observing certain rules, it is true, and perhaps *only after passing a fresh censorship*, though nonetheless without regard to the *Ucs.*" (1900a, p. 615; emphasis added). But the system *Pcs.* not only bars or permits access to consciousness; "it also controls access to the power of voluntary movement . . ." (p. 615). Furthermore, unlike the system *Ucs.*, the *Pcs.* system operates with *bound* energy and has as its mode of discharge the secondary process—a process that makes rational and ordered thinking possible and is indispensable for ordinary social intercourse.[2]

A word about the concept of consciousness is called for here. For at this point in Chapter VII of *The Interpretation of Dreams*, Freud asks:

> But what part is to be played in our scheme by consciousness, which was once so omnipotent and hid all else from view? *Only that of a sense-organ for the perception of psychical qualities.* [Freud's emphasis, but cf. 1940a (1938)]. In accordance with the ideas un-

---

[2] More is said of the primary and secondary processes in the brief comments to follow on the 1940 paper, even though it will be unnecessary for many readers.

derlying our attempt at a schematic picture, we can only regard conscious perception as the function proper to a particular system; and for this the abbreviation *Cs.* seems appropriate. In its mechanical properties we regard this system as resembling the perceptual systems *Pcpt.*: as being susceptible to excitation by qualities but incapable of retaining traces of alterations—that is to say, of having no memory. The psychical apparatus, which is turned towards the external world with its sense-organ of the *Pcpt.* systems, is itself the external world in relation to the sense-organ of the *Cs.*, whose teleological justification resides in this circumstance. Here we once again meet the principle of the hierarchy of agencies, which seems to govern the structure of the apparatus. Excitatory material flows in to the *Cs.* sense-organ from two directions: from the *Pcpt.* system, whose excitation, determined by qualities, is probably submitted to a fresh revision before it becomes a conscious sensation, and from the interior of the apparatus itself, whose quantitative processes are felt qualitatively in the pleasure-unpleasure series when, subject to certain modifications, they make their way to consciousness. [Freud, 1900a, pp. 615–616][3]

I hope these brief remarks and selected quotations will suffice for present purposes and be regarded as reminders, not expositions. To the same end, it seems justified to return to the concept of the "unconscious" from 1923 onwards and make some relevant observations on the preconscious and on consciousness too. Without a fairly clear knowledge of Freud's position and its modifications, it is not possible to call to account what I have already referred to as the threat to the psychoanalytic understanding of the "unconscious" itself.

The Ego and the Id (1923b) is generally regarded as a watershed in Freud's psychoanalytic thinking. While in some respects this is true, it does not put out of court or dismantle all that has gone before; and much of what seems new in it has already been anticipated or has its forerunners in his earlier writings. If we address the question posed in the early part of this paper, we would, with common knowledge, answer that Freud felt obliged to formulate his structural model on two grounds: the one theoretical, the other clinical. The theoretical reason was the problem of the location of the defences against drive expression: they could not be located in the system *Ucs.* without

---

[3] Mark Solms has made good use of these concepts in his papers on affect (1996) and consciousness (1997).

themselves becoming as inaccessible, as *unknowable*, as the mental content they were obliged to keep at bay. If that were indeed the case, what forces would *keep* them inaccessible? And to locate them in the system *Pcs.*, in the general sense of that word, would make them, with greater or lesser difficulty, accessible to consciousness, and to know one's defences would mean that one knew what one was defending against.

That was indeed a theoretical problem, but the clinical problem was just as compelling: it revealed itself in the *negative therapeutic reaction*. It will be in line with the general object of this chapter to assert at once that this expression, like *fantasy, transference, counter-transference*, and *acting out*, has lost the precision it once had before many subsequent years of misuse replaced clarity with ambiguity and confusion. Nowadays a "negative therapeutic reaction" is often taken to refer to a patient's failure to get better during analysis, what-ever the circumstances, whereas Freud was referring to the fact that, *in spite of good clinical work by both patient and analyst*, the analysand not only failed to improve, *he got worse*. That implied the operation of unconscious guilt, and with that understanding came the need to clarify and give a new status to the concept of the *superego*. The question that concerns us here, however, is this: what changes did this call for in the concepts of the unconscious, the preconscious, and perceptual consciousness?

Freud continues to use the terms *Ucs.*, *Pcs.*, and *Pcpt. Cs.* through-out his new work, but he now points out that "it is still true that all that is repressed is *Ucs.*, but not all that is *Ucs.* is repressed" (p. 18). The formulations at this stage of Freud's thinking can briefly be sum-marized as follows. The most superficial part of the mental apparatus is *Pcpt.-Cs.*, and the concept is essentially unchanged, though its mode of operation is enlarged on:

> Internal perceptions yield sensations of processes arising in the most diverse and certainly also in the deepest strata of the mental apparatus. Very little is known about these sensations and feel-ings; those belonging to the pleasure-unpleasure series may still be regarded as the best examples of them. They are more primor-dial, more elementary, than perceptions arising externally and they come about even when consciousness is clouded . . . [1923b, p. 22]

Freud enlarges on these observations, builds on concepts considered in *Beyond the Pleasure Principle* (1920g), and clarifies the relations between external and internal perception and the superficial system *Pcpt.Cs.* The *ego* starts out from this system, which forms its nucleus, "and begins by embracing the *Pcs.*, which is adjacent to the mnemic residues" (p. 23).

Freud then adopts a suggestion by Groddeck, who insisted that

> what we call our ego behaves essentially passively in life, and that as he [Groddeck] expresses it, we are "lived" by unknown and uncontrollable forces. We have all had impressions of the same kind, even though they may not have overwhelmed us to the exclusion of all others . . . I propose to take it [this view] into account by calling the entity which starts out from the system *Pcpt.* and begins by being *Pcs.* the "ego", and by following Groddeck in calling the other part of the mind, into which this entity extends and which behaves as though it were *Ucs.*, the "id". [Freud, 1920g, p. 23]

At this juncture I will make just two further points. (1) Freud retains, both in this paper and subsequently, the distinction between the two types of psychic energy (free and bound) and the two types of discharge (primary and secondary process) and thereby these crucial characteristics of, and distinctions between, the systems *Ucs.* and *Pcs.* (2) The major elaboration of the superego and the importance of its unconscious operations adds a substantial new dimension to our understanding of the factors motivating defence organization. It clarified much else, including the place of the *ego ideal* within what may legitimately be called the superego complex. A new era in the development of psychoanalysis is opened up by a new interest in the ego as just defined and by the fresh understanding of the superego, its structure, and its mode of operation.

That Freud's views on the operation of the primary and secondary processes were unchanged is particularly clear from his lucid and succinct account of them in the *Outline of Psychoanalysis* (1940a [1938]),[4] largely in his comments on dream formation. He stressed, in describing the laws of the unconscious, the process of condensation by

---

[4] This paper is, I believe, largely unread by students and perhaps by qualified analysts too. It was certainly not on the Freud reading list of the British Society three years ago, in spite of the fact that it adds pertinent points to almost everything Freud had said before about the structural model. This, by any standards, was a startling omission.

which mental elements that in everyday waking life are kept apart become combined, so that a single representation "stands for a whole number of latent dream-thoughts as though it were a combined allusion to all of them; and in general the compass of the manifest dream is extraordinarily small in comparison with the wealth of material from which it has sprung. Another peculiarity ... is the ease with which psychical intensities (cathexes) are *displaced* from one element to another" (pp. 167–168). Freud stresses the "archaic heritage" of the unconscious, thereby emphasizing its *timelessness*, and that in the dream things that had long been forgotten once more find expression. Logic carries no weight; contradictory aims exist side by side as if there were no such thing as contradiction; what grammarians call "particles" have no existence—there is no "and", "or", "but", or "not", so that negatives have no place there. Furthermore, in dreams, the operations of the unconscious that are carried forward into the preconscious *bring with them their own laws of operation*. All this is contrasted with the secondary process and the laws by which it makes logic attainable, provides speech and the thought that goes with it in embracing coherent thinking, can allow the free play of fantasy but still permit its distinction from memory and current reality, can order events in sequence and for this reason operate with the concept of time—it is unnecessary to go on.

It is impossible to touch on more than a few points in such an exiguous survey, including the importance of the revised drive theory for our understanding of the operations of the mental apparatus. But many questions were left unanswered in the 1923 paper and, long before he wrote the *Outline*, Freud had returned to the topic of the unconscious in the *New Introductory Lectures* (1933a). Here he re-emphasized that large parts of the ego and superego were and remained unconscious. He discussed the preconscious in terms already familiar and the unconscious in its descriptive *and* dynamic sense, adding: "we have come to understand the term 'unconscious' in a *topographical* or systematic sense as well" (1933a, p. 71, emphasis added). But he recognized the difficulties posed by these remarks, and added:

> ... we have used the word [system *Ucs.*] more and more to denote a mental province rather than a quality of what is mental. The discovery, actually an inconvenient one, that portions of the ego and super-ego as well are unconscious in the dynamic sense, comes as a relief—it makes possible the removal of a complication. [pp. 71–72]

Freud went on to say that "we have no right to name the region that is foreign to the ego 'the system *Ucs.'*, since the characteristic of being unconscious is not restricted to it . . . we will no longer use the term 'unconscious' in a systematic sense . . . " (pp. 71–72). Henceforth he proposed to give the region "a better name and one no longer open to misunderstanding"—that is, the "id". But he noted the dissatisfaction this might cause if things no longer fell neatly into place. The id was still "the dark, inaccessible part of the personality . . . we approach the id with analogies: we call it a chaos, a cauldron full of seething excitations . . ." (p. 73). And he went on, in all essentials, to describe the characteristics of the primary process in a way that, though succinct, was as clear as anything he wrote about the matter.

If the purpose of this chapter were simply to summarize Freud's thinking about the mental apparatus and his changing views about it, there would be a great deal more to say. But it may suffice for the present to add only one or two points. Freud contrasts the differences between the ego and the id, in popular parlance, with the comment that "we might say that the ego stands for reason and good sense while the id stands for the untamed passions" (Freud, 1933a, p. 76). But he reminds us that the ego is only a portion of the id, "a portion that has been expediently modified by the proximity of the external world and the threat of danger" (pp. 76–77). And he describes, lucidly, how the ego attempts to tame the id—for example, by identifying itself with actual or abandoned objects, the cathexes of which have sprung from the id's instinctual demands, and thereby "seeks to divert the id's libido on to itself" (p. 77). And it carries out the id's intentions by finding out how these demands can best be achieved.

But what about "repression" in its portmanteau sense? "There is one portion of the id from which the ego has separated itself by resistances due to repression. *But the repression is not carried over into the id: the repressed merges into the remainder of the id*" (Freud, 1933a, p. 77, emphasis added). These remarks find graphic expression in Freud's model of the mental apparatus depicted on page 78 of this work—a model that is in many way clearer than that put forward in the diagram to be found in *The Ego and the Id* (1923b). Nevertheless, for those still troubled by the conceptual status of repressing forces in the new model, and the relations between the parts of the apparatus, Freud ends with a warning:

In thinking of this division of the personality into an ego, a super-ego and an id, you will not, of course, have pictured sharp frontiers like the artificial ones drawn in political geography. We cannot do justice to the characteristics of the mind by linear outlines like those in a drawing or in primitive painting, but rather by areas of colour melting into one another as they are presented by modern artists. After making the separation we must allow what we have separated to merge together once more. You must not judge too harshly a first attempt at giving a pictorial representation of something so intangible as psychical processes. [1933a, p. 79]

Unfortunately, many of Freud's critics *do* judge too harshly—not only the pictorial representations but also the whole general approach of metapsychological theory. They seem unable to appreciate what I have referred to elsewhere as the remarkable combination of daring and modesty with which Freud puts forward his formulations.

Finally, *An Outline of Psycho-Analysis* (1940a [1938]) is a miracle of condensation and clarification, but it needs nowadays to be read with due reference to what Ilse Grubrich-Simitis has to say about it in her remarkable *Back to Freud's Texts* (1996) and her strongly supported discussion of far-reaching changes made in this posthumous publication in the interests of editorial lubricity. But what, with the necessary reservations, is to be especially noted is Freud's statement that the psychic is unconscious in itself, and (as previously mentioned) that "the processes with which it is concerned are in themselves just as unknowable as those dealt with by other sciences, by chemistry or physics, for example; but it is possible to establish the laws which they obey and to follow their mutual relations and interdependences unbroken over long stretches"—in short, to arrive at what is described as an "understanding" of the field of natural phenomena in question' (1940a [1938], p.158). Essentially, what is called "conscious" coincides with the consciousness of everyday opinion. "Everything else psychical is in our view 'the unconscious'" (p. 159).

There is a passage in this work which is of special interest from the point of view of topography and from the concept of feelings as motivators:

The process of something becoming conscious is above all linked with the perceptions which our sense organs receive from the external world. From *the topographical point of view*, therefore, it is a phenomenon which takes place in the outermost cortex of the ego. It is true that we also receive conscious information from the inside of the body—the feelings, which actually exercise a more

peremptory influence on our mental life than external perceptions; moreover, in certain circumstances the sense organs themselves transmit feelings, sensations of pain, in addition to the
sensations specific to them. [p. 161; emphasis added]

But here, "the body itself would take the place of the external world".

Two further remarks have importance for what is to follow: (1)
preconscious material can remain preconscious, and for a time may
be unable to gain access to consciousness; (2) preconscious mental
content can temporarily be put back into the unconscious state and
become subject to repression. But both these observations raise the
question of the censorship operating between the preconscious and
consciousness—a concept put forward in 1900 (1900a, pp. 541, 593)
and referred to above, as well as in the paper "The Unconscious"
(1915e, e.g. p. 193).

It may be irritating to those familiar with these concepts to be
presented with this kind of summary. But it seems to me the case that
the concepts *were* well known, but they have become, over the years,
increasingly lost to common psychoanalytic knowledge. However
this may be, it would not have been possible to tackle the task set for
this chapter without an attempt of this kind, however unsatisfactory.
And, indeed, I have left out of account the fact that many people have
been able to build on what Fred formulated without sacrificing his
basic principles. Anna Freud is a notable example, but there are, and
have been, many others. But perhaps enough has been said to convey
the orderly, painstaking, and comprehensive way in which Freud
tackled a subject that had never before been addressed in comparable
fashion and thereby set up a yardstick by which all subsequent attempts of this sort must be assessed. Above all, I hope this account is
sufficiently clear to allow a return to the contentions made at the start
of the chapter: namely, that Freud's formulations are not sufficiently
taught; that the contemporary custom of emphasizing the here-and-
now at the expense of personal history is particularly worrying; and
that the Freudian concept of "the unconscious" is itself endangered
and, I would add, endangered *without anything better being put in its
place.*

Now when we are told that there is a *past* unconscious and a
present unconscious, it is tempting to think that, whatever else, we are
dealing with a development in psychoanalysis that values both the
past and the present; that will no doubt emphasize how the one gives
rise to, or grows out of, the other; and thereby the importance of

personal history will be accorded full recognition. But if we are mindful of the multifarious ways in which psychoanalysis is under attack today—and particularly from within the movement itself—we should scrutinize any new formulation with particular care. And if, furthermore, in this instance, we are told that the new way of looking at Freudian psychology minimizes theoretical anomalies to be found within it, and which tend to limit its usefulness, we should cast the most wary of eyes upon the new presentation and see whether it really *does* do what it promises to do. Are we really looking at the mind in a more coherent, comprehensive, or convincing way than Freud himself did?

The first question that may occur to those confronted with a new model—or a substantial re-working of an existing one—is: what is wrong with the old one? Why were these changes called for? It is undeniably clear that the concept of unconscious mental processes gave Freud a great deal of trouble, that it is necessarily incomplete, and that it raises difficulties that are not yet fully resolved. So if we turn to Joseph and Anne-Marie Sandler, to whom the concept of a past and present unconscious is to be attributed, we can expect to find a clear indication of their reasons for putting forward their revisions. Their writings on the subject are already numerous (e.g. Sandler, 1989; Sandler & Sandler, 1984, 1987), but it may be well to look at one of the most recent (Sandler & Sandler, 1994) for their explanation. But before they come to this vital matter, we find a disarming disclaimer:

> What we shall describe is not a theory intended to replace other theories but rather a frame of reference to supplement other psychoanalytic models of mental functioning. It is a frame of reference aimed specifically at narrowing the gap between theory and practice. It is, of course, inevitable that in trying to do this we shall point to a few of the conceptual problems and contradictions that have hampered our psychoanalytic theories since the time of Freud. [Sandler & Sandler, 1994, p. 281]

It seems to me wise to be wary of such a disclaimer. What is a "frame of reference", expressed in these terms and in this context, if not a *clinical* theory? And if it is designed to narrow the gap between theory and practice, and if the authors were talking about Freud, as at first they appear to be, their theory would indicate either (1) that the clinical theory needs to be brought closer to Freud's theory of mind, or (2) that Freud's theory of mind is deficient—a point, in any case, suggested by the last sentence in the quotation. It seems clear, from the Sandlers' relevant writings, that Freud's theory is judged to be incapable of resolving its anomalies without radical revision. But one cannot simply respond to the authors' disclaimer in this way, because they say that their "frame of reference" is designed "to supplement *other* psychoanalytic models of mental functioning" (Sandler & Sandler, 1994). I find this hard to understand. For a clinical theory unrelated to a theory of mind is, quite simply, not worth its salt; and *the concepts of a past and present unconscious comprises a theory of mind with significant clinical implications.* So how the new theory can supplement *any* "psychoanalytic" theory of mind, whatever its nature, is difficult to see.[5]

It is far from clear to me what the Sandlers' disclaimer really amounts to (cf. Yorke, 1995, 1996b, following Freeman, 1995). But, having made it, they begin their *raison d'être* for their new formulations by stating that Freud's concepts of a "dynamic unconscious" and a "descriptive unconscious" have been a "source of endless confusion" (Sandler & Sandler, 1994, p. 282). They add that, "although many hoped that the structural theory would eliminate the problem, *the notion of the unconscious has not disappeared*[6] but has remained as a noun referring to all that is, descriptively speaking, unconscious".

These assertions are misleading; what has disappeared in Freud's final formulations is the *system* unconscious, as should be clear from what has been summarized above. But before saying more, it may be as well to look at the Sandlers' next objection—this time to the *preconscious* system. The authors refer to Merton Gill (1963) and Arlow and Brenner (1964) in support of their contention that the system *Pcs.* and "preconscious mental processes" have been a comparable source of confusion. Indeed, Arlow and Brenner appear to have thought it advisable to abandon the term "preconscious" altogether, though the Sandlers quote some remarks by Anna Freud that suggests that she moved between the topographical theory (with its systems *Ucs., Pcs.,* and *Pcpt.Cs*) and the structural theory (and its systems *id, ego,* and *superego*), and they support this statement with a quotation. I do not

---

[5] Eissler (1962) spoke of "an exaggeration of the differences that allegedly exist among Freud's theories, as they arose in the course of his development". His paper is insufficiently appreciated.

[6] If their "frame of reference" is not designed as an alternative to Freud, why did Sandler call his 1989 paper "The Id—or the Child Within"? Does that not suggest a choice to be argued?

doubt the accuracy of the quotation; but in conversations with her, over many years, about this issue I found Anna Freud—like many of her colleagues, particularly in the United States—in agreement with the notion that it was enough to add the topographical *point of view* (as opposed to the topographical *theory*) to the other points of view of the structural model (structural, dynamic, and economic). But perhaps that is to bring the discussion to a premature close.

However this may be, it *does* seem as if the Sandlers agree with Anna Freud that it would be a pity if the advantages of topography were lost. They do not propose a *return* to the topographical model but a *visit* to retrieve what has been forgone with the introduction of the structural model (Sandler & Sandler, 1994, p. 284).

It has to be said that the Sandlers *do* set about their task with some pertinent observations. One of these is that, in practice, many analysts *do* use alternative and supplementary models without generally recognizing the fact. "One example of this is the way [they] move quite unconsciously between an intrapsychic view and an interpersonal one", without realizing that this involves a change in the frames of reference (p. 282). It is argued that this practice is useful and even necessary. I would have thought it a result of confusion, brought about by those who think "object relations theory" is missing from Freud and fail to distinguish between *intrapsychic representations* and *interpersonal relationships*. (Pearl King, incidentally, has condemned a great deal of what passes for psychoanalysis today as "relationship therapy".) I have heard, like others, many less excusable examples of similar confusion: an analyst who still clings to some metapsychological concepts may say, "He's incapable of cathecting other people"—a sloppiness of expression easily avoided by saying, "He's incapable of being interested in anyone else." The first expression uses a term at a high level of abstraction, *involving a single mind,* and introduces it into a social context. That kind of error is neither useful nor necessary, but we can all fall into similar traps if our expressions lack rigour and we are off guard.

To my mind, there is no excuse for confusing the descriptive unconscious with the dynamic unconscious. The concept of the "id", even, does not do away with the fact that a great deal of mental content is unconscious only in the descriptive sense, and for all Freud's revisions of terms, the id is descriptively *and* dynamically unconscious too. The confusion can arise only if Freudian theory is badly taught or seriously misunderstood; but the Sandlers are on

more certain ground when they assert that it is not generally appreciated that Freud used the term "preconscious" in different ways. But it
ought to be so appreciated. The laws of the secondary process, the
common understanding equating the term preconscious with "capable of becoming conscious", the concept of preconscious material *that
is not freely accessible to consciousness,* may not be widely recognized,
but, as the brief summary above should make clear, it is all to be
found in Freud. In their discussion of these concepts the authors do
not mention Kris, whose paper "On Preconscious Mental Processes"
(1950) is a model of lucidity.

Kris freely acknowledges the complex issues involved in the concept of the preconscious and selects three of them for discussion: the
fact that not all preconscious content can reach consciousness with
equal ease; that preconscious processes differ widely in form and
kinds of content; and that when preconscious content *does* emerge
into consciousness it can do so silently (virtually unnoticed) or produce strong emotional reactions. And his attempt to account for these
phenomena is singularly thorough. It would go beyond the purposes
of this chapter to attempt any summary of the conclusions Kris
reaches and the metapsychological complexities involved in his arguments; but, on the issue of access to consciousness, it may be helpful
to mention just two of them. Ego dystonic preconscious content (i.e.,
content that derives from the system *Ucs.* and is also under the "pull"
of that system—my interpolation, but cf. Freud, 1915e, p. 193) often
reaches consciousness only with great difficulty but may do so if the
counter-cathexes at the border between the system *Cs.* and the system
Pcs. can be weakened. How may this happen? If the preconscious
succeeds in the recognition of associated material, links that allow
recall to follow may be forged. A second factor is the part played by
attention. If energy is withdrawn from the perception of outer reality
and used to augment the push of psychic material towards awareness, the concentration involved may be sufficient to ensure that the
hitherto unavailable content breaks through. Similarities between
these arguments and Freud's will be observed, but Kris does provide
helpful clarification.

The Sandlers rightly emphasize Freud's concept of a censorship
between the *Pcs.* and *Cs.* systems but seek to change its character by
interposing it between what they call the *present unconscious* and consciousness. They consider it clinically appropriate to regard resistance
at this border as basically motivated by the "avoidance of conscious

feelings of shame, embarrassment, and humiliation" (Sandler & Sandler, 1994, p. 284). In terms of development, "it can be linked first with the step of substituting conscious fantasying for play and the need to keep such fantasies secret". Elsewhere (Sandler & Sandler, 1983) they have remarked, in a passage quoted in the paper under consideration, that, as the child becomes able to anticipate shaming and humiliating reactions of others (augmented by his own projections), he himself begins to disapprove and "internalizes the social situation *in the form of the second censorship*" (Sandler & Sandler, 1994, p. 284, emphasis added). And they add: "only content that is acceptable will be permitted through to consciousness. It must be *plausible* and not ridiculous or 'silly'".

In spite of all his later modifications of the concept of the mental apparatus, Freud's account of the censorship at the border of consciousness, together with the clarifications brought by Kris, is perfectly lucid. It is true that the *development* of this censorship needs spelling out, and in this respect we once more regret the missing metapsychological paper on "attention". But the Sandlers' second censorship is a very different matter, and it is not at all easy to see how it can be expected to carry conviction. What is the evidence that supports their hypothesis of how it comes into being? If it were plausible, one would have to point out that plausibility is not at all the same thing as evidence. But is it even plausible, and plausible to a point that justifies the sacrifice of Freud's clarity? The young child, we would all agree, has shaming and humiliating experiences. The *memory* of these early experiences would certainly be shut out by the repression barriers, which becomes fully effective at the age of five or so, is responsible for childhood amnesia, and is, indeed, considered by the Sandlers later in their paper (1994). But if we look at the affect of shame and examine its characteristics and mode of operation, we find certain features that set it apart from other affects, as I have tried to show elsewhere (Yorke, 1990), For one thing, *a shaming experience is not easily forgotten* and when recalled, it is so powerful that it is re-experienced. It carries with it a strong feeling of exposure. Furthermore, it is always related to an awareness of an observer, a possible observer, a former observer, or a fantasized observer. How a fear of shame, humiliation, and related affects can promote a censorship system is highly problematic. Certainly, as the Sandlers say, a fear of being laughed at or thought "silly" can inhibit conversation *and inhibit verbalization in analysis*. It took a patient of mine, who in other respects worked hard in her analysis, two and a half years to tell me about a sexual escapade with a brother, but the memory of it was perfectly open to consciousness all the time. That fact has nothing to do with censorship: it is a fear of confession.

The difference between these views on the negotiation of a censorship barring the final path to consciousness (the Sandlers call it the second censorship) may lie in their concept of a *present unconscious* rather than a *preconscious*. What is this present unconscious, and what is the past unconscious?

I have examined the concepts of a past and present unconscious elsewhere (Yorke, 1996b): that was in another context and for a different purpose, and I have no wish to repeat here what was said quite fully there. But, for all that, certain points can be made again. The past unconscious, for its devisors, is regarded as "the child within". It has, they assert, all the characteristics of the mind of a child of five years of age or thereabouts, and in that respect it differs from the system *Ucs.* of the topographical model and the id of the structural model. (The age the authors have in mind is governed by the fact of the laying down in its final form of the repression barrier—mentioned above— and the age at which the oedipal conflict has been tackled and has led to the more established structure of the superego, *inter alia*.) As the Sandlers themselves pointed out (Sandler & Sandler, 1984), the "child within" cannot be the "id child": that would mean it was dominated by primary process functioning and had failed to pass through all the stages of development that a child of five has experienced. It gives form and structure to all the intrapsychic content that arises in the depths—in particular, to unconscious wishes and wishful fantasies. The "child within" is therefore comparatively sophisticated, but the unconscious content established in the child's mind "is modified in the present unconscious as it moves from the depths to the surface" (Sandler & Sandler, 1994, p. 281).

At this point the authors pause to explain that, in discussing unconscious fantasies as these appear in the present unconscious, they have in mind *all mental representations and their accompanying feeling states*. They do this "for the sake of convenience" and "for the time being at any rate" (Sandler & Sandler, 1994, p. 285). Since, for thirty years or more Joseph Sandler (Sandler & Nagera, 1963) had been very careful to delineate between the different ways in which the term "fantasy" was used and give it a very precise meaning, one cannot help wondering about the meaning of "convenience" and the duration of the "time being".

At any rate, fantasies derived, in varying degrees, from the past unconscious, "have to be dealt with *by the person of the present*, with the aim of maintaining equilibrium in the present" (Sandler & Sandler, 1994, p. 285). The fantasies differ in structure from those of early childhood: they are now closely linked with the representations of present-day people and are subject to more secondary-process functioning than would have been the case in the past. This has implications for unconscious transference fantasies (in the new sense): these exist in the present unconscious, not in the past unconscious, and inasmuch as they arouse conflict, it is there that they have to be modified, disguised, and defended against. Unconscious reactions and impulses arise in analysis as if the patient were a particular 5-year-old child. But these reactions "have to be dealt with in the present unconscious *by the person of the present*". The Sandlers add: "The censoring, if one can call it that, takes place throughout the present unconscious, with a final censorship or defensive transformation—Freud's second censorship—occurring before admission to conscious awareness." But this censorship is *not* Freud's second censorship, and it is the latter censorship one has to work around. One always did work around the second censorship, though it was the Freudian one, not the present authors' (cf. Yorke, 1965).

The concept of transference put forward by the Sandlers is particularly important for the purposes of the present chapter and a further quote from them seems necessary. "If an unconscious hostile wish toward the analyst arises in a patient's present unconscious, then it is not a death wish toward the father displaced on to the analyst in the transference. Rather, it is a hostile impulse arising in the here and now toward the analyst, quite possibly *modeled on* the inner child's hostile wishes towards the father" (Sandler & Sandler, 1994, p. 290). And lastly: "If, in certain cases, it may be necessary to refer to the past *before* speaking of the present, this should be done *with the aim of showing the patent what is going on in the present*" (emphasis in original).

A great deal more could be said about the past and present unconscious; but it would not perhaps add very much to the points that need to be made here. For the views put forward in the Sandlers' series of papers on this subject can only be welcomed by those who put the present before everything else in the psychoanalytic understanding of what goes on in the treatment-room. Many who subscribe to the here-and-now school of thought will find a fresh rationale for their clinical practice in these arguments. I do not find it a very sound rationale: on the one hand it is asserted that the patient on the couch behaves like the "child within", but it is not the unconscious of the 5-year-old that is to be addressed—it is that of the present adult. Even if this seeming anomaly could be reconciled, as the Sandlers believe it can, the fact is that a "child" on the couch does not behave, except at times, as a 5-year-old but has periods of regression and progression. Regression is virtually done away with in the new theory; and although the child never regresses in all respects (he or she has to become an adult or older child again in order to comprehend and make use of the analyst's interpretations), it is important to analyse the ways in which he or she does.

The new concepts will certainly be welcomed by those who consider that Freud's psychology, and the mainstream developments that have built on it, are old hat. The Sandlers do not say this in so many words. But they make far too much of the supposed dichotomy between the structural and topographical views of the mental apparatus (cf. Eissler, 1962), and the assertion that the structural theory is already showing signs of "creaking at the edges" is not followed by acceptable suggestions for stabilization. And if there are some difficulties still awaiting resolution in Freudian theory, I hope my summary of its development will show that it has *not* been replaced by anything approaching its power and lucidity. It seems to me that a thorough knowledge of Freud would be enough to point to the implausible nature of the theory of a past and present unconscious.

But the new system is not designed simply as an alternative to Freud: it is supposed to supplement *other* clinical and conceptual theories. How it can do that, when so many of these viewpoints are incompatible with each other in so many respects, is difficult to see. When it comes to the couch, for example, there are still many analysts who regard the "child" recumbent upon it as a baby, not as a 5-year-old, and I am not only thinking of those Kleinians who have not kept up with changes in Kleinian thinking, but of some baby observation theorists as well. At any rate, the new approach will be welcomed by those who believe that it is justifiable for psychoanalysts to live in a pluralistic age and still be called psychoanalysts, irrespective of whether or not basic Freudian principles governing views of the unconscious have been distorted or sacrificed altogether. So it seems appropriate to recall that Pearl King is not among them; and that is certainly why I, personally, have always been delighted when she has agreed to supervise one of my analysands. As for the *future unconscious*, one can only hope there *is* one and that it restores something of what has been increasingly lost over the years. Whatever the outcome, there is no choice but to work to that end.

REFERENCES

Abraham, K. (1919). The applicability of psycho-analytic treatment to patients at an advanced age. In: *Selected Papers on Psycho-Analysis* (pp. 312–317). New York: Brunner/Mazel, 1979.

Abraham, K. (1924). A short study of the development of the libido, viewed in the light of mental disorders. In: *Selected Papers* (chap. 26). London: Hogarth Press, 1927.

Ahumada, J. L. (1997). Counterinduction in psychoanalytic practice: espistemic and technical aspects. In: J. L. Ahumada, J. Olagaray, A. K. Richards, & A. D. Richards (Eds.), *The Perverse Transference and Other Matters* (chap. 11). Northvale, NJ/London: Jason Aronson.

Alberoni, F. (1987). *L'Erotisme*. Paris: Ramsay.

Álvarez Lince, B. (1996). *La interpretación psicoanalítica: método and creación*. Santafé de Bogotá: Editorial Grijalbo.

Arlow, J. A., & Brenner, C. (1964). *Psychoanalytic Concepts and the Structural Model*. New York: International Universities Press.

Austin, J. L. (1962). *How to Do Things with Words*. Oxford: Clarendon Press.

Bergmann, M. S. (1987). *The Anatomy of Loving*. New York: Columbia University Press.

Bergmann, M. V. (1982). Thoughts on superego pathology of survivors and their children. In: M. S. Bergmann & M. E. Jucovy (Eds.), *Generations of the Holocaust*. New York: Basic Books.

Bianchedi, E. T. de (1991). Psychic change: the "becoming" of an inquiry. *International Journal of Psycho-Analysis, 72*: 6–15, 1991.

Bion, W. R. (1957). Differentiation of the psychotic from the non-psychotic personalities. *International Journal of Psycho-Analysis, 38*: 266–275.

Bion, W. R. (1963). *Elements of Psychoanalysis*. New York: Basic Books.

Bion, W. R. (1967). *Second Thoughts*. London: Karnac Books.

Bion, W. R. (1970). *Attention and Interpretation*. London: Karnac Books.

Bion, W. R. (1977). *Seven Servants*. New York: Jason Aronson.

Blakiston, N. (1975). *A Romantic Friendship: The Letters of Cyril Connolly to Noel Blakiston*. London: Constable.

Bleger, J. (1967). *Simbiosis y Ambigüedad*. Buenos Aires: Paidós.

Blos, P. (1962). *On Adolescence*. New York: Free Press.

Blos, P. (1967). The second individuation process of adolescence. *Psychoanalytic Study of the Child, 22*: 162–186.

Blum, H. (1974). The borderline childhood of the Wolf-Man. *Journal of the American Psychoanalytic Association, 22*: 721–742.

Blum, H. (1985). Superego formation, adolescent transformation, and the adult neurosis. *Journal of the American Psychoanalytic Association, 33*: 887–910.

Blum, H. (1994). *Reconstruction in Psychoanalysis: Childhood Revisited and Recreated*. New York: International Universities Press.

Braunschweig, D., & Fain, M. (1971). *Eros et Anteros*. Paris: Petite Bibliothéque Payot.

Brenner, C. (1980). Metapsychology and psychoanalytic theory. *Psychoanalytic Quarterly, 49*: 189–214.

Brierley, M. (1939). A preparatory note on internalized objects. In: *Trends in Psycho-Analysis*. London: Hogarth Press and The Institute of Psycho-Analysis, 1951.

Brierley, M. (1942). Internal objects and theory. In: *Trends in Psycho-Analysis*. London: Hogarth Press and The Institute of Psycho-Analysis, 1951.

Britton, R., & Steiner, J. (1994). Interpretation: selected fact or overvalued idea. *International Journal of Psycho-Analysis, 75*: 1069–1078.

Chasseguet-Smirgel, J. (1975). *The Ego Ideal: A Psychoanalytic Essay on the Malady of the Ideal*. London: Free Association Books, 1984.

Chasseguet-Smirgel, J. (1993). Some thoughts on Freud's attitude during the Nazi period. In: D. Meghnagi (Ed.), *Freud and Judaism*. London: Karnac Books.

Coltart, N. (1991). Analysis of an elderly patient. *International Journal of Psycho-Analysis, 72*: 209–219.

Connolly, C. (1945). *The Unquiet Grave*. London/New York: Harper & Brothers.

Davidson, D. (1984). *Inquiries into Truth and Interpretation*. Oxford: Oxford University Press.

Dorey, R. (1991). Introducción. El sujeto de la ciencia y el sujeto del inconciente. In: R. Dorey, C. Castoriadis, E. Enriquez, et al., *El inconciente y la ciencia*. Buenos Aires: Amorrortu Editores, 1993. [Original in French: *L'Inconscient et la science*. Paris: Dunod.]

Dorey, R., Castoriadis, C., Enriquez, E., et al. (1991). *El inconciente y la ciencia*. Buenos Aires: Amorrortu Editores, 1993. [Original in French: *L'Inconscient et la science*. Paris: Dunod.]

Edelson, M. (1984). *Hypothesis and Evidence in Psychoanalysis*. Chicago, IL/London: University of Chicago Press.

Edgcumbe, R. (1993). Developmental disturbances in adolescence and their implications for transference and technique. *Bulletin of the Anna Freud Centre, 16*: 107.

Edgcumbe, R. (1995). The history of Anna Freud's thinking on developmental disturbances. *Bulletin of the Anna Freud Centre, 18*: 1.

Eissler, K. R. (1962). On the metapsychology of the preconscious: a contribution to psychoanalytic morphology. *Psychoanalytic Study of the Child, 17*: 9–41.

Erikson, E. (1959). *Identity and the Life Cycle. Psychological Issues, Monograph I*. New York: International Universities Press.

Etchegoyen, R. H. (1989). On interpretation and its testing. In: H. P. Blum, E. M. Weinshel, & F. R. Rodman (Eds.), *The Psychoanalytic Core: Essays in Honour of Leo Rangell* (chap. 20). Madison, CT: International Universities Press.

Etchegoyen, R. H. (1993). Das Junktim von Forschen und Heilen in der Psychoanalyse. *Psyche, 47*: 241–260.

Etchegoyen, R. H. (1994). Validation in the clinical process. *International Journal of Psycho-Analysis*: 83–92. (Precirculated paper for the 75th Anniversary Celebration Conference at West Point, NY, April 8–10.)

Fenichel, O. (1941). *Problems of Psychoanalytic Technique*. New York: Psychoanalytic Quarterly.

Ferenczi, S. (1913). Stages in the development of the sense of reality. In:

First Contributions to Psycho-Analysis (chap. 8). New York: Brunner/ Mazel, 1980.

Ferenczi, S. (1927). Book review of *Technik der Psychoanalyse: I. Die Analytische Situation*, by Dr. Otto Rank, 1926. *International Journal of Psycho-Analysis, 8*: 93–100.

Ferenczi, S. (1980). *First Contributions to Psycho-Analysis*. New York: Brunner/Mazel.

Fisher, C. (1966). Dreaming and sexuality. In: R. M. Loewenstein, L. M. Newman, M. Schur, & A.J. Solnit (Eds.), *Psychoanalysis: A General Psychology* (pp. 537–569). New York: International Universities Press.

Fisher, C. (1978). Experimental and clinical approaches to the mind–body problem through recent research in sleep and dreaming. In: N. Rosenzweig & H. Griscom (Eds.), *Psychopharmacology and Psychotherapy: Synthesis or Antithesis?* (pp. 61–99). New York: Human Sciences Press.

Fonagy, P., Moran, G., Edgcumbe, R., Kennedy, H., & Target, M. (1993). The roles of mental representations and mental processes in therapeutic action. *Psychoanalytic Study of the Child, 48*: 9–48.

Freeman, T. (1995). "On the Formal Aspects of Psychotic Phenomena." Unpublished paper.

Freud, A. (1936). *The Ego and the Mechanisms of Defence*. New York: International Universities Press, 1946.

Freud, A. (1958). Adolescence. *Psychoanalytic Study of the Child, 13*: 255–278.

Freud, A. (1965). *Normality and Pathology in Childhood: Assessments of Development. Writings, Vol. 6*. New York: International Universities Press.

Freud, A. (1971). Foreword. In: M. Gardiner (Ed.), *The Wolf-Man by the Wolf-Man*. New York: Basic Books.

Freud, S. (1895d) (with Breuer, J.). *Studies on Hysteria. S.E., 2*.

Freud, S. (1899a). Screen memories. *S.E., 3*.

Freud, S. (1900a). *The Interpretation of Dreams. S.E., 4–5*.

Freud, S. (1904a). Freud's psycho-analytic procedure. *S.E., 7*.

Freud, S. (1905a). On psychotherapy. *S.E., 7*.

Freud, S. (1905e [1901]). Fragment of an analysis of a case of hysteria. *S.E., 7*.

Freud, S. (1909d). Notes upon a case of obsessional neurosis. *S.E., 10*.

Freud, S. (1911b). Formulations on to the two principles of mental functioning. *S.E., 12*:.

Freud, S. (1912e). Recommendations to physicians practising psychoanalysis. *S.E., 12*:.

Freud, S. (1912g). A note on the unconscious in psycho-analysis. *S.E., 12.*

Freud, S. (1913i). The disposition to obsessional neurosis. *S.E., 12.*

Freud, S. (1914c). On narcissism: an introduction. *S.E., 14.*

Freud, S. (1914g). Remembering, repeating and working-through. (Further recommendations on the technique of psychoanalysis, II). *S.E., 12:.*

Freud, S. (1915e). The unconscious. *S. E., 14.*

Freud, S. (1916–17). *Introductory Lectures on Psychoanalysis. S.E., 15–16.*

Freud, S. (1918b [1914]). From the history of an infantile neurosis. *S.E., 17.*

Freud, S. (1920g). *Beyond the Pleasure Principle. S.E., 18.*

Freud, S. (1921c). *Group Psychology and the Analysis of the Ego. S.E., 18.*

Freud, S. (1923a [1922]). Two encyclopaedia articles. *S.E., 18.*

Freud, S. (1923b). *The Ego and the Id. S.E., 19.*

Freud, S. (1926d [1925]). *Inhibitions, Symptoms and Anxiety. S.E., 20.*

Freud, S. (1926e). *The Question of Lay Analysis. S.E., 20.*

Freud, S. (1927a). "Postscript" to *The Question of Lay Analysis. S.E., 20.*

Freud, S. (1933a). *New Introductory Lectures on Psycho-Analysis. S.E., 22.*

Freud, S. (1937c). Analysis terminable and interminable. *S.E., 23.*

Freud, S. (1937d). Constructions in analysis. *S.E., 23.*

Freud, S. (1940a [1938]). *An Outline of Psycho-Analysis. S.E., 23.*

Freud, S. (1950 [1895]). Project for a scientific psychology. *S.E., 1.*

García, M. G. (1985). *El amor en las tiempos del colera.* Buenos Aires: Editorial Sudamericana.

Gardiner, M. (Ed.) (1971). *The Wolf-Man by the Wolf-Man.* New York: Basic Books.

Gill, M. M. (1963). *Topography and Systems in Psychoanalytic Theory: Psychological Issues, Monograph 10.* New York: International Universities Press.

Gill, M. M. (1967). Introduction to "Some Metapsychological Considerations Concerning Activity and Passivity". In: *The Collected Papers of David Rapaport* (pp. 530–532), ed. M. M. Gill. New York: Basic Books, 1967.

Giovacchini, P. L. (1969). The influence of interpretation upon schizophrenic patients. *International Journal of Psycho-Analysis, 50:* 179–186.

Gitelson, M. (1952). The emotional position of the analyst in the psychoanalytic situation. *International Journal of Psycho-Analysis, 33:* 1–10.

Glymour, C. (1974). Freud, Kepler, and the clinical evidence. In: R. Wollheim & J. Hopkins (Eds.), *Philosophical Essays on Freud* (pp. 12–29). Cambridge: Cambridge University Press, 1982.

Glymour, C. (1980). *Theory and Evidence*. Princeton, NJ: Princeton University Press.

Glymour, C. (1982). Afterword to "Freud, Kepler and the Clinical Evidence". In: R. Wollheim & J. Hopkins (Ed.), *Philosophical Essays on Freud* (pp. 29–31). Cambridge: Cambridge University Press.

Goldhagen, D. J. (1996). *Hitler's Willing Executioners: Ordinary Germans and the Holocaust*. London: Little Brown.

Goldman, D. (1993). Introduction. In: *In One's Bones: The Clinical Genius of Winnicott*. Northvale, NJ: Jason Aronson.

Green, A. (1991). Desconocimiento del inconciente (ciencia y psicoanálisis). In: R. Dorey, C. Castoriadis, E. Enriquez, et al., *El inconciente y la ciencia*. Buenos Aires: Amorrortu Editores, 1993. [Original in French: "Méconnaissance de l'inconscient", in: *L'Inconscient et la science*. Paris: Dunod.]

Greenaway, P. (1987). *The Belly of an Architect*. West Hollywood, CA: Hemdale Film Corporation.

Grinberg, L. (1956). Sobre algunos problemas de técnica psicoanalíticas determinados por la identificación and contraidentificación proyectivas. *Revista de Psicoanálisis, 13*: 507–511.

Grubrich-Simitis, I. (1996). *Back to Freud's Texts: Making Silent Documents Speak*. New Haven, CT/London: Yale University Press.

Grünbaum, A. (1984). *The Foundations of Psychoanalysis: A Philosophical Critique*. Berkeley, CA: University of California Press.

Grünbaum, A. (1990). "Meaning" connections and causal connections in the human sciences: the poverty of hermeneutic philosophy. *Journal of the American Psychoanalytic Association, 38*: 559–577.

Grunberger, B. (1964). Outline for a study of narcissism in female sexuality. In: J. Chasseguet-Smirgel (Ed.), *Female Sexuality*. Ann Arbor, MI: University of Michigan Press, 1970.

Guntrip, H. (1975). My experience of analysis with Fairbairn and Winnicott (how complete a result does psycho-analytic therapy achieve?). *International Review of Psychoanalysis, 2*: 145–156.

Habermas, J. (1968). *Erkenntnis und Interesse*. Frankfurt: Suhrkamp Verlag. [*Knowledge and Human Interest*. Boston: Beacon Press, 1972.]

Hanly, C. M. T. (1992). *The Problem of Truth in Applied Psychoanalysis*. New York: Guilford Press.

Hanly, C. M. T. (1997). Psychoanalysis and the uses of philosophy. In: J. L. Ahumada, J. Olagaray, A. K. Richards, & A. David Richards (Eds.), *The Perverse Transference and Other Matters* (chap. 17). Northvale, NJ/London: Jason Aronson.

Hartmann, H. (1939). *Ego Psychology and the Problem of Adaptation*, trans. D. Rapaport. New York: International Universities Press, 1958.

Hartmann, H. (1947). On rational and irrational action. In: *Essays on Ego Psychology: Selected Problems in Psychoanalytic Theory* (pp. 37–68). New York: International Universities Press, 1964.

Hartmann, H. (1950). Comments on the psychoanalytic theory of the ego. *Psychoanalytic Study of the Child, 5*: 74–96.

Hartmann, H. (1951). Technical implications of ego psychology. *Psychoanalytic Quarterly, 20*: 31–43. [Also in: *Essays on Ego Psychology* (chap. 8). New York: International Universities Press, 1964.]

Hayman, A. (1989). What do we mean by phantasy? *International Journal of Psycho-Analysis, 70*: 105–114.

Hayman, A. (1994). Some remarks about the "Controversial Discussions". *International Journal of Psycho-Analysis, 75*: 343–358.

Heaney, S. (1995). A torchlight procession of one: on Hugh McDiarmid. In: *The Redress of Poetry*. London: Faber & Faber.

Heimann, P. (1950). On countertransference. *International Journal of Psycho-Analysis, 31*: 81–84.

Hodges, J., & Edgcumbe, R. (1990). Mixed feelings. *Bulletin of the Anna Freud Centre, 13*: 3.

Hurry, A. (Ed.) (1998). *Psychoanalysis and Developmental Therapy*. London: Karnac Books.

Isaacs, S. (1943). The nature and function of phantasy. In: P. King & R. Steiner (Eds.), *The Freud-Klein Controversies, 1941–45* (pp. 265–314). London: Routledge, 1991.

Jaspers, K. (1913). *Allgemeine Psychopatologie*. Heidelberg: Springer. [*General Psychopathology*. Manchester: Manchester University Press, 1963.]

Jones, E. (1925). Introduction to the Congress Symposium on "The Relation of Psychoanalytic Theory to Psychoanalytic Technique". *International Journal of Psycho-Analysis, 6*: 1–4.

Joseph, B. (1989). Transference, the total situation. In: E. B Spillius & M. Feldman (Eds.), *Psychic Equilibrium and Psychic Change* (pp. 156–167). London: Tavistock/Routledge.

Kandel, E. R. (1998). A new intellectual framework for psychiatry. *American Journal of Psychiatry, 155*: 457–469.

Karpf, A. (1996). *The War After: Living with the Holocaust*. London: Heinemann.

Kernberg, O. (1995). *Love Relations: Normality and Pathology*. New Haven, CT: Yale University Press.

Kestenberg, J. S. (1993). What a psychoanalyst learned from the Holocaust and genocide. *International Journal of Psycho-Analysis, 74*: 117–1129.

Kestenberg, J. S., & Brenner, I. (1996). *The Last Witness: The Child Survivor of the Holocaust.* London: American Psychiatric Press.

Kety, S. S. (1960). A biologist examines the mind and behaviour. *Science, 132*: 1861.

Khan, M. M. R. (1986). Introduction. In: D. W. Winnicott, *Holding and Interpretation: Fragment of an Analysis.* London: Hogarth Press.

King, P. (1964). International Psychoanalytical Association, 24th Bulletin. *International Journal of Psycho-Analysis, 45*: 460–466.

King, P. (1973). The therapist–patient relationship. *Journal of Analytical Psychology, 18*: 1–10.

King, P. (1978). Affective response of the analyst to the patient's communications. *International Journal of Psycho-Analysis, 59*: 329–340.

King, P. (1979). The contribution of Ernest Jones to the British Psycho-Analytical Society. *International Journal of Psycho-Analysis, 60*: 280–284.

King, P. (1980). The life cycle as indicated by the nature of the transference in the psychoanalysis of the middle-aged and elderly. *International Journal of Psycho-Analysis, 61*: 153–160.

King, P. (1981). The education of a psychoanalyst: the British experience." *British Psychoanalytical Society Bulletin,* No. 2 (revised 1991).

King, P. (1994). The evolution of controversial issues. *International Journal of Psycho-Analysis, 75*: 335–342.

King, P. (1995). Adam Limentani: commemorative meeting. *British Psychoanalytical Society Bulletin,* No. 5.

King, P. (1996). "What Has Happened to Psychoanalysis in the British Society?" Unpublished paper prepared for discussion in *The Forum,* 31 January.

King, P., & Steiner, R. (1991). *The Freud–Klein Controversies, 1941–45.* London: Tavistock/Routledge.

Klein, G. S. (1973). Two theories or one? *Bulletin of the Menninger Clinic, 37*: 102–132.

Klein, G. S. (1976). *Psychoanalytic Theory: An Exploration of Essentials.* New York: International Universities Press.

Klein, M. (1932). *The Psycho-Analysis of Children: The Writings of Melanie Klein, Vol. 2.* London: Hogarth Press, 1975.

Klein, M. (1943). Memorandum on her technique. In: P. King & R. Steiner (Eds.), *The Freud-Klein Controversies, 1941–45* (pp. 635–638). London: Routledge, 1991.

Klein, M. (1946). Notes on some schizoid mechanisms. *International Journal of Psycho-Analysis*, 27: 99–110. [Also in: *Envy and Gratitude and Other Works, 1946–1963* (chap. 1). *The Writings of Melanie Klein, Vol. 3*. London: Hogarth Press, 1975.]

Klimovsky, G. (1980). Ciencia y anticiencia en psicología. Conferencia dictada en la Asociación Argentina de Investigaciones Psicológicas (ADIP). In: G. Klimovsky, M. Aguinis, L. Chiozza, et al., *Opiniones sobre la psicología* (pp. 11–48). Buenos Aires: Ediciones ADIP, 1986.

Klimovsky, G. (1986). Epistemological aspects of psychoanalytic interpretation. In: R. H. Etchegoyen, *The Fundamentals of Psychoanalytic Technique* (chap. 35). London: Karnac Books, 1991; revised edition, 1999.

Klimovsky, G. (1989). "La epistemología de Sigmund Freud." Paper presented at the 36th IPAC, Rome.

Klimovsky, G. (1994). *Las Desventuras del Conocimiento Científico. Una Introducción a la Epistemología*. Buenos Aires: A–Z Editor.

Kogan, I. (1995). *The Cry of Mute Children: A Psychoanalytic Perspective of the Second Generation of the Holocaust*. London: Free Association Books.

Kohut, H. (1971). *The Analysis of the Self*. New York: International Universities Press.

Kohut, H. (1977). *The Restoration of the Self*. New York: International Universities Press.

Krell, R., & Sherman, M. I. (Eds.) (1997). *Medical and Psychological Effects of Concentration Camps on Holocaust Survivors*. London: Transaction Publishers.

Kris, E. (1950). On preconscious mental processes. *Psychoanalytic Quarterly, 19*: 540–560.

Lacan, J. (1957). L'instance de la lettre dans l'inconscient ou la raison depuis Freud. In: *Écrits* (pp. 493–528). Paris: Seuil.

Lacan, J. (1966). *Écrits*. Paris: Seuil.

Lagache, D. (1964). Symposium on fantasy. *International Journal of Psycho-Analysis, 45*: 180–189.

Laing, A. C. (1994). *R. D. Laing: A Biography*. London/Chester Springs, PA: Peter Owen.

Laing, R. D. (1960a). *The Divided Self*. London: Tavistock Publications.

Laing, R. D. (1960b). *Self and Others*. London: Tavistock Publications.

Laing, R. D. (1967). *The Politics of Experience and the Bird of Paradise*. Harmondsworth: Penguin.

Laing, R. D., & Esterson, A. (1998), *Sanity Madness and the Family*. London: Routledge.

Laufer, M., & Laufer, M. E. (1984). *Adolescence and Developmental Breakdown: A Psychoanalytic View*. New Haven, CT/London: Yale University Press.

Levin, S., & Kahana, R. (Eds.) (1967). *Psychodynamic Studies on Ageing*. New York: International Universities Press.

Liberman, D. (1962). *La comunicación en terapéutica psicoanalítica*. Buenos Aires: EUDEBA.

Liberman, D. (1970–72). *Lingüística, interacción comunicativa y proceso psicoanalítico, Vols. 1–3*. Buenos Aires: Galerna.

Lifton, R. J. (1993). *The Protean Self: Human Resilience in an Age of Fragmentation*. Chicago, IL: University of Chicago Press, 1999.

Loewald, H. W. (1978). *Psychoanalysis and the History of the Individual*. New Haven, CT: Yale University Press.

Mahler, M., Pine, F., & Bergman, A. (1975). *The Psychological Birth of the Human Infant*. London: Hutchinson.

Mahony, P. J. (1984). *Cries of the Wolf Man*. New York: International Universities Press.

Mahony, P. J. (1986). *Freud and the Rat Man*. New Haven, CT/London: Yale University Press.

Mayer-Gross, W., Slater, E., & Roth, M. (1969). *Clinical Psychiatry* (3rd ed.). London: Bailliere, Tindall & Cassell.

Meltzer, D., & Williams, M. H. (1988). *The Apprehension of Beauty*. Old Ballechin, Strathtay: Clunie Press.

Mijolla, A. de (Ed.) (1981). *Les visiteurs du moi, fantasmes d'identification* (3rd edition*)*. Paris: Les Belle Lettres, 1996.

Mijolla, A. de (1982). La psychanalyse en France (1893–1965). In: R. Jaccard (Ed.), *Histoire de la psychanalyse, Vol. 2*. Paris: Hachette.

Mijolla, A. de (1984). Quelques avatars de la psychanalyse en France. Lecture du Disque Vert (juin 1924). *L'Evolution Psychiatrique, 49*: 773–795.

Mijolla, A. de (1987). Unconscious identification fantasies and family prehistory, *International Journal of Psycho-Analysis, 68*: 397–403.

Mijolla, A. de (1988a). La psychanalyse et les psychanalystes en France entre 1939 et 1945. *Revue Internationale de l'Histoire de Psychanalyse, 1*: 167–223.

Mijolla, A. de (1988b). Quelques aperçus sur le role de la princesse Marie Bonaparte dans la création de la Société Psychanalytique de Paris. *Revue Française de Psychanalyse, 52*: 1197–1214.

Mijolla, A. de (Ed.) (1989). Collection of articles on the history of psychoanalytic training in France. *Revue Internationale de l'Histoire de Psych-analyse*, 2: 293–417.

Mijolla, A. de, & Mijolla, M. S. de (1996). *Psychanalyse*. Paris: Presses Universitaires de France.

Miller, J.-A. (1976). La scission de 1953. *Ornicar?*, 7.

Miller, J.-A. (1977). L'excommunication. *Ornicar?*, 8.

Milner, M. (1952). Aspects of symbolism in comprehension of the not-self. *International Journal of Psycho-Analysis*, 33: 181–194.

Money-Kyrle, R. E. (1968). Cognitive development. *International Journal of Psycho-Analysis*, 49: 691–698. [Also in: *Collected Papers* (chap. 31). Perthshire: Clunie Press, 1978.]

Money-Kyrle, R. E. (1971). The aim of psycho-analysis. *International Journal of Psycho-Analysis*, 52: 103–107. [Also in: *Collected Papers* (chap. 33). Perthshire: Clunie Press, 1978.]

Nemiroff, R., & Colarusso, C. (1985). *The Race against Time: Psychotherapy and Psychoanalysis in the Second Half of Life*. New York: Basic Books.

Obholzer, K. (1980). *Gespräche mit dem Wolfsmann*. Hamburg, Germany: Rowohlt.

Painceira, A. (1993). Algunas ideas acerca del proceso analitico y la acti-tud del psicoanalista en la obra de Winnicott. In: *Il encuentro Latino-americano sobre el pensamiento de Winnicott*. Montevideo: Enfoques Teorico-Tecnicas.

Parker, T. (1985). *The People of Providence*. London: Pan Books.

Pines, D. (1993a). Working with women survivors of the Holocaust. In: *A Woman's Unconscious Use of Her Body*. London: Virago.

Pines, D. (1993b). The impact of the holocaust on the second generation. In: *A Woman's Unconscious Use of Her Body*. London: Virago.

Popper, K. R. (1953) La ciencia. In: *El Desarrollo del Conocimiento Científico* (pp. 43–79). Buenos Aires: Paidós, 1967.

Popper, K. R. (1962) *Conjectures and Refutations*. London: Routledge & Kegan Paul.

Racker, H. (1960). *Transference and Countertransference*. London: Hogarth Press, 1968.

Radcliffe, M. (1975). Before the Barbarians. *The Times* (London), 18 December 1975.

Rangell, L. (1955). On the psychoanalytic theory of anxiety: a statement of a unitary theory. *Journal of the American Psychoanalytic Association*, 3: 389–414.

Rangell, L. (1959). The nature of conversion. *Journal of the American Psychoanalytic Association*, 7: 632–662.

Rangell, L. (1967). Psychoanalysis, affects, and the "human core": On the relationship of psychoanalysis to the behavioral sciences. *Psychoanalytic Quarterly*, 36: 172–202.

Rangell, L. (1968). A further attempt to resolve "the problem of anxiety". *Journal of the American Psychoanalytic Association*, 16: 371–404.

Rangell, L. (1969a). The intrapsychic process and its analysis: a recent line of thought and its current implications. *International Journal of Psycho-Analysis*, 50: 65–77.

Rangell, L. (1969b). Choice-conflict and the decision-making function of the ego. A psychoanalytic contribution to decision theory. *International Journal of Psycho-Analysis*, 50: 599–602.

Rangell, L. (1971). The decision-making process. A contribution from psychoanalysis. *Psychoanalytic Study of the Child*, 26: 425–452.

Rangell, L. (1974). A psychoanalytic perspective leading currently to the syndrome of the compromise of integrity. *International Journal of Psycho-Analysis*, 55: 3–12.

Rangell, L. (1976). Lessons from Watergate: a derivative for psychoanalysis. *Psychoanalytic Quarterly*, 45: 37–61.

Rangell, L. (1986). The executive functions of the ego: an extension of the concept of ego autonomy. *Psychoanalytic Study of the Child*, 41: 1–37.

Rangell, L. (1987). A core process in psychoanalytic treatment. *Psychoanalytic Quarterly*, 56: 222–249.

Rangell, L. (1997). Into the second psychoanalytic century: one theory or many? The unitary theory of Leo Rangell, M.D. *Journal of Clinical Psychoanalysis*, 6: 451–612.

Rank, O. (1926). *Technik der Psychoanalyse: I. Die analytische Situation*. Leipzig & Vienna: Franz Deuticke.

Rapaport, D. (1951). The autonomy of the ego. *Bulletin of the Menninger Clinic*, 15: 113–123.

Rapaport, D. (1953a). On the psychoanalytic theory of affects. *International Journal of Psycho-Analysis*, 34: 177–198.

Rapaport, D. (1953b). Some metapsychological considerations concerning activity and passivity. In: *The Collected Papers of David Rapaport* (pp. 530–568), ed. M. M. Gill. New York: Basic Books, 1967.

Rapaport, D. (1958). The theory of ego autonomy: a generalization. *Bulletin of the Menninger Clinic*, 22: 13–35.

Reich, A. (1951). On counter-transference. *International Journal of Psycho-Analysis*, 32: 25–31.

Rosenfeld, D. (1980). The handling of resistances in adult patients. *International Journal of Psycho-Analysis*, 61: 71–83.

Rosenfeld, H. (1987). *Impasse and Interpretation*. London: Tavistock Publications.

Roudinesco, E. (1982). *La bataille de cent ans, Vol. 1*. Paris: Ramsay.

Roudinesco, E. (1986). *Histoire de la psychanalyse en France, Vol. 2: 1925–1985*. Paris: Seuil.

Rubinstein, M. A. (1993). Algunas reflexiones surgidas de la reflectura de un texto de D. W. Winnicott. In: *Il encuentro latinoamericano sobre el pensamiento de Winnicott*. Montevideo: Enfoques Teorico-Tecnicas.

Sandler, A.-M. (1984). Problems of the development and adaptation in an elderly patient. *Psychoanalytic Study of the Child*, 39: 471—489.

Sandler, J. (1976). Countertransference and role-responsiveness. *International Review of Psychoanalysis*, 3: 43–47.

Sandler, J. (1989). The id—or the child within. In: J. Sandler (Ed.), *Dimensions of Psychoanalysis*. London: Karnac Books.

Sandler, J., Dare, C., & Holder, A. (1973). *The Patient and the Analyst*. London: Allen & Unwin.

Sandler, J., & Nagera, H. (1963). Aspects of the metapsychology of fantasy. *Psychoanalytic Study of the Child*, 18: 159–194.

Sandler, J., & Sandler, A.-M. (1983). The "second censorship", the "three-box model" and some technical implications. *International Journal of Psycho-Analysis*, 64: 413–425.

Sandler, J., & Sandler, A.-M. (1984). The past unconscious, the present unconscious and interpretation of the transference. *Psychoanalytic Inquiry*, 4: 367–399.

Sandler, J., & Sandler, A.-M. (1987). The past unconscious, the present unconscious and the vicissitudes of guilt. *International Journal of Psycho-Analysis*, 68: 331–341.

Sandler, J., & Sandler, A.-M. (1994). The past unconscious and the present unconscious: a contribution to a technical frame of reference. *Psychoanalytic Study of the Child*, 49: 278–292.

Schafer, R. (1976). *A New Language for Psychoanalysis*. New Haven, CT: Yale University Press.

Searle, J. R. (1969). *Speech Acts: An Essay in the Philosophy of Language*. Cambridge: Cambridge University Press.

Segal, F. (1993). D. W. Winnicott: clasico o moderno? In: *Il encuentro latinoamericano sobre el pensamiento de Winnicott*. Uruguay: Enfoques Teorico-Tecnicas.

Selye, H. (1950). *Stress*. Montreal: Acta.

Sereny, G. (1995). *Albert Speer: His Battle with Truth*. London: Macmillan.

Settlage, C. (1996). Transcending old age. *International Journal of Psycho-Analysis, 77*: 549–564.

Solms, M. (1996). Was sind Affekte? *Psyche, 50*: 485–522.

Solms, M. (1997). What is consciousness? *Journal of the American Psychoanalytic Association, 45*: 601–703.

Stoller, R. (1969). *Sex and Gender*. New York: Science House.

Storr, A. (1968). *Human Aggression*. London: Allen Lane, Penguin Press.

Strachey, J. (1934). The nature of the therapeutic action of psycho-analysis. *International Journal of Psycho-Analysis, 15*: 127–152.

Tausk, V. (1919). On the origin of the "influencing machine" in schizophrenia. *Psychoanalytic Quarterly, 2*: 519–556, 1933. [Also in: R. Fliess (Ed.), *The Psychoanalytic Reader*. London: Hogarth Press, 1950.]

Thomä, H., & Kächele, H. (1985). *Psychoanalytic Practice, Vol. 1: Principles*. Berlin-Heidelberg: Springer Verlag, 1987.

Tyson, A. (1975). Homage to Catalonia. *New York Review of Books*, 11 February 1971.

Valenstein, A. (2000). The older patient in psychoanalysis. *Journal of the American Psychoanalytic Association, 48*: 1563–1589.

Waelder, R. (1967). *Progress and Revolution: A Study of the Issues of Our Age*. New York: International Universities Press.

Wallerstein, R. S. (1986). *Forty-Two Lives in Treatment: A Study of Psychoanalysis and Psychotherapy*. New York/London: Guilford Press.

Wallerstein, R. S. (1998). The IPA and the American Psychoanalytic Association: a perspective on the regional association agreement. *International Journal of Psycho-Analysis, 79*: 553–564.

Wardi, D. (1992). *Memorial Candles: Children of the Holocaust*. London: Routledge.

Weinshel, E. (1988). Structural change in psychoanalysis. *Journal of the American Psychoanalytic Association, 36* (Suppl.): 263–280.

Winnicott, D. W. (1952). Psychoses and child care. In: *Through Paediatrics to Psychoanalysis*. London: Hogarth Press, 1975.

Winnicott, D. W. (1954a). Metapsychological and clinical aspects of regression within the psychoanalytical set-up. In: *Through Paediatrics to Psychoanalysis*. London: Hogarth Press, 1975.

Winnicott, D. W. (1954b). Withdrawal and regression. In: *Through Paediatrics to Psychoanalysis*. London: Hogarth Press, 1975.

Winnicott, D. W. (1955). Clinical varieties of transference. In: *Through Paediatrics to Psychoanalysis*. London: Hogarth Press, 1975.

Winnicott, D. W. (1960). Ego distortion in terms of true and false self. In:

The Maturational Processes and the Facilitating Environment. London: Hogarth Press, 1965.

Winnicott. D. W. (1962). Ego integration in child development. In: *The Maturational Processes and the Facilitating Environment.* London: Hogarth Press and The Institute of Psycho-Analysis, 1965.

Winnicott, D. W. (1963). Dependence in infant-care, child care and in the psychoanalytic setting. In: *The Maturational Processes and the Facilitating Environment.* London: Hogarth Press, 1965.

Wisdom, J. O. (1956). Psychoanalytic technology. In: L. Paul et al. (Eds.), *Psychoanalytic Clinical Interpretation* (pp. 143–161). London: Collier-Macmillan, 1964.

Wisdom, J. O. (1967). Testing an interpretation within a session. *International Journal of Psycho-Analysis, 48*: 44–52.

Yorke, C. (1965). Some metapsychological aspects of interpretation. *British Journal of Medical Psychology, 38*: 27–42.

Yorke, C. (1990). The development and functioning of the sense of shame. [In collaboration with T. Balogh, P. Cohen, J. Davids, A. Gavshon, M. McCutcheon, D. McLean, J. Miller, & J. Szydlo.] *Psychoanalytic Study of the Child, 45*: 377–409.

Yorke, C. (1995). Freud's psychology: can it survive? *Psychoanalytic Study of the Child, 50*: 3–31.

Yorke, C. (1996a). Diagnosis in clinical practice: its relationship to psychoanalytic theory. *Psychoanalytic Study of the Child, 51*: 190–214.

Yorke, C. (1996b). Childhood and the unconscious. *American Imago, 53*: 227–256.

Zac, J. (1971). Un enfoque metodológico del establecimiento del encuadre. *Revista de Psicoanálisis, 28*: 593–610.

Zinberg, N., & Kaufman, I. (Eds.) (1978). *Normal Psychology of the Aging Process.* New York: International Universities Press.

INDEX

transference (*passim*):
  analysis, 117
  breaking of, 19
  concept of, 249
    different meanings of, 165–169,
      172, 176
  epidemiological study of, 150
  explanatory value of, 163
  fantasies, unconscious, 249
  and Freud's model of representation,
    34
  and genetic reconstruction, 210
  here-and-now, 29–38, 165, 166
  historical dimension of, 35–38
  interpretations, 37–38
  Klein on, 30–31
  life-cycle manifested in, 127
  of middle-aged patients, 129–139
  monitoring of, 140
  negative, 160
    analysis of, 22
  neurosis, 19, 109
  object, analyst as, 117
  positive, 160
  psychotic, 123, 125
  vs. relationship, 31
  repetition, 151, 155
  scientific credentials of, 151
  suggestion in, 32
  and time, 33
transitional object, 32
transitional states, 174
transposition, and Holocaust survivors,
  106–107
trans-sexualism, 226
transvestism, 226
true self and false self [Winnicott on],
  123, 174
Turquet, P., 3, 4, 13, 15
Tyson, A., 49
Tyson, R., 76

unconscious, the:
  Freud's theory of:
    teaching of, 230
    timelessness of, 33
  future, 251
  past: *see* past unconscious
  present: *see* present unconscious
unconscious choice and responsibility,
  193–204
unthinkable anxiety, 123, 175

Valabrega, J.-P., 14, 20
Valenstein, A., 110
van der Leeuw, P., 13
Vincent, M., 46, 52

Waelder, R., 67, 199
Wallace, A. R., 175
Wallace, W., 48
Wallerstein, R. S., 77, 147
Wardi, D., 101, 102
Weinshel, E., 150
Widlöcher, D., 15
will, ego, 198–199
Williams, C., 7
Williams, M. H., 181
Winkley, L., 93
Winnicott, D. W., xvi, 11, 32, 38, 41,
    121–126, 135, 167, 170
  on ego and id, 169, 173–174
  unthinkable anxiety, 123, 175
Wisdom, J. O., 157, 162
wish-fulfilment, hallucinatory, 169
"Wolf Man", 33, 109–113

Yorke, C., xiv, xvi, 230–251
young adult, analysis of, 127–140
  clinical vignette, 129–139

Zac, J., 151
Zinberg, N., 110